The Least You Should Know about English

The Least You Should Know about English

FORM C
Writing Skills

NINTH EDITION

Paige Wilson
Pasadena City College

Teresa Ferster Glazier
Late, Western Illinois University

Australia Brazil Canada Mexico Singapore Spain United Kingdom United States

The Least You Should Know about English, Writing Skills, Form C, Ninth Edition
Paige Wilson/Teresa Ferster Glazier, Late

Publisher: *Lyn Uhl*
Acquisitions Editor: *Annie Todd*
Editorial Assistant: *Dan DeBonis*
Senior Technology Project Manager: *Stephanie Gregoire*
Marketing Manager: *Kate Edwards*
Marketing Assistant: *Kate Remsberg*
Advertising Project Manager: *Darlene Amidon-Brent*
Content Project Manager: *Sarah Sherman*
Senior Art Director: *Cate Rickard Barr*
Print Buyer: *Betsy Donaghey*
Rights Acquisition Account Manager: *Mardell Glinski Schultz*
Production Service/Compositor: *ICC Macmillan Inc.*
Cover Designer: *Gina Petti*
Printer: *Edward Brothers*

Printed in the United States of America
1 2 3 4 5 6 7 09 08 07

Library of Congress Control Number: 2007921435

ISBN-10: 1-4130-2935-3
ISBN-13: 978-1-4130-2935-2

Thomson Higher Education
25 Thomson Place
Boston, MA 02210-1202
USA

CONTENTS

To the Instructor

This book is for students who need to review basic English skills and who may profit from a simplified "least you should know" approach. Parts 1 to 3 cover the essentials of word choice and spelling, sentence structure, punctuation, and capitalization. Part 4 on writing teaches students the basic structures of the paragraph and the essay, along with the writing skills necessary to produce them.

The "least you should know" approach attempts to avoid the use of linguistic terminology whenever possible. Students work with words they know instead of learning a vocabulary they may never use again.

Abundant exercises include practice writing sentences and proofreading paragraphs. Diligent students learn to use the rules automatically and thus *carry their new skills over into their writing.* Most exercises consist of sets of ten thematically related, informative sentences on both timely and timeless subjects—anything from stone age dentists and medieval toys to the therapeutic effects of virtual earthquakes. Such exercises reinforce the need for coherence and details in student writing. With answers provided at the back of the book, students can correct their own work and progress at their own pace.

The ninth edition includes a new section in Part 1 devoted to Adjectives and Adverbs. In Part 2, the format of exercises to correct Clichés, Awkward Phrasing, and Wordiness has changed from sentences to paragraphs. In addition, comma exercises in Part 3 now allow students to practice using individual comma rules before combining them. Finally, in Part 4, the Writing section, students will find a contemporary poem to read and respond to, along with several other new student and professional sample paragraphs and essays. As always, the Writing section outlines the writing process and stresses the development of the student's written "voice." Writing assignments follow each discussion. Students improve their reading by learning to find main ideas and their writing by learning to write meaningful reactions and concise summaries.

The Least You Should Know about English functions equally well in the classroom and at home as a self-tutoring text. The simple explanations, ample exercises, and answers at the back of the book provide students with everything they need to progress on their own. Students who have previously been overwhelmed by the complexities of English should, through mastering simple rules and through writing and rewriting simple papers, gain enough competence to succeed in further composition courses.

As in all previous editions, **Form C** differs from **Forms A and B** in its exercises, writing samples, and assignments; however, the explanatory sections are the same.

A **Test Booklet** with additional exercises and ready-to-photocopy tests accompanies this text and is available to instructors.

Acknowledgments

For their thoughtful commentary on the book, we would like to thank the following reviewers:

Brenda J. L. Trottman
Katherine Gibbs School, New York

Michael W. Keathley
Ivy Tech State College

Greta Anderson
Kirkwood Community College

David P. Gonzales
Los Angeles Pierce College

In addition, thanks to our publishing team for their expertise and hard work: Annie Todd, Acquisitions Editor; Dan DeBonis, Editorial Assistant; Elise Kaiser, Director of Production.

For their specific contributions to Form C, we extend our gratitude to the following student writers: Eric Coffey, Christine Foy, Amanda Gomez, Sherika McPeters, Ruby Warren, and InYoung Yang.

As always, we are especially indebted to our families and friends for their support and encouragement.

Paige Wilson
Teresa Ferster Glazier (1907–2004)

This edition is dedicated to the memory of Teresa Ferster Glazier. In creating *The Least You Should Know about English,* she discovered a way to teach grammar and writing that students have actually enjoyed for nearly thirty years. Her explanations and approaches have been constant sources of inspiration for this and the past two coauthored editions, as they will be for all future editions of her text.

What Is the Least You Should Know?

Most English textbooks try to teach you more than you need to know. This book will teach you the least you should know—and still help you learn to write clearly and acceptably. You won't have to deal with grammatical terms like *gerund, modal auxiliary verb,* or *demonstrative pronoun.* You can get along without knowing such technical labels if you learn a few key concepts. You *should* know about the parts of speech and how to use and spell common words; you *should* be able to recognize subjects and verbs; you *should* know the basics of sentence structure and punctuation—but rules, as such, will be kept to a minimum.

The English you'll learn in this book is sometimes called Standard Written English, and it may differ slightly or greatly from the spoken English you use. Standard Written English is the form of writing accepted in business and the professions. So no matter how you speak, you will communicate better in writing when you use Standard Written English. You might *say* something like "That's a whole nother problem," and everyone will understand, but you would probably want to *write,* "That's a completely different problem." Knowing the difference between spoken English and Standard Written English is essential in college, in business, and in life.

Until you learn the least you should know, you'll probably have difficulty communicating in writing. Take this sentence, for example:

I hope that the film school will except my application for admission.

We assume that the writer used the *sound,* not the meaning, of the word *except* to choose it and in so doing used the wrong word. If the sentence had read

I hope that the film school will *accept* my application for admission.

then the writer would have communicated clearly. Or take this sentence:

The film school accepted Beth and Hector and I will try again next year.

This sentence includes two statements and therefore needs punctuation, a comma in this case:

> The film school accepted Beth and Hector, and I will try again next year.

But perhaps the writer meant

> The film school accepted Beth, and Hector and I will try again next year.

Punctuation makes all the difference, especially for Hector. With the help of this text, we hope you'll learn to make your writing so clear that no one will misunderstand it.

As you make your way through the book, it's important to remember information after you learn it because many concepts and structures build upon others. For example, once you can identify subjects and verbs, you'll be better able to recognize fragments, understand subject-verb agreement, and use correct punctuation. Explanations and examples are brief and clear, and it shouldn't be difficult to learn from them—*if you want to*. But you have to want to!

How to Learn the Least You Should Know

1. Read each explanatory section carefully (aloud, if possible).
2. Do the first exercise. Compare your answers with those at the back of the book. If they don't match, study the explanation again to find out why.
3. Do the second exercise and correct it. If you miss a single answer, go back once more to the explanation. You must have missed something. Be tough on yourself. Don't just think, "Maybe I'll get it right next time." Reread the examples, and *then* try the next exercise. It's important to correct each group of ten sentences before moving on so that you'll discover your mistakes early.
4. You may be tempted to quit after you do one or two exercises perfectly. Instead, make yourself finish another exercise. It's not enough to *understand* a concept or structure. You have to *practice* using it.
5. If you're positive, however, after doing several exercises, that you've learned a concept or structure, take the next exercise as a test. If you miss even one answer, you should do all the rest of the questions. Then move on to the proofreading and sentence composing exercises so that your understanding carries over into your writing.

Learning the basics of word choice and spelling, sentence structure, and punctuation does take time. Generally, college students must study a couple of hours outside of class for each hour in class. You may need to study more. Undoubtedly, the more time you spend, the more your writing will improve.

PART 1

Word Choice and Spelling

Anyone can learn to use words more effectively and become a better speller. You can eliminate most of your word choice and spelling errors if you want to. It's just a matter of deciding you're going to do it. If you really intend to improve your word choice and spelling, study each of the following nine sections until you make no mistakes in the exercises.

- Your Own List of Misspelled Words
- Words Often Confused (Sets 1 and 2)
- The Eight Parts of Speech
- Adjectives and Adverbs
- Contractions
- Possessives
- Words That Can Be Broken into Parts
- Rule for Doubling a Final Letter
- Using a Dictionary

Your Own List of Misspelled Words

On the inside cover of your English notebook or in some other obvious place, write correctly all the misspelled words from your previously graded papers. Review the correct spellings until you're sure of them, and edit your papers to find and correct repeated errors.

Words Often Confused (Set 1)

Learning the differences between these often-confused words will help you overcome many of your spelling problems. Study the words carefully, with their examples, before trying the exercises.

a, an

Use *an* before a word that begins with a vowel *sound* (*a, e, i,* and *o,* plus *u* when it sounds like *uh*) or silent *h*. Note that it's not the letter but the *sound* of the letter that matters.

an apple, *an* essay, *an* inch, *an* onion

an umpire, *an* ugly design (The *u*'s sound like *uh*.)

an hour, *an* honest person (The *h*'s are silent.)

Use *a* before a word that begins with a consonant sound (all the sounds except the vowels, plus *u* or *eu* when they sound like *you*).

a chart, *a* pie, *a* history book (The *h* is not silent in *history*.)

a union, *a* uniform, *a* unit (The *u*'s sound like *you*.)

a European vacation, *a* euphemism (*Eu* sounds like *you*.)

accept, except

Accept means "to receive willingly."

I *accept* your apology.

Except means "excluding" or "but."

Everyone arrived on time *except* him.

advise, advice

Advise is a verb. (Pronounce the *s* like a *z*.)

I *advise* you to take your time finding the right job.

Advice is a noun. (It rhymes with *rice*.)

My counselor gave me good *advice*.

affect, effect

Affect is a verb and means "to alter or influence."

All quizzes will *affect* the final grade.

The happy ending *affected* the mood of the audience.

Effect is most commonly used as a noun and means "a result." If *a, an,* or *the* is in front of the word, then you'll know it isn't a verb and will use *effect*.

The strong coffee had a powerful *effect* on me.

We studied the *effects* of sleep deprivation in my psychology class.

all ready, already If you can leave out the *all* and the sentence still makes sense, then *all ready* is the form to use.

We're *all ready* for our trip. (*We're ready for our trip* makes sense.)

The banquet is *all ready.* (*The banquet is ready* makes sense.)

But if you can't leave out the *all* and still have a sentence that makes sense, then use *already* (the form in which the *al* has to stay in the word).

They've *already* eaten. (*They've ready eaten* doesn't make sense.)

We have seen that movie *already.*

are, our *Are* is a verb.

We *are* going to Colorado Springs.

Our shows we possess something.

We painted *our* fence to match the house.

brake, break *Brake* used as a verb means "to slow or stop motion." It's also the name of the device that slows or stops motion.

I had to *brake* quickly to avoid an accident.

Luckily I just had my *brakes* fixed.

Break used as a verb means "to shatter" or "to split." It's also the name of an interruption, as in "a coffee break."

She never thought she would *break* a world record.

Enjoy your spring *break.*

choose, chose The difference here is one of time. Use *choose* for present and future; use *chose* for past.

I will *choose* a new major this semester.

We *chose* the wrong time of year to get married.

clothes, cloths *Clothes* are something you wear; *cloths* are pieces of material you might clean or polish something with.

I love the *clothes* that characters wear in movies.

The car wash workers use special *cloths* to dry the cars.

coarse, course *Coarse* describes a rough texture.

I used *coarse* sandpaper to smooth the surface of the board.

Course is used for all other meanings.

Of *course* we saw the golf *course* when we went to Pebble Beach.

complement, compliment The one spelled with an *e* means to complete something or bring it to perfection.

Use a color wheel to find a *complement* for purple.

Juliet's personality *complements* Romeo's: she is practical, and he is a dreamer.

The one spelled with an *i* has to do with praise. Remember "*I* like compliments," and you'll remember to use the *i* spelling when you mean praise.

My evaluation included a really nice *compliment* from my coworkers.

We *complimented* them on their new home.

conscious, conscience *Conscious* means "aware."

They weren't *conscious* of any problems before the accident.

Conscience means that inner voice of right and wrong. The extra *n* in *conscience* should remind you of *No,* which is what your conscience often says to you.

My *conscience* told me not to keep the expensive watch I found.

dessert, desert *Dessert* is the sweet one, the one people like two helpings of. So give it two helpings of *s.*

We had a whole chocolate cheesecake for *dessert.*

The other one, *desert,* is used for all other meanings and has two pronunciations.

I promise that I won't *desert* you at the party.

The snake slithered slowly across the *desert.*

do, due

Do is a verb, an action. You *do* something.

I always *do* my best work at night.

But a payment or an assignment is *due;* it is scheduled for a certain time.

Our first essay is *due* tomorrow.

Due can also be used before *to* in a phrase that means *because of.*

The outdoor concert was canceled *due to* rain.

feel, fill

Feel describes *feel*ings.

Whenever I stay up late, I *feel* sleepy in class.

Fill is the action of pouring into or packing a container fully.

Why did he *fill* the pitcher to the top?

fourth, forth

The word *fourth* has *four* in it. (But note that *forty* does not. Remember the word *forty-fourth.*)

This is our *fourth* quiz in two weeks.

My grandparents celebrated their *forty-fourth* anniversary.

If you don't mean a number, use *forth.*

We wrote back and *forth* many times during my trip.

have, of

Have is a verb. Sometimes, in a contraction, it sounds like *of.* When you say *could've,* the *have* may sound like *of,* but it is not written that way. Always write *could have, would have, should have, might have.*

We should *have* planned our vacation sooner.

Then we could *have* used our coupon for a free one-way ticket.

Use *of* only in a prepositional phrase. (See p. 67).

She sent me a box *of* chocolates for my birthday.

hear, here

The last three letters of *hear* spell "ear." You *hear* with your ear.

When I listen to a sea shell, I *hear* ocean sounds.

The other spelling *here* tells "where." Note that the three words indicating a place or pointing out something all have *here* in them: *here, there, where.*

I'll be *here* for three more weeks.

it's, its *It's* is a contraction and means "it is" or "it has."

It's hot. (*It is* hot.)

It's been hot all week. (*It has* been hot all week.)

Its is a possessive. (Words such as *its, yours, hers, ours, theirs,* and *whose* are already possessive forms and never need an apostrophe. See p. 43.)

The jury had made *its* decision.

The dog pulled at *its* leash.

knew, new *Knew* has to do with knowledge. Both start with *k.*

New means "not old."

Her friends *knew* that she wanted a *new* bike.

know, no *Know* has to do with knowledge. Both start with *k.*

By Friday, I must *know* all the state capitals.

No means "not any" or the opposite of "yes."

My boss has *no* patience. *No,* I am not exaggerating.

EXERCISES

Circle the correct words in parentheses. Don't guess! If you aren't sure, turn back to the explanatory pages. When you've finished ten sentences, compare your answers with those at the back of the book. Correct each set of ten sentences before continuing so you'll catch your mistakes early.

Exercise 1

1. Soon we may have a (knew, new) way to buy books.
2. (It's, Its) all (do, due) to a device called the Espresso Book Machine.
3. A customer can (choose, chose) a title from (a, an) online list and send the data to the "Espresso" machine.
4. This machine is capable of printing (a, an) 300-page book in only three minutes; it reproduces (it's, its) pages and binds them in a paper cover.

5. One bookstore in Washington, D.C., (all ready, already) has this unique kind of Espresso machine.
6. Libraries could use these instant printers to (complement, compliment) the books in their regular holdings.
7. People might (choose, chose) to print books that have been translated into different languages or ones that have gone out of print.
8. (It's, Its) hard to (know, no) whether customers will (accept, except) the idea of instant books.
9. Once they (hear, here) about the Espresso Book Machine, many people will probably want to try it.
10. The cost of printing (a, an) instant book is reasonable, too; (it's, its) about one penny a page.

Source: Newsweek, July 31, 2006

Exercise 2

1. (It's, Its) never too late to learn something (knew, new).
2. After living for nearly one hundred years without knowing how to read or write, George Dawson could (have, of) just (accepted, excepted) his life as it was.
3. But he never did (feel, fill) good about hiding his illiteracy from his children or signing his name with (a, an) X.
4. In 1996, George Dawson (choose, chose) to start school for the first time at the age of ninety-eight.
5. Dawson, who was (all ready, already) in his teens when the *Titanic* sank, worked all of his life to support his family and even outlived his (fourth, forth) wife.
6. He had enough memories to (feel, fill) a book, (accept, except) he wouldn't (have, of) been able to read it.
7. When a man in Seattle came to (hear, here) of Dawson's long life and strong desire for (a, an) education, he gave Dawson some (advise, advice).
8. Richard Glaubman, a teacher himself, suggested that Dawson share his experiences in a book; they (are, our) now coauthors of Dawson's autobiography.

9. In the (coarse, course) of his life as an African-American man and the grandson of slaves, Dawson witnessed and felt the (affects, effects) of racism and oppression.

10. But Dawson always believed that the joyful moments in life more than (complemented, complimented) the painful ones, and he titled his book *Life Is So Good.*

Source: Jet, April 17, 2000

Exercise 3

1. If you wear any (clothes, cloths) made of polyester, you may be wearing what used to be (a, an) old movie print.

2. (Do, Due) to the huge numbers of reels of film needed to meet the demands of today's movie audiences, recycling is (a, an) necessary part of the motion picture industry.

3. Companies such as Warner Bros. and New Line Cinema (accept, except) the responsibility for film recycling.

4. Of (coarse, course), the best prints of movies are saved for the future, but there (are, our) usually thousands of leftover copies (all ready, already) to be turned into something else.

5. The recycling process begins by chopping the film into (course, coarse) pieces, then transforming the rubble into a (knew, new) substance, such as polyester fabric.

6. Movie distributors are (conscious, conscience) that collectors and other interested parties would love to get their hands on these extra movie prints.

7. Therefore, security is (a, an) essential part of the movie-recycling process.

8. Someone trying to (brake, break) into a warehouse in search of last month's hottest release would (feel, fill) very disappointed.

9. The five to six reels of each film would (have, of) (all ready, already) been separated and mixed together with other films' reels.

10. (It's, Its) (know, no) surprise that movie companies want to protect their interests.

Source: Los Angeles Times, February 17, 2003

Exercise 4

1. I've been out of high school for two years, and I (all ready, already) miss it.
2. While I was still in high school, my parents bought my (clothes, cloths) and took care of all my necessities.
3. When my car needed to have (it's, its) (brakes, breaks) fixed, they paid the repair bills.
4. Every time I had to (choose, chose) a new elective or a summer activity, my family gave me the best (advise, advice).
5. One summer, I spent a spectacular week in the (dessert, desert) with my school's geology club.
6. That firsthand experience with nature strongly (affected, effected) me, especially the sight of the brilliant blue sky and the feeling of the (coarse, course), rocky sand.
7. Now that I am (hear, here) at college, I am (conscious, conscience) of a change in my parents' attitude.
8. (It's, Its) as if they (feel, fill) that (are, our) lives should grow apart.
9. I didn't (know, no) that this change was coming, or I would (have, of) tried to prepare myself for it.
10. Now I go back and (fourth, forth) between wishing for the past and trying to (accept, except) the future.

Exercise 5

1. Dentists (are, our) hardworking professionals, but most of us don't want to visit them.
2. Almost all of us hate to have (are, our) teeth drilled.
3. Most of us do, however, (accept, except) the need for dental work as a part of modern life.
4. (It's, Its) surprising to learn that dentists used drills on their patients 9,000 years ago.
5. (Knew, New) scientific discoveries have brought (fourth, forth) the remains of nomads who lived in the Stone Age.

6. Amazingly, many of their teeth revealed the (affects, effects) of drilling to eliminate decay.
7. Scientists don't (know, no) exactly what substance was used to (feel, fill) the cavities.
8. (It's, Its) also unclear whether patients were given anything so that they didn't (feel, fill) pain.
9. Based on the drilling patterns, scientists believe that some Stone Age people took advantage of the holes in their teeth for a decorative (affect, effect).
10. They may have used precious stones to (feel, fill) these holes as (a, an) ancient form of "mouth bling."

Source: National Geographic News, April 4, 2006

PROOFREADING EXERCISE

Find and correct the ten errors contained in the following student paragraph. All of the errors involve Words Often Confused (Set 1).

In the middle of a debate in my speech class last week, I suddenly became very self-conscience. My heart started beating faster, and I didn't no what to due. I looked around to see if my show of nerves was having a affect on the audience. Of coarse, they could here my voice trembling. The topic that we were debating involved whether it would be best to eliminate letter grades in college, and everyone else was doing so well. But for some reason, my face turned red, and I would of left the room if the door had been closer. After the debate, my classmates tried to give me complements, but I new that they were just trying to make me feel better.

SENTENCE WRITING

The surest way to learn these Words Often Confused is to use them immediately in your own writing. Choose the five pairs or groups of words that you most often confuse from Set 1. Then use each of them correctly in a new sentence. No answers are provided at the back of the book, but you can see if you are using the words correctly by comparing your sentences to the examples in the explanations. Use your own paper, and keep all of your sentence writing results in a folder.

Words Often Confused (Set 2)

Study this second set of words carefully, with their examples, before attempting the exercises. Knowing all of the word groups in these two sets will take care of many of your spelling problems.

lead, led

Lead is the metal that rhymes with *head.*

Old paint is dangerous because it often contains *lead.*

The past form of the verb "to lead" is *led.*

What factors *led* to your decision?

I *led* our school's debating team to victory last year.

If you don't mean past time, use *lead,* which rhymes with *bead.*

I will *lead* the debating team again this year.

loose, lose

Loose means "not tight." Note how *l o o s e* that word is. It has plenty of room for two *o*'s.

My dog has a *loose* tooth.

Lose is the opposite of win.

If we *lose* this game, we will be out for the season.

passed, past

The past form of the verb "to pass" is *passed.*

She easily *passed* her math class.

The runner *passed* the baton to her teammate.

I *passed* your house on my way to the store.

Use *past* when it's not a verb.

I drove *past* your house. (Meaning "I drove *by* your house.")

I try to learn from *past* experiences.

In the *past,* he worked for a small company.

personal, personnel

Pronounce these two correctly, and you won't confuse them—*pérsonal, personnél.*

She shared her *personal* views as a parent.

Personnel means "a group of employees."

I had an appointment in the *personnel* office.

piece, peace Remember "piece of pie." The one meaning "a *piece* of something" always begins with *pie.*

Some children asked for an extra *piece* of candy.

The other one, *peace,* is the opposite of war.

The two sides finally signed a *peace* treaty.

principal, principle *Principal* means "main." Both words have *a* in them: princip*a*l, m*a*in.

The *principal* concern is safety. (main concern)

We paid both *principal* and interest. (main amount of money)

Also, think of a school's "princi*pal*" as your "*pal.*"

An elementary school *principal* must be kind. (main administrator)

A *principle* is a "rule." Both words end in *le*: princip*le*, ru*le.*

I am proud of my *principles.* (rules of conduct)

We value the *principle* of truth in advertising. (rule)

quiet, quite Pronounce these two correctly, and you won't confuse them. *Quiet* means "free from noise" and rhymes with *diet.*

Tennis players need *quiet* in order to concentrate.

Quite means "very" and rhymes with *bite.*

It was *quite* hot in the auditorium.

right, write *Right* means "correct" or "proper."

You will find your keys if you look in the *right* place.

It also means in the exact location, position, or moment.

Your keys are *right* where you left them.

Let's go *right* now.

Write means to compose sentences, poems, essays, and so forth.

I asked my teacher to *write* a letter of recommendation for me.

than, then *Than* compares two things.

I am taller *than* my sister.

Then tells when. (*Then* and *when* rhyme, and both have *e* in them.)

I always write a rough draft of a paper first; *then* I revise it.

their, there, they're

Their is a possessive, meaning belonging to them.

Their cars have always been red.

There points out something. (Remember that the three words indicating a place or pointing out something all have *here* in them: *here, there, where.*)

I know that I haven't been *there* before.

There was a rainbow in the sky.

They're is a contraction and means "they are."

They're living in Canada now. (*They are* living in Canada now.)

threw, through

Threw is the past form of "to throw."

We *threw* snowballs at each other.

I *threw* away my application for a scholarship.

If you don't mean "to throw something," use *through.*

We could see our beautiful view *through* the new curtains.

They worked *through* their differences.

two, too, to

Two is a number.

We have written *two* papers so far in my English class.

Too means "extra" or "also," and so it has an extra *o.*

The movie was *too* long and *too* violent. (extra)

They are enrolled in that biology class, *too.* (also)

Use *to* for all other meanings.

They like *to* ski. They're going *to* the mountains.

weather, whether

Weather refers to conditions of the atmosphere.

Snowy *weather* is too cold for me.

Whether means "if."

I don't know *whether* it is snowing there or not.

Whether I travel with you or not depends on the weather.

were, wear, where These words are pronounced differently but are often confused in writing.

Were is the past form of the verb "to be."

We *were* interns at the time.

Wear means to have on, as in wearing clothes.

I always *wear* a scarf in winter.

Where refers to a place. (Remember that the three words indicating a place or pointing out something all have *here* in them: *here, there, where.*)

Where is the mailbox? There it is.

Where are the closing papers? Here they are.

who's, whose *Who's* is a contraction and means "who is" or "who has."

Who's responsible for signing the checks? (*Who is* responsible?)

Who's been reading my journal? (*Who has* been reading my journal?)

Whose is a possessive. (Words such as *whose, its, yours, hers, ours,* and *theirs* are already possessive forms and never need an apostrophe. See p. 43.)

Whose keys are these?

woman, women The difference here is one of number: wo*man* refers to one adult female; wo*men* refers to two or more adult females.

I know a *woman* who has bowled a perfect game.

I bowl with a group of *women* from my work.

you're, your *You're* is a contraction and means "you are."

You're as smart as I am. (*You are* as smart as I am.)

Your is a possessive meaning belonging to you.

I borrowed *your* lab book.

EXERCISES

Circle the correct words in parentheses. When you've finished ten sentences, compare your answers with those at the back of the book. Do only ten sentences at a time so that you will catch your mistakes early.

Exercise 1

1. (Their, There, They're) is a new way to prepare children for earthquakes.
2. Researchers use current technology to put kids (threw, through) a simulated earthquake using virtual reality headphones and goggles.
3. Children in Greece have been the first (two, too, to) receive the training.
4. (Their, There, They're) very likely to experience a real earthquake, according to scientists.
5. The (personal, personnel) who teach students with special needs have seen very positive results from earthquake training.
6. In the (passed, past), children with Down syndrome, for example, would (loose, lose) control and panic during a frightening event such as an earthquake.
7. In a twist of fate, (their, there, they're) was an earthquake in Greece just a few months after some children were trained.
8. After being (lead, led) (through, threw) an artificial quake using virtual reality, the children with Down syndrome (were, wear, where) able to remain calm and follow directions.
9. In fact, all of the children who had experienced a virtual earthquake coped with the event better (than, then) those who hadn't.
10. It's unclear (weather, whether) virtual earthquake training will work as well with adults.

Source: Science News, August 5, 2006

Exercise 2

1. As a student on financial aid, I was advised to work on campus or (loose, lose) some of my benefits.
2. At first I didn't know (were, wear, where) to work.

3. It definitely needed to be a (quiet, quite) place so that I could study or (right, write) a paper in my free time.
4. I finally chose to take a job in the (personal, personnel) office.
5. Now that I have been working (their, there, they're) for (two, too, to) months, I know that I made the (right, write) decision.
6. My (principal, principle) duties include filing documents and stuffing envelopes.
7. However, when the receptionist takes a break, I am the one (who's, whose) at the front desk.
8. Once I was sitting up front when the (principal, principle) of my old high school came in to apply for a job at the college.
9. I didn't know (weather, whether) to show that I recognized her or to keep (quiet, quite) about the (passed, past).
10. As a student, I like working on campus for financial-aid benefits better (than, then) working off campus for a tiny paycheck.

Exercise 3

1. (You're, Your) not alone if you don't know (were, wear, where) to shop for pants anymore.
2. (Weather, Whether) (you're, your) a man or a (woman, women), it isn't easy to decide on the best pants to (were, wear, where).
3. The styles are often (two, too, to) (loose, lose) or (two, too, to) tight.
4. (Their, There, They're) never (quiet, quite) (right, write).
5. Anyone (who's, whose) tried to find the perfect pair of jeans, for instance, knows that the fabric is often more important (than, then) the fit.
6. Fabric choice can be a matter of (personal, personnel) taste.
7. You like (you're, your) jeans to be either light or dark, or (you're, your) the kind of person (who's, whose) able to (were, wear, where) both.
8. I have (passed, past) whole rows of dark-colored jeans on my quest for a lighter pair with just the (right, write) amount of fading.

9. I have a friend (who's, whose) wardrobe consists of nothing but vintage jeans and T-shirts.
10. She's a (woman, women) who dresses the same way in every kind of (weather, whether) and for every occasion.

Exercise 4

1. Recently, several countries have produced life-size androids that are (quiet, quite) remarkable.
2. (Their, There, They're) are (two, too, to) that look exactly like real (woman, women).
3. The (principal, principle) reason for creating these two robots has been to get as close to real human expressions as possible.
4. Both androids are in permanent seated positions, and (their, there, they're) unable to move (their, there, they're) lower bodies.
5. Scientists at Osaka University first introduced Repliee Q1, (who's, whose) life-like appearance and actions amazed visitors to the 2005 World Expo in Japan.
6. Q1 looks like a real human being and uses her head and upper body (two, too, to) react as a real (woman, women) would.
7. Q1 speaks, appears to breathe, and uses her arms to block the impact of objects headed (right, write) at her.
8. South Korean scientists have created a similar female android called EveR-1, (who's, whose) got longer hair (than, then) Q1.
9. EveR-1 speaks, (two, too, to), and can use 400 words in conversation.
10. EveR-1 can make eye contact and can change her expression from happy (two, too, to) sad or mad due (two, too, to) fifteen motors hidden beneath her "skin."

Source: National Geographic News, June 6, 2005

Exercise 5

1. One beautiful morning, you may receive a phone call that changes (you're, your) life.

2. The caller will tell you that (you're, your) half a million dollars richer and that you don't have to do anything other (than, then) be yourself to deserve the money.

3. You might wonder (weather, whether) it is a real or a crank call.

4. Believe it or not, this wonderful (piece, peace) of news is delivered to between twenty and thirty special men and (woman, women) in America every year.

5. (Their, There, They're) unofficially called the "Genius Awards," but (their, there, they're) real title is the MacArthur Fellowships.

6. The MacArthur Foundation awards its fellowships each year based on the (principal, principle) that forward-thinking people deserve an opportunity to pursue their ideas freely and without obligation to anyone.

7. No application is necessary (two, too, to) receive the gift of $100,000 a year plus health insurance for five years, and no particular field of work receives more consideration (than, then) another.

8. The (principal, principle) characteristic that MacArthur Fellows share is (their, there, they're) creative potential—in any area.

9. Each year, the MacArthur Foundation sends about one hundred "scouts" across the country looking for people with untapped potential (two, too, to) nominate; (than, then) another anonymous group selects the year's recipients.

10. The nominees don't even know that (their, there, they're) going (threw, through) the process until the phone rings on that fateful morning one day.

PROOFREADING EXERCISE

See if you can correct the ten errors in this student paragraph. All errors involve Words Often Confused (Set 2).

Sometimes it's hard to find the write place to study on campus. The library used too be the principle location for students to do they're difficult course work, weather it was preparing research papers or writing critical essays. But now, most library resources are available online, two. This change has lead students to use campus computer labs and cafés as study halls. There, students can go online, get up-to-date sources, write their reports, and have peace and quite without the stuffy atmosphere of the library. The only problem with doing research online is that it's easier to loose a piece of information on the computer then it is to lose a hard copy in the library.

SENTENCE WRITING

Write several sentences using any words you missed in the exercises for Words Often Confused (Set 2).

Sentence writing is a good idea not only because it will help you remember these Words Often Confused, but also because it will be a storehouse for ideas you can later use in writing papers. Here are some topics you might consider writing your sentences about:

- Something you would like to accomplish this year
- Qualities of a good friend
- All-time favorite songs or movies
- Places you would like to know more about
- Reasons why you're in school

Use your own paper, and keep all of your sentence writing results in a folder.

The Eight Parts of Speech

Choosing the right word is an important aspect of writing. Some words sound alike but are spelled differently and have different meanings (*past* and *passed,* for instance), and some words are spelled the same but sound different and mean different things (*lead,* for the action of "leading," and *lead,* for the stuff inside pencils).

One way to choose words more carefully is to understand the roles that words play in sentences. Just as one actor can play many different parts in movies (a hero, a villain, a humorous sidekick), single words can play different parts in sentences (a noun, a verb, an adjective). These are called the *eight parts of speech,* briefly defined with examples below.

1. **Nouns** name some*one, thing, place,* or *idea* and are used as subjects and objects in sentences. (See pp. 61, 67, and 135 for more about nouns as subjects and objects.)

   The **technician** installed the **computers** in the **lab.**

2. **Pronouns** are special words—such as *I, she, him, it, they,* and *us*—that replace nouns to avoid repeating them. (See p. 153 for more about pronouns.)

   She (the technician) installed **them** (the computers) in **it** (the lab).

3. **Adjectives** add description to nouns and pronouns—telling *which one, how many, what kind, color,* or *shape* they are. (See p. 28 for more about adjectives.)

   The **best** technician installed **thirty new** computers in the **writing** lab.

   The words *a, an,* and *the* are special forms of adjectives called **articles.** They always point to a noun or a pronoun. They are used so often that there is no need to label them.

4. **Verbs** show action or state of being. (See p. 61 for more about verbs.)

   The technician **installed** the new computers in the writing lab; Terri **is** the technician's name.

5. **Adverbs** add information—such as *when, where, why,* or *how*—to verbs, adjectives, and other adverbs. (See p. 29 for more about adverbs.)

   Yesterday, Terri **quickly** installed the **brand** new computers in the writing lab.

6. **Prepositions** show position in *space* and *time* and are followed by noun objects to form prepositional phrases. (See p. 67 for more about prepositions.)

   The computers arrived **in** the writing lab **at** noon.

7. **Conjunctions** are connecting words—such as *and, but,* and *or*—and words that begin dependent clauses—such as *because, since, when, while,* and *although.* (See p. 73 and p. 87 for more about conjunctions.)

   Students still visited the lab **and** the media center **while** Terri installed the computers.

8. **Interjections** interrupt a sentence to show surprise or other emotions and are rarely used in Standard Written English.

   Wow, Terri is a valuable employee.

To find out what parts of speech an individual word can play, look it up in a good dictionary. (See p. 53.) A list of definitions beginning with an abbreviated part of speech (*n, adj, prep,* and so on) will catalog its uses. However, seeing how a word is used in a particular sentence is the best way to identify its part of speech. Look at these examples:

> Our **train** arrived at exactly three o'clock.
>
> (*Train* is a noun in this sentence, naming the vehicle we call a "train.")
>
> Sammy and Helen **train** dolphins at Sea World.
>
> (*Train* is a verb in this example, expressing the action of teaching skills we call "training.")
>
> Doug's parents drove him to the **train** station.
>
> (*Train* is acting as an adjective here, adding description to the noun "station," telling what *kind* of station it is.)

All of the words in a sentence work together to create meaning, but each one serves its own purpose by playing a part of speech. Think about how each of the words in the following sentence plays the particular part of speech labeled:

> n prep adj n adv v adj n prep n conj v
> Students at community colleges often attend several classes in a day and are
>
> adv adj conj pro adv v adv
> very tired when they finally go home.

Below, you'll find an explanation for each label:

Students	n (*names the people* who are the subject of the sentence)
at	prep (*begins a prepositional phrase* showing position in space)
community	adj (*adds description* to the noun *colleges,* telling what kind)
colleges	n (*names the place* that is the object of the preposition *at*)
often	adv (*adds to the verb,* telling when students attend classes)
attend	v (*shows an action,* telling what the students do)

several adj (*adds description* to the noun *classes,* telling how many)

classes n (*names the things* that the students *attend*)

in prep (*begins a prepositional phrase* showing position in time)

a no label (an article that *points to the noun day*)

day n (*names the thing* that is the object of the preposition *in*)

and conj (*joins* the two verbs *attend* and *are*)

are v (*shows a state of being,* linking the subject *students* with the descriptive word *tired*)

very adv (*adds to the adjective tired,* telling how tired the students are)

tired adj (*describes the noun* subject *students*)

when conj (*begins a dependent clause*)

they pro (*replaces* the word *students* as a new subject to avoid repetition)

finally adv (*adds to the verb,* telling when they *go* home)

go v (*shows an action,* telling what they do)

home. adv (*adds to the verb,* telling where they *go*)

Familiarizing yourself with the parts of speech will help you spell better now and understand phrases and clauses better later. Each of the eight parts of speech has characteristics that distinguish it from the other seven, but it takes practice to learn them.

EXERCISES

Label the parts of speech above all of the words in the following sentences using the abbreviations **n, pro, adj, v, adv, prep, conj,** and **interj.** For clarity's sake, the sentences here are very brief, and you may ignore the words *a, an,* and *the.*

Refer back to the definitions and examples of the parts of speech whenever necessary. When in doubt, leave a word unmarked until you check the answers at the back of the book after each set of ten sentences.

Exercise 1

1. Good movies entertain people.
2. They also educate and motivate people.
3. Well-written characters seem real on the screen.
4. Their downfalls or successes have lasting effects on the audience.
5. A person sees a movie with a wild character in it.
6. She or he learns about wildness.
7. Often, the story revolves around a secret.
8. Someone discovers the secret and reveals it in the end.
9. The story usually moves ahead when the main character changes.
10. Such changes are not always positive.

Exercise 2

1. Clyde Tombaugh discovered the ninth "planet," Pluto, in 1930.
2. Tombaugh died in 1997 at the age of 90.
3. Scientists loaded Tombaugh's ashes onto New Horizons, a space probe that was launched in January of 2006.
4. New Horizons will arrive near Pluto in 2015.
5. After the launch of New Horizons, astronomers deleted Pluto from the list of real planets.
6. They determined that real planets must control their own orbits.
7. Pluto is an icy ball under the influence of Neptune's orbit.
8. Astronomers put Pluto into a new category.
9. Therefore, the official number of planets has changed.
10. Wow! That is an amazing development.

Source: Newsweek, September 4, 2006

Exercise 3

1. Mechanical pencils are delicate instruments.
2. I see other students with them.
3. Then I buy one.
4. I open the package.
5. I load the pencil with the tiny shaft of lead.
6. As I put the pencil tip down on the paper, the lead snaps off.
7. Am I an unrefined clod?
8. I believe that I am.
9. Now I know my limitations.
10. Ballpoint pens and wooden pencils are the only writing tools for me.

Exercise 4

1. The following old sayings still have meaning today.
2. A penny saved is a penny earned.
3. A stitch in time saves nine.
4. Haste makes waste.
5. Love me, love my dog.
6. A picture is worth a thousand words.
7. He or she who hesitates is lost.
8. Time flies when you are having fun.
9. The grass is always greener on the other side of the fence.
10. The truth of many old sayings lies beneath their surfaces.

Exercise 5

1. Some people collect rare coins and paper money.
2. The Del Monte twenty-dollar bill is very famous.
3. The mint made a mistake when it printed this bill.

4. A sticker from a banana accidentally attached itself to the paper during the printing process.
5. The round green and red sticker became a part of the bill.
6. Such mistakes usually lead to a bill's destruction.
7. This flawed note, however, left the mint with the normal twenties.
8. Experts immediately authenticated its rare status.
9. The bill first sold on eBay for $10,000.
10. Eventually, a couple from Texas paid $25,000 for this one-of-a-kind note.

Source: www.delmontenote.com, and *USA Today,* January 6, 2006

PARAGRAPH EXERCISE

Here is a challenging little exercise. Read the following excerpt from a book called *American Yesterday,* by Eric Sloane. This paragraph, which comes from the chapter "Grandfather's Town," discusses some memorable street names that we still recognize. Label the parts of speech above as many of the words as you can before checking your answers at the back of the book. Remember that proper nouns (those that name particular people and places) are capitalized and can include more than one word.

Some of the richest American street names live only in people's minds. They are permanent because they are not on the map and therefore cannot be stricken from it. Hell's Kitchen, Back Bay, The Gas House District, The Loop, Harlem, Chinatown, and thousands of others will live on long after the place has changed character entirely. Like the great men of the past, their names remain long after all else has vanished.

SENTENCE WRITING

Write ten sentences imitating those in Exercises 1–5. Keep your sentences short (under 10 words each), and avoid using "to ______" forms of verbs. Label the parts of speech above the words in your imitation sentences. Use your own paper, and keep all of your sentence writing results in a folder.

Adjectives and Adverbs

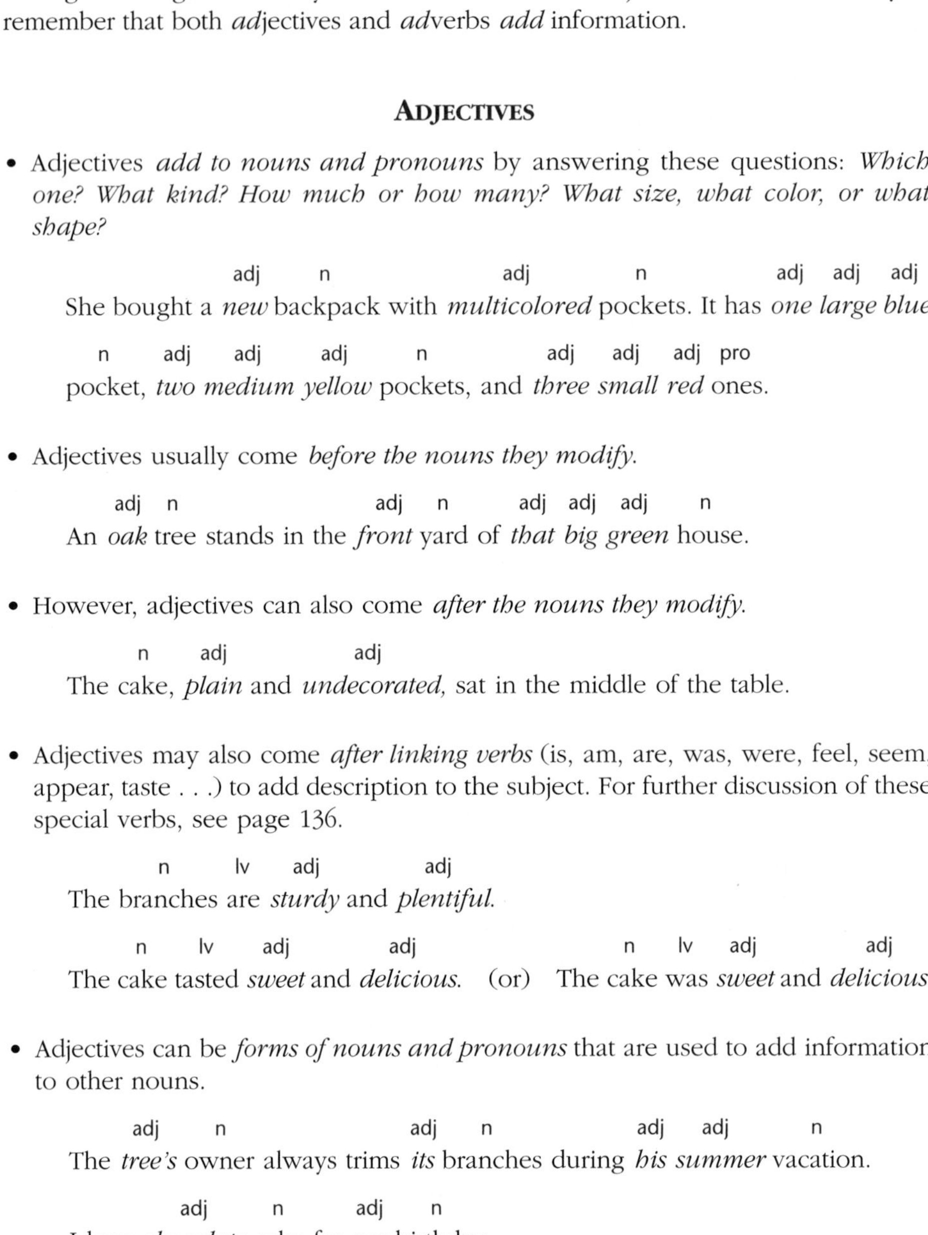

Two of the eight parts of speech, adjectives and adverbs, are used to *add* information to other words. "To modify" means to change or improve something, usually by adding to it. English has only two kinds of modifiers: adjectives and adverbs. Try to remember that both *ad*jectives and *ad*verbs *add* information.

ADJECTIVES

- Adjectives *add to nouns and pronouns* by answering these questions: *Which one? What kind? How much or how many? What size, what color, or what shape?*

  adj n adj n adj adj adj
  She bought a *new* backpack with *multicolored* pockets. It has *one large blue*

  n adj adj adj n adj adj adj pro
  pocket, *two medium yellow* pockets, and *three small red* ones.

- Adjectives usually come *before the nouns they modify.*

  adj n adj n adj adj adj n
  An *oak* tree stands in the *front* yard of *that big green* house.

- However, adjectives can also come *after the nouns they modify.*

  n adj adj
  The cake, *plain* and *undecorated,* sat in the middle of the table.

- Adjectives may also come *after linking verbs* (is, am, are, was, were, feel, seem, appear, taste . . .) to add description to the subject. For further discussion of these special verbs, see page 136.

  n lv adj adj
  The branches are *sturdy* and *plentiful.*

  n lv adj adj n lv adj adj
  The cake tasted *sweet* and *delicious.* (or) The cake was *sweet* and *delicious.*

- Adjectives can be *forms of nouns and pronouns* that are used to add information to other nouns.

  adj n adj n adj adj n
  The *tree's* owner always trims *its* branches during *his summer* vacation.

  adj n adj n
  I love *chocolate* cake for *my* birthday.

ADVERBS

- Adverbs *add to verbs, adjectives, and other adverbs* by answering these questions: *How? In what way? When? Where? Why?*

  adv v adv v
  I *quickly* called my sister, who *sleepily* answered her cell phone.

  v adv v
  She did *not* recognize my voice at first.

  adv adj n
  He wore his *light* blue shirt to the party.

  adv adj n
  It was an *extremely* tall tree.

  adv adj adv adj
  Its branches were *very* sturdy and *quite* plentiful.

  adv adv adv
  People *often* drive *really fast* in the rain.

- Unlike adjectives, some adverbs can move around in sentences without changing the meaning.

  adv
  Now I have enough money for a vacation.

  adv
  I *now* have enough money for a vacation.

  adv
  I have enough money *now* for a vacation.

  adv
  I have enough money for a vacation *now*.

Notice that many—but not all—adverbs end in *ly*. Be aware, however, that adjectives can also end in *ly*. Remember that a word's part of speech is determined by how the word is used in a particular sentence. For instance, in the old saying "The early bird catches the worm," *early* adds to the noun, telling which bird. *Early* is acting as an adjective. However, in the sentence "The teacher arrived early," *early* adds to the verb, telling when the teacher arrived. *Early* is an adverb.

Now that you've read about adjectives and adverbs, try to identify the question that each modifier (adj or adv) answers in the following example. Refer back to the questions listed under Adjectives and Adverbs.

> adj n adj n adv adv v
> My family and I went to the farmer's market yesterday. We excitedly watched the
>
> adj adj n adv v adv adj
> decoration of a huge wedding cake. The baker skillfully squeezed out colorful

n adj n adv adj adj n adj adj
flowers, leaf patterns, and pale pink curving letters made of smooth, creamy

n
frosting.

> **NOTE**—Although we discuss only single-word adjectives and adverbs here, phrases and clauses can also function as adjectives and adverbs following the same patterns.

CHOOSING BETWEEN ADJECTIVES AND ADVERBS

Knowing how to choose between adjectives and adverbs is important, especially in certain kinds of sentences. See if you can make the correct choices in these three sentences:

We did (good, well) on that test.

I feel (bad, badly) about quitting my job.

She speaks (really clear/really clearly).

Did you choose *well, bad,* and *really clearly?* If you missed *bad,* you're not alone. You might have reasoned that *badly* adds to the verb *feel,* but *feel* is acting in a special way here—not naming the action of feeling with your fingertips (as in "I *feel* (v) the fabric *carefully* (adv)"), but describing the feeling of it (as in "The *fabric* (n) feels *smooth* (adj)"). To test your understanding of this concept, try substituting "I feel (happy, happily)" instead of "I feel (bad, badly)" and note how easy it is to choose.

Another way that adjectives and adverbs work is to compare two or more things by describing them in relation to one another. The *er* ending is added to both adjectives and adverbs when comparing two items, and the *est* ending is added when comparing three or more items.

adj n adj adj n adj adj n
The red pockets are *big*. The yellow pockets are *bigger*. The blue pocket is

adj pro
the *biggest* one of all.

v adv v adv v adv
She works *hard*. He works *harder*. I work *hardest*.

In some cases, such comparisons require the addition of a word (*more* or *most, less* or *least*) instead of a change in the ending from *er* to *est*. Longer adjectives and adverbs usually require these extra adverbs to help with comparisons.

adj adv adj adv adj
Food is *expensive.* Gas is *more expensive.* Rent is *most expensive.*

adv adv adv adv adv
You danced *gracefully.* They danced *less gracefully.* We danced *least gracefully.*

EXERCISES

Remember that adjectives add to nouns and pronouns, while adverbs add to verbs, adjectives, and other adverbs. Check your answers frequently.

Exercise 1

Identify whether each *italicized* word is used as an adjective or an adverb in the sentence.

1. We have *several* beautiful buildings on our campus. (adjective, adverb)
2. The library and the auditorium are *especially* pretty. (adjective, adverb)
3. Huge *carved* letters spell out Latin phrases over their doorways. (adjective, adverb)
4. These old buildings have such *thick* walls. (adjective, adverb)
5. Modern buildings are *usually* constructed of lighter materials. (adjective, adverb)
6. Gardeners take *special* pride in landscaping around old buildings. (adjective, adverb)
7. I like to sit in front of the library in the *early* afternoon. (adjective, adverb)
8. *Then* the shade from two huge trees falls over the courtyard. (adjective, adverb)
9. I am *very* happy whenever I sit in the shade. (adjective, adverb)
10. The library courtyard will *always* be my favorite spot on campus. (adjective, adverb)

Exercise 2

Identify whether the word *only* is used as an adjective or an adverb in the following sentences. In each sentence, try to link the word *only* with another word to figure out if *only* is an adjective (adding to a noun or pronoun) or an adverb (adding to a verb, adjective, or other adverb). Have fun with this exercise!

1. As soon as I arrive at school, I reach into my backpack and pull out my *only* textbook.
2. I have *only* one textbook this semester.
3. *Only* I have a new copy of the textbook for my biology class.
4. Some students buy *only* used textbooks, not new ones.
5. I buy *only* new textbooks.
6. I am not the *only* one who prefers a new book over a used one.
7. *Only* the students who use new textbooks understand.
8. My best friend buys *only* heavily marked books.
9. She spends *only* a fraction of what I spend.
10. She is the *only* one I know who trusts other students' notes more than her own.

Exercise 3

Choose the correct adjective or adverb form required to complete each sentence.

1. I have many (close, closely) friends who live in the area.
2. I've discovered that I am (close, closely) related to some important people in history.
3. During hard times, I feel (close, closely) to everyone in my family.
4. My aunt suffered (bad, badly) after her root canal.
5. She felt (bad, badly) about taking pain medication.
6. Her jaw hurt really (bad, badly) for the first two days.
7. Our landlord runs (very happy, very happily) around the park every evening.
8. We are always (very happy, very happily) to have the building to ourselves.
9. I received a (good, well) grade on my paper about fast food.
10. I worked (good, well) with my partner from class.

Exercise 4

Choose the correct adjective or adverb form required to complete each sentence.

1. Of all my friends' dogs, Josh's is (small, smaller, the smallest).
2. Diane has (a small, a smaller, the smallest) dog, too.
3. Her dog is (small, smaller, smallest) than mine.
4. Keith bought his phone last week, so it's (a new, a newer, the newest) one.
5. Mine has (new, newer, newest) features than Keith's, but I bought mine a month ago.
6. Jack's phone is (new, newer, newest) than Rohan's.
7. I want a car with (good, better, best) gas mileage than my old one.
8. Of course, tiny cars get (good, better, the best) gas mileage of all.
9. Rohan gets (good, better, best) gas mileage now that his car has new tires.
10. Gas mileage is (important, more important, most important) than it used to be.

Exercise 5

Label all of the adjectives (adj) and adverbs (adv) in the following sentences. Mark the ones you are sure of; then check your answers at the back of the book and find the ones you missed.

1. I took a very unusual acting class over the summer.
2. The title of the summer seminar was "Clowning and Physical Acting."
3. It was a special class for students majoring in theater arts.
4. We usually started with warm-up exercises.
5. Then we experimented with unique movements and crazy combinations.
6. Sometimes, we would combine "happy knees" with "curious elbows."
7. Next, we added costume elements, such as padded leggings or strange hats.
8. Some of us transformed into totally unrecognizable characters.
9. I was very happy with my progress as a clown.
10. We learned many valuable skills during our first clown seminar.

PROOFREADING EXERCISE

Correct the five errors in the use of adjectives and adverbs in the following student paragraph. Then try to label all of the adjectives (adj) and adverbs (adv) in the paragraph for practice.

I didn't do very good during my first semester at community college. I feel badly whenever I think of it. I skipped classes and turned in sloppy work. My counselor warned me about my negative attitude, but I was real stubborn. I dropped out for a year and a half. Now that I have come back to college, I am even stubborner than before. I go to every class and do my best. Now, a college degree is only my goal.

SENTENCE WRITING

Write a short paragraph (five to seven sentences) describing your favorite subject in grade school or high school. Then go back through the paragraph and label your single-word adjectives and adverbs. Use your own paper, and keep all of your sentence writing results in a folder.

Contractions

When two words are shortened into one, the result is called a *contraction:*

is not ········➤	isn't	you have ········➤	you've

The letter or letters that are left out are replaced with an apostrophe. For example, if the two words *do not* are shortened into one, an apostrophe is put where the second *o* is left out.

do not	don't

Note how the apostrophe goes in the exact place where the letter or letters are left out in these contractions:

I am	I'm
I have	I've
I shall, I will	I'll
I would	I'd
you are	you're
you have	you've
you will	you'll
she is, she has	she's
he is, he has	he's
it is, it has	it's
we are	we're
we have	we've
we will, we shall	we'll
they are	they're
they have	they've
are not	aren't
cannot	can't
do not	don't
does not	doesn't
have not	haven't

let us	let's
who is, who has	who's
where is	where's
were not	weren't
would not	wouldn't
could not	couldn't
should not	shouldn't
would have	would've
could have	could've
should have	should've
that is	that's
there is	there's
what is	what's

One contraction does not follow this rule: *will not* becomes *won't.*

In all other contractions that you're likely to use, the apostrophe goes exactly where the letter or letters are left out. Note especially that *it's, they're, who's,* and *you're* are contractions. Use them when you mean *two* words. (See p. 43 for more about the possessive forms—*its, their, whose,* and *your*—which *don't* need apostrophes.)

EXERCISES

Add the missing apostrophes to any contractions in the following sentences. Then compare your answers with those at the back of the book. Be sure to correct each exercise before going on to the next so you'll catch your mistakes early.

Exercise 1

1. I bet youve never heard of a "geep"; I hadnt either until I read about it in a library book.
2. The geep is an animal thats half goat and half sheep.
3. Its not one that occurs naturally.
4. But a number of geep were produced in the early 1980s.

5. Scientists created this strange beast by combining a goat's cells with a sheep's cells at their earliest stages of development.
6. What many people couldnt believe was that the resulting geep's cells still kept either their goat or sheep qualities intact.
7. Therefore, the geep had long straight goat hair on parts of its body and fluffy sheep's wool on other parts.
8. Theres a picture of a geep in the book that I read.
9. Its so weird to look at a goat's head surrounded by curled sheep horns.
10. Lets hope that scientists dont try to make a "cog" or a "dat" in the same way.

Source: Mysteries of Planet Earth (Carlton Books, 1999)

Exercise 2

1. "Music wasnt made to make us wise, but better natured." Josh Billings
2. "Give me a laundry list, and Ill set it to music." Rossini
3. "I know only two tunes. One of them is 'Yankee Doodle'—and the other one isnt." Ulysses S. Grant
4. "Its not me. Its the songs. Im just the postman. I deliver the songs." Bob Dylan
5. "If you think youve hit a false note, sing loud. When in doubt, sing loud." Robert Merrill
6. "I dont know anything about music. In my line, you dont have to." Elvis Presley
7. "If the king loves music, theres little wrong in the land." Mencius
8. "When you got to ask what jazz is, youll never get to know." Louis Armstrong
9. "I havent understood a bar of music in my life, but I have felt it." Igor Stravinsky
10. "There are more love songs than anything else. If songs could make you do something, wed all love one another." Frank Zappa

Source: Music: A Book of Quotations (Dover, 2001)

Exercise 3

1. Theres an old tongue twister thats getting a new twist these days.
2. "Fuzzy Wuzzy was a bear. Fuzzy Wuzzy had no hair. Fuzzy Wuzzy wasnt fuzzy, was he?"
3. Some black bears in Florida dont have any hair, and its not funny.
4. The bears' fur has been falling out, and it isnt growing back.
5. The hairless animals dont even look like bears anymore.
6. Without their hair, the bears arent as prepared for cold temperatures.
7. Theyre also prone to scratches on their skin, which is usually protected by fur.
8. Bear experts havent been able to find a cure for the bears' balding.
9. Theyve identified the problem as mange, a condition common to dogs.
10. But theyre not sure why some bears have it while others dont.

Source: National Geographic News, January 14, 2003

Exercise 4

1. The new bleachers in the gymnasium arent ready to be used yet.
2. Theyre made of unfinished wood that isnt smooth.
3. This weekend, were all meeting in the gym to paint on the varnish.
4. I hope it doesnt take long for the varnish to dry.
5. I dont know why the boards werent sealed before the bleachers were assembled.
6. Thats one question that nobodys asking.
7. If the planks dont dry in time, our fans wont get to watch our first game on Monday.
8. Of course, therell be more games in the future.
9. However, the first game of the season should be memorable, shouldnt it?
10. Lets hope its not memorable because no one gets to see it.

Exercise 5

1. This week, Im helping my sister with her research paper, and shes chosen chocolate as her topic.
2. Weve been surprised by some of the things weve discovered.
3. First, the cocoa beans arent very appetizing in their natural form.
4. They grow inside an odd-shaped, alien-looking pod, and theyre surrounded by white mushy pulp.
5. After cocoa beans have been removed from the pods, theyre dried, blended almost like coffee beans, and processed into the many types of chocolate foods available.
6. In fact, the Aztecs enjoyed chocolate as a heavily spiced hot drink that was more like coffee than the sweet, creamy chocolate thats popular today.
7. Weve also learned that white chocolate cant be called chocolate at all since it doesnt contain any cocoa solids, only cocoa butter.
8. With an interest in organic foods, wed assumed that organic chocolate would be better than conventional chocolate.
9. But thats not true either because its got to be grown on pesticide-free trees, and theyre the strongest but not the tastiest sources of chocolate.
10. Unfortunately, the best cocoa trees are also the most vulnerable to disease, so it isnt easy to grow them organically.

Source: The Chocolate Companion (Simon & Schuster, 1995)

PROOFREADING EXERCISE

Add apostrophes to the ten contractions used in the following paragraph.

Jokes affect people differently based on their content and the way theyre told. No two individuals tell jokes in the same way or react to them in the same way. Thats why using humor at work or with people we dont know isnt usually a good idea. I have an Irish friend, Grace, whos very good at making people laugh.

It isnt that her jokes are so funny; its the way she tells them. For instance, shell ask someone, "What comes from Ireland and stays outside all night?" While shes waiting for the person to answer, shell tilt her head and look at the person with a twinkle in her eye. Just as the person is about to take a guess, Grace will blurt out, "Patio furniture! Get it? Patty O'Furniture?" The expression on Grace's face after she tells the joke is often funnier than its punch line.

SENTENCE WRITING

Doing exercises will help you learn a rule, but even more helpful is using the rule in writing. Write ten sentences using contractions. You might write about your own ability (or inability) to tell jokes and make people laugh, or you can choose your own subject. Use your own paper, and keep your sentence writing results in a folder.

Possessives

Words that clarify ownership are called *possessives.* The trick in writing possessives is to ask the question "Who (or what) does the item belong to?" Modern usage has made *who* acceptable when it begins a question. More correctly, of course, the phrasing should be "*Whom* does the item belong to?" or even "*To whom* does the item belong?"

In any case, if the answer to this question does not end in *s* (e.g., *player, person, people, children, month*), simply add an apostrophe and *s* to show the possessive. Look at the first five examples in the following chart.

However, if the answer to the question already ends in *s* (e.g., *players, Brahms*), add only an apostrophe after the *s* to show the possessive. See the next two examples in the chart, and say them aloud to hear that their sound does not change.

Finally, some *s*-ending words need another sound to make the possessive clear. If you need another *s* sound when you *say* the possessive (e.g., *boss* made possessive is *boss's*), add the apostrophe and another *s* to show the added sound.

a player (uniform)	Whom does the uniform belong to?	a player	Add '*s*	a player's uniform
a person (clothes)	Whom do the clothes belong to?	a person	Add '*s*	a person's clothes
people (clothes)	Whom do the clothes belong to?	people	Add '*s*	people's clothes
children (games)	Whom do the games belong to?	children	Add '*s*	children's games
a month (pay)	What does the pay belong to?	a month	Add '*s*	a month's pay
players (uniforms)	Whom do the uniforms belong to?	players	Add '	players' uniforms
Brahms (Lullaby)	Whom does the Lullaby belong to?	Brahms	Add '	Brahms' Lullaby
my boss (office)	Whom does the office belong to?	my boss	Add '*s*	my boss's office

The trick of asking "Whom does the item belong to?" will always work, but you must ask the question every time. Remember that the key word is *belong.* If you ask the question another way, you may get an answer that won't help you. Also, notice that the trick does not depend on whether the answer is *singular* or *plural,* but on whether it ends in *s* or not.

TO MAKE A POSSESSIVE

1. Ask "Whom (or what) does the item belong to?"
2. If the answer doesn't end in *s*, add an apostrophe and *s*.
3. If the answer already ends in *s*, add just an apostrophe *or* an apostrophe and *s* if you need an extra sound to show the possessive (as in *boss's office*).

EXERCISES

Follow the directions carefully for each of the following exercises. Because possessives can be tricky, we include explanations in some exercises to help you understand them better.

Exercise 1

Cover the right column and see if you can write the following possessives correctly. Ask the question "Whom (or what) does the item belong to?" each time. Don't look at the answer before you try!

1. people (opinions) _______________ people's opinions
2. a jury (verdict) _______________ a jury's verdict
3. Chris (GPA) _______________ Chris' or Chris's GPA
4. Tiffany (scholarship) _______________ Tiffany's scholarship
5. the Jacksons (new roof) _______________ the Jacksons' new roof
6. Dr. Moss (advice) _______________ Dr. Moss's advice
7. patients (rights) _______________ patients' rights
8. a fish (gills) _______________ a fish's gills
9. a car (windshield) _______________ a car's windshield
10. many cars (windshields) _______________ many cars' windshields

(Sometimes you may see a couple of choices when the word ends in *s*. *Chris' GPA* may be written *Chris's GPA*. That is also correct, depending on how you want your reader to say it. Be consistent when given such choices.)

> **CAUTION**—Don't assume that every word that ends in *s* is a possessive. The *s* may indicate more than one of something, a plural noun. Make sure the word actually possesses something before you add an apostrophe.

A few commonly used words have their own possessive forms and don't need apostrophes added to them. Memorize this list:

our, ours	its
your, yours	their, theirs
his, her, hers	whose

Note particularly *its, their, whose,* and *your.* They are already possessive and don't take an apostrophe. (These words sound just like *it's, they're, who's,* and *you're,* which are *contractions* that use an apostrophe in place of their missing letters.)

Exercise 2

Cover the right column and see if you can write the required form. The answer might be a *contraction* or a *possessive.* If you miss any, go back and review the explanations.

1. Yes, (that) the one I ordered.	that's
2. (He) saving his money for summer.	He's
3. Does (you) dog bark at night?	your
4. I don't know (who) backpack that is.	whose
5. (You) been summoned for jury duty?	You've
6. My cat is so old that (it) going bald.	it's
7. (They) taking classes together this spring.	They're
8. My car's paint is losing (it) shine.	its
9. We welcomed (they) suggestions.	their
10. (Who) visiting us this weekend?	Who's

Exercise 3

Here's another chance to check your progress with possessives. Cover the right column again as you did in Exercises 1 and 2, and add apostrophes correctly to any possessives. Each answer is followed by an explanation.

Sentence	Answer
1. My twin brothers are members of our schools orchestra.	school's (You didn't add an apostrophe to *brothers* or *members,* did you? The brothers and members don't possess anything.)
2. The cashier asked to see my friends identification, too.	friend's (if it is one friend) friends' (two or more friends)
3. Both mens and womens tennis are exciting to watch.	men's, women's (Did you use the "Whom does it belong to" test?)
4. I bought a bad textbook; half of its pages were printed upside down.	No apostrophe. *Its* needs no apostrophe unless it means "it is" or "it has."
5. Julias grades were higher than yours.	Julia's (*Yours* is already possessive and doesn't take an apostrophe.)
6. I decided to quit my job and gave my boss two weeks notice.	weeks' (The notice belongs to *two weeks,* and since *weeks* ends in *s,* the apostrophe goes after the *s.*)
7. The Taylors porch light burned out while they were still on vacation.	Taylors' (The light belongs to the Taylors.)
8. It is every citizens duty to vote in national elections.	citizen's (The duty belongs to *every citizen,* and since *citizen* doesn't end in *s,* we add an apostrophe and *s.*)
9. The chemistry students evaluated each others results as they cleaned up after the experiment.	each other's (*Students* is plural, not possessive.)
10. During a long trip, flight attendants attitudes can greatly affect an airline passengers experience.	attendants', passenger's (Did you use the "Whom do they belong to" test?)

Exercises 4 and 5

Now you're ready to add apostrophes to the possessives that follow. But be careful. *First,* make sure the word really possesses something; not every word ending in *s* is a possessive. *Second,* remember that certain words already have possessive forms and don't use apostrophes. *Third,* even though a word ends in *s,* you can't tell where the apostrophe goes until you ask the question "Whom (or what) does the item belong to?" The apostrophe or apostrophe and *s* should follow the answer to that question. Check your answers at the back of the book after the first set.

Exercise 4

1. The vampire bats habit of sucking an animals blood is aided by a substance that stops the blood from clotting.
2. This same substance might come to a stroke patients aid very soon.
3. Sometimes a persons brain function becomes blocked by a blood clot.
4. This conditions medical label is "ischemic stroke."
5. Obviously, the vampire bats ability to unclot its victims blood would come in handy.
6. Luckily for stroke patients, the substance would be removed from the bat first.
7. Doctors believe that if stroke patients families could get them to the hospital fast enough, the bats enzyme could reduce the clot to avoid brain damage.
8. The enzymes technical name is DSPA.
9. Researchers have tested DSPAs abilities on mice with great success.
10. Perhaps the vampire bats bad reputation will change with the discovery of its healing powers.

Source: The American Heart Association's "Stroke Journal Report," January 9, 2003

Exercise 5

1. The pencils history began in the 1500s.
2. A source of graphite was discovered in one of Englands many valleys.
3. The valleys name was Borrowdale.

4. For hundreds of years, the Borrowdale mine was the worlds main source for pure graphite.
5. Writing with any other form of lead or graphite made an artists or a writers experience less successful.
6. In the late 1700s, Nicolas Jacques Conte learned how to combine graphite and clay to allow manufacturers to vary the hardness of pencils points.
7. After Contes discovery came the mass-production of pencils.
8. The modern pencils yellow color originally had symbolic meanings.
9. The pencils physical design varied over the years, but its hexagonal shape became common.
10. At first, teachers felt that if erasers were added to pencils, their students work would become sloppy.

Source: Invention & Technology, Fall 2004

PROOFREADING EXERCISE

Find and correct the five errors in the following paragraph. All of the errors involve missing or misused apostrophes to form possessives.

I have a cat named Shelby who always keeps me company when I do my homework. Shelbys' favorite spot to lie down is right in the middle of my desk. Whenever she can, she makes herself comfortable on top of my actual homework. All of my books pages have Shelbys fur on them. Many people are allergic to cat's fur, so I wipe off my assignment sheets before I turn them in to my teachers'. Shelby's purring noise helps me relax when I'm working on a difficult math problem or starting a new writing assignment.

SENTENCE WRITING

Write ten sentences using the possessive forms of the names of your family members or the names of your friends. You could write about a recent event that brought your family or friends together. Just tell the story of what happened that day. Use your own paper, and keep all of your sentence writing results in a folder.

REVIEW OF CONTRACTIONS AND POSSESSIVES

Here are two review exercises. First, add the necessary apostrophes to the following sentences. Try not to make the mistake of placing an apostrophe where it isn't needed. Don't excuse an error by saying, "Oh, that was just a careless mistake." A mistake is a mistake. Be tough on yourself.

1. According to artist Eric Sloane, it isnt easy to draw or paint clouds.
2. A clouds shape is difficult to capture because its always moving.
3. Clouds arent static bumps that float in the sky.
4. Theyre like living things—constantly building up or disintegrating.
5. Sloanes suggestions for capturing clouds beauty make good sense.
6. Artists shouldnt forget that clouds are "wet air in action."
7. Theyre not solid; theyre transparent.
8. Color choices will affect an artists ability to recreate clouds on paper or canvas.
9. An artist who wants to paint a cloudy sky mustnt rely on blue and white alone.
10. Its better to use gray, yellow, and pink to capture a cloudscapes full effect.

Source: Skies and the Artist (Dover, 2006)

Second, add the necessary apostrophes to the following short student essay.

A Journal of My Own

Ive been keeping a journal ever since I was in high school. I dont write it for my teachers sake. I wouldnt turn it in even if they asked me to. Its mine, and it helps me remember all of the changes Ive gone through so far in my life. The way I see it, a diarys purpose isnt just to record the facts; its to capture my true feelings.

When I record the days events in my journal, they arent written in minute-by-minute details. Instead, if Ive been staying at a friends house for the weekend, Ill write something like this: "Sharons the only friend I have who listens to my whole sentence before starting hers. Shes never in a hurry to end a good conversation. Today we talked for an hour or so about the pets wed had when we were kids. We agreed that were both 'dog people.' We cant imagine our lives without dogs. Her favorites are Pomeranians, and mine are golden retrievers." Thats the kind of an entry Id make in my journal. It doesnt mean much to anyone but me, and thats the way it should be.

I know that another persons diary would be different from mine and that most people dont even keep one. Im glad that writing comes easily to me. I dont think Ill ever stop writing in my journal because it helps me believe in myself and value others beliefs as well.

Words That Can Be Broken into Parts

Breaking words into their parts will often help you spell them correctly. Each of the following words is made up of two shorter words. Note that the word then contains all the letters of the two shorter words.

chalk board	. . .	chalkboard	room mate	. . .	roommate
over due	. . .	overdue	home work	. . .	homework
super market	. . .	supermarket	under line	. . .	underline

Becoming aware of prefixes such as *dis, inter, mis,* and *un* is also helpful. When you add a prefix to a word, note that no letters are dropped, either from the prefix or from the word.

dis appear	disappear	mis represent	misrepresent
dis appoint	disappoint	mis spell	misspell
dis approve	disapprove	mis understood	misunderstood
dis satisfy	dissatisfy	un aware	unaware
inter act	interact	un involved	uninvolved
inter active	interactive	un necessary	unnecessary
inter related	interrelated	un sure	unsure

Have someone dictate the preceding list for you to write and then mark any words you miss. Memorize the correct spellings by noting how each word is made up of a prefix and a word.

Rule for Doubling a Final Letter

Most spelling rules have so many exceptions that they aren't much help. But here's one worth learning because it has very few exceptions.

Double a final letter (consonants only) when adding an ending that begins with a vowel (such as *ing, ed, er*) if all three of the following are true:

1. The word ends in a single consonant,

2. which is preceded by a single vowel (the vowels are *a, e, i, o, u*),

3. and the accent is on the last syllable (or the word only has one syllable).

We'll try the rule on a few words to which we'll add *ing, ed,* or *er.*

begin
1. It ends in a single consonant—*n,*
2. preceded by a single vowel—*i,*
3. and the accent is on the last syllable—be *gín.*

Therefore, we double the final consonant and write *beginning, beginner.*

stop
1. It ends in a single consonant—*p,*
2. preceded by a single vowel—*o,*
3. and the accent is on the last syllable (only one).

Therefore, we double the final consonant and write *stopping, stopped, stopper.*

filter
1. It ends in a single consonant—*r,*
2. preceded by a single vowel—*e,*
3. But the accent isn't on the last syllable. It's on the first—*fíl* ter.

Therefore, we don't double the final consonant. We write *filtering, filtered.*

keep
1. It ends in a single consonant—*p,*
2. but it isn't preceded by a single vowel. There are two *e*'s.

Therefore, we don't double the final consonant. We write *keeping, keeper.*

NOTE 1—Be aware that *qu* is treated as a consonant because *q* is almost never written without *u.* Think of it as *kw.* In words like *equip* and *quit,* the *qu* acts as a consonant. Therefore, *equip* and *quit* both end in a single consonant preceded by a single vowel, and the final consonant is doubled in *equipped* and *quitting.*

NOTE 2—The final consonants *w, x,* and *y* do not follow this rule and are not doubled when adding *ing, ed,* or *er* to a word (as in *bowing, fixing,* and *enjoying*).

EXERCISES

Add *ing* to these words. Correct each group of ten before continuing so you'll catch any errors early.

Exercise 1

1. bet
2. quit
3. wait
4. park
5. skim
6. admit
7. slap
8. think
9. tap
10. hit

Exercise 2

1. tow
2. rip
3. peel
4. refer
5. invest
6. order
7. profit
8. scream
9. slip
10. predict

Exercise 3

1. box
2. munch
3. roll
4. mop
5. flavor
6. cash
7. beep
8. talk
9. travel
10. play

Exercise 4

1. paint
2. row
3. shiver
4. defend
5. trim
6. press
7. deal
8. knit
9. blunder
10. chug

Exercise 5

1. shout
2. deploy
3. refer
4. equal
5. dig
6. mix
7. drip
8. send
9. hem
10. tax

PROGRESS TEST

This test covers everything you've studied so far. One sentence in each pair is correct. The other is incorrect. Read both sentences carefully before you decide. Then write the letter of the incorrect sentence in the blank. Try to isolate and correct the error if you can.

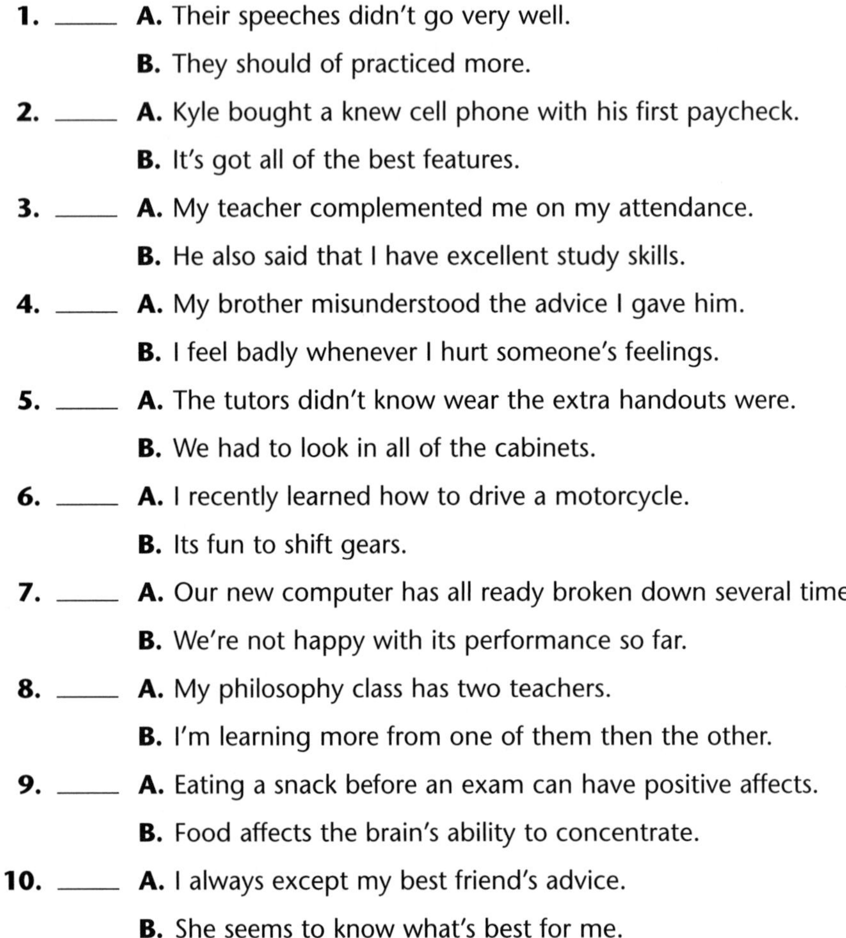

1. _____ **A.** Their speeches didn't go very well.

B. They should of practiced more.

2. _____ **A.** Kyle bought a knew cell phone with his first paycheck.

B. It's got all of the best features.

3. _____ **A.** My teacher complemented me on my attendance.

B. He also said that I have excellent study skills.

4. _____ **A.** My brother misunderstood the advice I gave him.

B. I feel badly whenever I hurt someone's feelings.

5. _____ **A.** The tutors didn't know wear the extra handouts were.

B. We had to look in all of the cabinets.

6. _____ **A.** I recently learned how to drive a motorcycle.

B. Its fun to shift gears.

7. _____ **A.** Our new computer has all ready broken down several times.

B. We're not happy with its performance so far.

8. _____ **A.** My philosophy class has two teachers.

B. I'm learning more from one of them then the other.

9. _____ **A.** Eating a snack before an exam can have positive affects.

B. Food affects the brain's ability to concentrate.

10. _____ **A.** I always except my best friend's advice.

B. She seems to know what's best for me.

Using a Dictionary

Some dictionaries are more helpful than others. A tiny pocket-sized dictionary or one that fits on a single sheet in your notebook might help you find the spelling of very common words, but for all other uses, you will need a complete, recently published dictionary. Spend some time at a bookstore looking through the dictionaries to find one that you feel comfortable reading. Look up a word that you have had trouble with in the past, and see if you understand the definition. Try looking up the same word in another dictionary and compare.

Complete the following exercises using a good dictionary. Then you will understand what a valuable resource it is.

1. Pronunciation

Look up the word *punctuate,* and copy the pronunciation here.

___

___

For help with pronunciation of the syllables, you'll probably find key words at the bottom of one of the two dictionary pages open before you. Note especially that the upside-down *e* (ə) always has the sound of *uh* like the *a* in *ago* or *about*. Remember that sound because it's found in many words.

Slowly pronounce *punctuate,* giving each syllable the same sound as its key word.

Note which syllable has the heavy accent mark. (In most dictionaries, the accent mark points to the stressed syllable, but in others, it is in front of the stressed syllable.) The stressed syllable in *punctuate* is *punc*. Now say the word, letting the full force of your voice fall on that syllable.

When more than one pronunciation is given, the first is preferred. If the complete pronunciation of a word isn't given, look at the word above it to find the pronunciation.

Find the pronunciation of these words, using the key words at the bottom of the dictionary page to help you pronounce each syllable. Then note which syllable has the heavy accent mark, and say the word aloud.

justify produce fixate comprehend

2. Definitions

The dictionary may give more than one meaning for a word. Read all the meanings for each italicized word, and then write a definition appropriate to the sentence.

1. Our neighbors taught their dog to *heel.* ____________________

____

2. He made himself a cup of *instant* coffee. ____________________

____

3. When we *land,* I will call my parents. ____________________

____

4. The battery was leaking at one of its *poles.* ____________________

____

3. Spelling

By making yourself look up each word you aren't sure how to spell, you'll soon become a better speller. When two spellings are given in the dictionary, the first one (or the one with the definition) is preferred.

Use a dictionary to find the preferred spelling for each of these words.

moustache, mustache ____________ wagon, waggon ____________

judgement, judgment ____________ cancelled, canceled ____________

4. Parts of Speech

English has eight parts of speech: noun, pronoun, verb, adjective, adverb, preposition, conjunction, and interjection. At the beginning of each definition for a word, you'll find an abbreviation for the part of speech that the word is performing when so defined (n, pron, v, adj, adv, prep, conj, interj). For more discussion of parts of speech, see page 22.

Identify the parts of speech listed in all the definitions for each of the following words.

band ____________ several ____________

tank ____________ during ____________

5. Compound Words

If you want to find out whether two words are written separately, written with a hyphen between them, or written as one word, consult your dictionary. Look at these examples:

half sister	written as two words
father-in-law	hyphenated
stepson	written as one word

Write each of the following as listed in the dictionary (as two words, as a hyphenated word, or as one word):

film maker ____________ draw bridge ____________

play off ____________ in house ____________

6. Capitalization

If a word is capitalized in the dictionary, that means it should always be capitalized. If it is not capitalized in the dictionary, then it may or may not be capitalized, depending on how it is used (see p. 196). For example, *American* is always capitalized, but *college* is capitalized or not, according to how it is used.

Last year, she graduated from college.

Last year, she graduated from Monterey Peninsula College.

Write the following words as they're given in the dictionary (with or without a capital) to show whether they must always be capitalized or not. Take a guess before looking them up.

europe ____________ pacific ____________

mars ____________ grammy ____________

7. Usage

Just because a word is in the dictionary doesn't mean that it's in standard use. The following labels indicate whether a word is used today and, if so, where and by whom.

obsolete	no longer used
archaic	not currently used in ordinary language but still found in some Biblical, literary, and legal expressions

colloquial, informal	used in informal conversation but not in formal writing
dialectal, regional	used in some localities but not everywhere
slang	popular but nonstandard expression
nonstandard, substandard	not used in Standard Written English

Look up each italicized word and write the label indicating its usage. Dictionaries differ. One may list a word as slang, whereas another will call it colloquial. Still another dictionary may give no designation, thus indicating that it considers the word in standard use.

1. Please *gimme* some of that popcorn. ____________________

2. His *deadpan* delivery of the joke is what made it so funny. ____________

3. What are the *specs* on that computer? ____________________

4. Our teacher *freaked out* when we said that we needed more time. ________

5. *Alas,* the deadline has been postponed. ____________________

8. Derivations

The derivations or stories behind words will often help you remember the current meanings. For example, if you read that someone is *narcissistic* and you consult your dictionary, you'll find that *narcissism* is a condition named after Narcissus, who was a handsome young man in Greek mythology. One day, Narcissus fell in love with his own reflection in a pool, but when he tried to get closer to it, he fell in the water and drowned. A flower that grew nearby is now named for Narcissus. And *narcissistic* has come to mean "in love with oneself."

Look up the derivation of each of these words. You'll find it in square brackets either just before or just after the definition.

Murphy bed ____________________

Chihuahua ____________________

goody two-shoes ____________________

silhouette ____________________

9. Synonyms

At the end of a definition, a group of synonyms is sometimes given. For example, at the end of the definition of *injure,* you'll find several synonyms, such as *damage* or *harm*. And if you look up *damage* or *harm*, you'll be referred to the same synonyms listed under *injure*.

List the synonyms given for the following words.

profess ______________________________

weep ______________________________

dodge ______________________________

10. Abbreviations

Find the meaning of the following abbreviations.

DVD ______________ HMO ______________

UN ______________ ATM ______________

11. Names of People

The names of famous people will be found either in the main part of your dictionary or in a separate biographical names section at the back.

Identify the following famous people.

Anna Ivanovna ______________________________

Gabriel García Marquez ______________________________

Grace Hopper ______________________________

Frederick Douglass ______________________________

12. Names of Places

The names of places will be found either in the main part of your dictionary or in a separate geographical names section at the back.

Identify the following places.

Killiecrankie ______________________________

Chernobyl ______________________________

Mauritius ______________________________

Zanzibar ______________________________

13. Foreign Words and Phrases

Find the language and the meaning of the italicized expressions.

1. The *hors d'oeuvres* at the party were delicious. ____________________

____

2. I hope to graduate *magna cum laude*. ____________________

____

3. My new sheet music said that it should be played *all' otava*. ____________

____

4. Beverly's projects were always considered the *crème de la crème*. ________

____

14. Miscellaneous Information

Find these miscellaneous bits of information in a good dictionary.

1. What duty is a *devil's advocate* supposed to perform? ____________________

____

2. In what country would you measure liquid by *mutchkin*? ________________

____

3. Under what circumstances should someone be given *ipecac*? ______________

____

4. Is a *macaroon* something to eat or something to wear? __________________

____

5. What part of speech is the expression *yoo-hoo*? ______________________

____

P A R T 2

Sentence Structure

Sentence structure refers to the way sentences are built using words, phrases, and clauses. Words are single units, and words link up in sentences to form clauses and phrases. Clauses are word groups *with* subjects and verbs, and phrases are word groups *without* subjects and verbs. Clauses are the most important because they make statements—they tell who did what (or what something is) in a sentence. Look at the following sentence for example:

> We bought oranges at the farmer's market on Main Street.

It contains ten words, each playing its own part in the meaning of the sentence. But which of the words together tell who did what? *We bought oranges* is correct. That word group is a clause. Notice that *at the farmer's market* and *on Main Street* also link up as word groups but don't have somebody (subject) doing something (verb). Instead, they are phrases to clarify *where* we bought the oranges.

Importantly, you could leave out one or both of the phrases and still have a sentence—*We bought oranges.* However, you cannot leave the clause out. Then you would just have *At the farmer's market on Main Street.* Remember, every sentence needs at least one clause that can stand by itself.

Learning about the structure of sentences helps you control your own. Once you know more about sentence structure, then you can understand writing errors and learn how to correct them.

Among the most common errors in writing are fragments, run-ons, and awkward phrasing.

Here are some fragments:

> Wandering around the mall all afternoon.
>
> Because I tried to do too many things at once.
>
> By interviewing the applicants in groups.

They don't make complete statements—not one has a clause that can stand by itself. Who was *wandering?* What happened *because you tried to do too many things at once?* What was the result of *interviewing the applicants in groups?* These incomplete sentence structures fail to communicate a complete thought.

In contrast, here are some run-ons:

Computer prices are dropping they're still beyond my budget.

The forecast calls for rain I'll wait to wash my car.

A truck parked in front of my driveway I couldn't get to school.

Unlike fragments, run-ons make complete statements, but the trouble is they make *two* complete statements; the first *runs on* to the second without correct punctuation. The reader has to go back to see where there should have been a break.

So fragments don't include enough information, and run-ons include too much. Another problem occurs when the information in a sentence just doesn't make sense.

Here are a few sentences with awkward phrasing:

The problem from my grades started to end.

It was a time at the picnic.

She won me at chess.

Try to find the word groups that show who did what, that is, the clauses. Once you find them, then try to put the clauses and phrases together to form a precise meaning. It's difficult, isn't it? You'll see that many of the words themselves are misused or unclear, such as *from, it,* and *won.* These sentences don't communicate clearly because the clauses, phrases, and even words don't work together. They suffer from awkward phrasing.

Fragments, run-ons, awkward phrasing, and other sentence structure errors confuse the reader. Not until you get rid of them will your writing be clearer and easier to read. Unfortunately, there is no quick, effortless way to learn to avoid errors in sentence structure. First, you need to understand how clear sentences are built. Then you will be able to avoid common errors in your own writing.

This section will describe areas of sentence structure one at a time and then explain how to correct errors associated with the different areas. For instance, we start by helping you find subjects and verbs and understand dependent clauses; then we show you how to avoid fragments. You can go through the whole section yourself to learn all of the concepts and structures. Or your teacher may assign only parts based on errors the class is making.

Finding Subjects and Verbs

The most important words in sentences are those that make up its independent clause—the subject and the verb. When you write a sentence, you write about a noun or pronoun (a person, place, thing, or idea). That's the *subject.* Then you write what the subject *does* or *is.* That's the *verb.*

Lightning strikes.

The word *Lightning* is the thing you are writing about. It's the subject, and we'll underline all subjects once. *Strikes* tells what the subject does. It shows the action in the sentence. It's the verb, and we'll underline all of them twice. Most sentences do not include only two words (the subject and the verb). However, these two words still make up the core of the sentence even if other words and phrases are included with them.

Lightning strikes back and forth from the clouds to the ground very quickly.

It often strikes people on golf courses or in boats.

When many words appear in sentences, the subject and verb can be harder to find. Because the verb often shows action, it's easier to spot than the subject. Therefore, always look for it first. For example, take this sentence:

The neighborhood cat folded its paws under its chest.

Which word shows the action? The action word is folded. It's the verb, so we'll underline it twice. Now ask yourself who or what folded? The answer is cat. That's the subject, so we'll underline it once.

Study the following sentences until you understand how to pick out subjects and verbs.

Tomorrow our school celebrates its fiftieth anniversary. (Which word shows the action? The action word is celebrates. It's the verb, so we'll underline it twice. Who or what celebrates? The school does. It's the subject. We'll underline it once.)

The team members ate several boxes of chocolates. (Which word shows the action? Ate shows the action. Who or what ate? Members ate.)

Internet users crowd the popular services. (Which word shows the action? The verb is crowd. Who or what crowd? Users crowd.)

Often the verb doesn't show action but merely tells what the subject *is* or *was.* Learn to spot such verbs—*is, am, are, was, were, seems, feels, appears, becomes, looks* . . . . (For more information on these special verbs, see the discussion of sentence patterns on p. 136).

> Marshall is a neon artist. (First spot the verb is. Then ask who or what is? Marshall is.)
>
> The bread appears moldy. (First spot the verb appears. Then ask who or what appears? Bread appears.)

Sometimes the subject comes after the verb, especially when a word like *there* or *here* begins the sentence without being a real subject. It's best not to start sentences with "There is . . . " or "There are . . . " for this reason.

> In the audience were two reviewers from the *Times.* (Who or what were in the audience? Two reviewers from the *Times* were in the audience.)
>
> There was a fortune-teller at the carnival. (Who or what was there? A fortune-teller was there at the carnival.)
>
> There were name tags for all the participants. (Who or what were there? Name tags were there for all the participants.)
>
> Here are the contracts. (Who or what are here? The contracts are here.)

NOTE—Remember that *there* and *here* (as used in the last three sentences) are not subjects. They simply point to something.

In commands, often the subject is not expressed. An unwritten *you* is understood by the reader.

> Sit down. (You sit down.)
>
> Place flap A into slot B. (You place flap A into slot B.)
>
> Meet me at 7:00. (You meet me at 7:00.)

Commonly, a sentence may have more than one subject.

> Toys and memorabilia from the 1950s are high-priced collectibles.
>
> Celebrity dolls, board games, and even cereal boxes from that decade line the shelves of antique stores.

A sentence may also have more than one verb.

> Water boils at a consistent temperature and freezes at another.
>
> The ice tray fell out of my hand, skidded across the floor, and landed under the table.

EXERCISES

Underline the subjects once and the verbs twice in the following sentences. When you've finished the first set, compare your answers carefully with those at the back of the book.

Exercise 1

1. The summer heat causes many problems for people.
2. Food spoils more quickly in the summer.
3. Insects and other pests seek shelter inside.
4. There are power outages due to excessive use of air conditioners and fans.
5. In some areas, smog levels increase dramatically in the summer.
6. Schoolchildren suffer in overheated classrooms.
7. On the worst days, everyone searches for a swimming pool or drives to the beach.
8. Sleeping comfortably becomes impossible.
9. No activity seems worth the effort.
10. But the heat of summer fades in our minds at the first real break in the weather.

Exercise 2

1. I got an actual letter in the mail last month.
2. It came from my aunt Leone in England.
3. She used real stationery and wrote her thoughts with an ink pen.
4. I read the letter several times and really enjoyed its one-of-a-kind qualities.
5. My aunt's personality and voice came through her letter.
6. She crossed out her mistakes and added little notes and drawings in the margins.
7. It felt like an original artwork in my hands.
8. Until recently, I wrote only e-mails or sent only preprinted cards to my friends and relatives.
9. Leone's letter changed my habits.
10. Nothing captures an artistic personality better than paper and pen.

Exercise 3

1. Katharine M. Rogers recently published her biography of L. Frank Baum.
2. Most people know Baum's work but not his name.
3. L. Frank Baum wrote *The Wonderful Wizard of Oz* and many other children's books and stories.
4. Of course, filmmakers used Baum's tale of the Wizard of Oz in the classic movie of the same name.
5. Baum's memorable character of the Scarecrow has an interesting story behind him.
6. During Baum's childhood, his father bought some farmland.
7. Baum saw scarecrows in the fields and found them fascinating.
8. Unfortunately, his keen imagination led to bad dreams about a scarecrow.

9. The scarecrow in his dreams ran after him but always fell into a heap of straw just in time.
10. As a writer, Baum brought the Scarecrow to life in his Oz stories and made him less of a nightmare and more of a friend.

Source: L. Frank Baum: Creator of Oz (St. Martin's Press, 2002)

Exercise 4

1. In 1940, four teenagers took a walk and discovered something marvelous.
2. They entered an underground cavern in Lascaux, France, and found vivid images of animals on its walls.
3. There were horses, deer, bulls, cats, and oxen.
4. The prehistoric artists also left tracings of their handprints on the walls.
5. Scientists dated the paintings and engravings at approximately 17,000 years old.
6. After its discovery, the Lascaux cave became a popular tourist attraction.
7. Twelve hundred people visited the site daily.
8. These visitors had a negative impact on the cave's prehistoric artwork.
9. They breathed carbon dioxide into the cave and increased its humidity.
10. French officials closed the Lascaux cave to the public in 1963.

Sources: The Writer's Almanac, September 12, 2006, and *The Cave of Lascaux* official Web site (http://www.culture.gouv.fr:80/culture/arcnat/lascaux/en/)

Exercise 5

1. Movies and television programs often include real dogs as actors.
2. Disney's live-action *101 Dalmatians* is just one example.
3. *Snow Dogs, Eight Below,* and *The Shaggy Dog* are three other dog-friendly films.
4. According to experts, dogs in films both help and hurt certain dog breeds.

5. For instance, sales and adoptions of Dalmatians rose dramatically after the Disney movie's popularity.
6. The other films caused the same effect for Siberian huskies and bearded collies.
7. However, these breeds are not good choices for everyone.
8. Many people become unhappy with them and put them up for adoption.
9. Disney now attaches warning labels to their DVDs of dog-related films.
10. The labels caution the public about the choice of dogs based on their movie roles.

Source: Newsweek, August 14, 2006

PARAGRAPH EXERCISE

Underline the subjects once and the verbs twice in the following student paragraph.

I was on the volleyball team in high school, so my high school gym was a special place for me. It was an ordinary gym with bleachers on both sides. There were basketball court lines on the floors and the school's mascot in the center. We stretched a net across the middle for our volleyball games. The pale wooden floors sparkled, sometimes with sweat and sometimes with tears. The gym had a distinct stuffy smell of grimy socks, stale potato chips, and sticky sodas. I liked the smell and remember it fondly. Songs from dances and screams and cheers from games echoed throughout the big old building. In the gym during those high school years, I felt a sense of privacy and community.

SENTENCE WRITING

Write ten sentences about any subject—your favorite movie snacks, for instance. Keeping your subject matter simple in these sentence-writing exercises will make it easier to find your sentence structures later. After you have written your sentences, go back and underline your subjects once and your verbs twice. Use your own paper, and keep your sentence writing results in a folder.

Locating Prepositional Phrases

Prepositional phrases are among the easiest structures in English to learn. Remember that a phrase is just a group of related words (at least two) without a subject and a verb. And don't let a term like *prepositional* scare you. If you look in the middle of that long word, you'll find a familiar one—*position*. In English, we tell the *positions* of people and things in sentences using prepositional phrases.

Look at the following sentence with its prepositional phrases in parentheses:

Our field trip (to the desert) begins (at 6:00) (in the morning) (on Friday).

One phrase tells where the field trip is going (*to the desert*), and three phrases tell when the trip begins (*at 6:00, in the morning,* and *on Friday*). As you can see, prepositional phrases show the position of someone or something in space or in time.

Here is a list of some prepositions that can show positions in space:

under	across	next to	against
around	by	inside	at
through	beyond	over	beneath
above	among	on	in
below	near	behind	past
between	without	from	to

Here are some prepositions that can show positions in time:

before	throughout	past	within
after	by	until	in
since	at	during	for

These lists include only individual words, *not phrases*. Remember, a preposition must be followed by a noun or pronoun object—a person, place, thing, or idea—to create a prepositional phrase. Notice that in the added prepositional phrases that follow, the position of the balloon in relation to the object, *the clouds,* changes completely:

The hot-air balloon floated *above the clouds.*
below the clouds.
within the clouds.
between the clouds.
past the clouds.
around the clouds.

Now notice the different positions in time:

The balloon landed *at 3:30.*
by 3:30.
past 3:30.
before the thunderstorm.
during the thunderstorm.
after the thunderstorm.

> **NOTE**—A few words—*of, as,* and *like*—are prepositions that do not fit neatly into either the space or time category, yet they are very common prepositions (box *of candy,* note *of apology,* type *of bicycle;* act *as a substitute,* use *as an example,* testified *as an expert;* sounds *like a computer,* acts *like a child,* moves *like a snake*).

By locating prepositional phrases, you will be able to find subjects and verbs more easily. For example, you might have difficulty finding the subject and verb in a long sentence like this:

> During the rainy season, one of the windows in the attic leaked at the corners of its molding.

But if you put parentheses around all the prepositional phrases like this

> (During the rainy season), one (of the windows) (in the attic) leaked (at the corners) (of its molding).

then you have only two words left—the subject and the verb. Even in short sentences like the following, you might pick the wrong word as the subject if you don't put parentheses around the prepositional phrases first.

> Two (of the characters) lied (to each other) (throughout the play).

> The waves (around the ship) looked real.

> **NOTE**—Don't mistake *to* plus a verb for a prepositional phrase. Special forms of verbals always start with *to,* but they are not prepositional phrases (see p. 125). For example, in the sentence "I like to run to the beach," *to run* is a verbal, not a prepositional phrase. However, *to the beach* is a prepositional phrase because it begins with a preposition (to), ends with a noun (beach), and shows position in space.

EXERCISES

Put parentheses around the prepositional phrases in the following sentences. Be sure to start with the preposition itself (*in, on, to, at, of . . .*) and include the word or words that go with it (*in the morning, on our sidewalk, to Hawaii . . .*). Then underline the sentences' subjects once and verbs twice. Remember that subjects and verbs are not found inside prepositional phrases, so if you locate the prepositional phrases *first,* the subjects and verbs will be much easier to find. Review the answers given at the back for each set of ten sentences before continuing.

Exercise 1

1. Everyone worries about identity theft.
2. Thieves search for certain pieces of information.
3. These facts are names, addresses, dates of birth, and social security numbers.
4. With these facts, thieves attempt to access people's accounts.
5. There are some new forms of protection on the Internet.
6. One program checks the Web for groupings of people's most valuable information.
7. The name of the program is Identity Angel.
8. Carnegie Mellon University in Pittsburgh created the program.
9. Identity Angel sends e-mail warnings to vulnerable people.
10. It warns them about possible identity theft.

Source: CNET News.com, August 10, 2006

Exercise 2

1. One fact about William Shakespeare and his work always surprises people.
2. There are no copies of his original manuscripts.
3. No museum or library has even one page from a Shakespeare play in Shakespeare's own handwriting.
4. Museums and libraries have copies of the First Folio instead.
5. After Shakespeare's death in 1616, actors from his company gathered the texts of his plays and published them as one book, the First Folio, in 1623.

6. They printed approximately 750 copies at the time.
7. Currently, there are 230 known copies of the First Folio in the world.
8. Many owners of the Folio remain anonymous by choice.
9. One woman inherited her copy of the Folio from a distant relative.
10. Another copy of the First Folio recently sold for five million dollars.

Source: Smithsonian, September 2006

Exercise 3

1. Twiggy the Squirrel is a star in the world of trained animals.
2. Twiggy performs on a pair of tiny water skis and delights crowds at boat shows and other events.
3. Like many other famous animal entertainers, the current Twiggy is not the original.
4. The Twiggy of today is fifth in the line of Twiggys.
5. Lou Ann Best is Twiggy's trainer and continues the work begun by her husband Chuck during the 1970s.
6. In his time, Chuck Best convinced many types of animals to ride on water skis.
7. He had success with everything from a dog to a frog.
8. But Twiggy the Squirrel was a hit with crowds from the beginning.
9. All of the Twiggys seemed happy with their show-biz lifestyles.
10. In fact, the Bests received four of the Twiggys from the Humane Society.

Source: Current Science, May 2, 2003

Exercise 4

1. At 2 A.M. on the second Sunday in March, something happens to nearly everyone in America: Daylight Saving Time.
2. But few people are awake at two in the morning.

3. So we set the hands or digits of our clocks ahead one hour on Saturday night in preparation for it.
4. And before bed on the first Saturday in November, we turn them back again.
5. For days after both events, I have trouble with my sleep patterns and my mood.
6. In spring, the feeling is one of loss.
7. That Saturday-night sleep into Sunday is one hour shorter than usual.
8. But in fall, I gain a false sense of security about time.
9. That endless Sunday morning quickly melts into the start of a hectic week like the other fifty-one in the year.
10. All of this upheaval is due to the Uniform Time Act of 1966.

Exercise 5

1. I saw a news story about an art exhibit with a unique focus and message.
2. All of the pieces in the art show started with the same basic materials.
3. The materials were all of the parts of a huge English oak tree.
4. Most of a tree usually becomes waste except the large trunk section.
5. But in the case of this tree, artists took every last bit and made "art" with it as a tribute to the tree.
6. One artist even made clothes from some of the smallest pieces—tiny branches, sawdust, and leaves.
7. Another artist used thousands of bits of the tree in a kind of mosaic painting.
8. Still another turned one hunk of the tree's timber into a pig sculpture.
9. Other chunks, branches, and even the roots became abstract pieces of art.
10. The tree lives on as art and as a new tree with the sprouting of an acorn in its old location.

PARAGRAPH EXERCISE

Put parentheses around the prepositional phrases in this modified excerpt from *A Day in a Medieval City,* by Chiara Frugoni.

A whole collection of clay toys was discovered during the nineteenth century in Strasbourgh, in the workshop of a thirteenth-century potter. Since then, we know more about medieval children's games: bird-shaped whistles, miniature tiles and pitchers, tiny moneyboxes, little dolls, and diminutive horses with riders on their backs. Children fought battles with wooden swords, competed in play tournaments, played games with balls and wooden sticks in a remote precursor to modern field hockey.

In families with more means, there were "educational toys," such as an alphabet wheel in gesso from the fourteenth century or a covered pewter cup decorated with the entire alphabet. The letter A, the first the child would pronounce, is on the knob. We find out about the instruction of children primarily from images of family life.

SENTENCE WRITING

Write ten sentences describing your favorite type of vacation—or choose any topic you like. When you go back over your sentences, put parentheses around your prepositional phrases and underline your subjects once and your verbs twice. Use your own paper, and keep all of your sentence writing results in a folder.

Understanding Dependent Clauses

All clauses contain a subject and a verb, yet there are two kinds of clauses: *independent* and *dependent.* Independent clauses have a subject and a verb and make complete statements by themselves. Dependent clauses have a subject and a verb but don't make complete statements because of the words they begin with. Here are some of the words (conjunctions) that begin dependent clauses:

after	since	where
although	so that	whereas
as	than	wherever
as if	that	whether
because	though	which
before	unless	whichever
even if	until	while
even though	what	who
ever since	whatever	whom
how	when	whose
if	whenever	why

When a clause starts with one of these dependent words, it is usually a dependent clause. To see the difference between an independent and a dependent clause, look at this example of an independent clause:

We ate dinner together.

It has a subject (We) and a verb (ate), and it makes a complete statement. But as soon as we put one of the dependent words in front of it, the clause becomes *dependent* because it no longer makes a complete statement:

After we ate dinner together . . .
Although we ate dinner together . . .
As we ate dinner together . . .
Before we ate dinner together . . .
Since we ate dinner together . . .
That we ate dinner together . . .
When we ate dinner together . . .
While we ate dinner together . . .

Each of these dependent clauses leaves the reader expecting something more. Each would depend on another clause—an independent clause—to make a sentence. For the rest of this discussion, we'll place a broken line beneath dependent clauses.

After we ate dinner together, we went to the evening seminar.

We went to the evening seminar *after* we ate dinner together.

The speaker didn't know *that* we ate dinner together.

While we ate dinner together, the restaurant became crowded.

As you can see in these examples, *when a dependent clause comes before an independent clause, it is followed by a comma.* Often the comma prevents misreading, as in the following sentence:

When he returned, the DVD was on the floor.

Without a comma after *returned,* the reader would read *When he returned the DVD* before realizing that this was not what the author meant. The comma prevents misreading. Sometimes if the dependent clause is short and there is no danger of misreading, the comma can be left off, but it's safer simply to follow the rule that a dependent clause coming before an independent clause is followed by a comma. You'll learn more about the punctuation of dependent clauses on page 175, but right now just remember the previous rule.

Note that a few of the dependent words (*that, who, which, what*) can do "double duty" as both the dependent word and the subject of the dependent clause:

Thelma wrote a poetry book *that* sold a thousand copies.

The manager saw *what* happened.

Sometimes the dependent clause is in the middle of the independent clause:

The book *that* sold a thousand copies was Thelma's.

The events *that* followed the parade delighted everyone.

The dependent clause can even be the subject of the entire sentence:

What you do also affects me.

How your project looks counts for ten percent of the grade.

Also note that sometimes the *that* of a dependent clause is omitted:

I know *that* you feel strongly about this issue.

I know you feel strongly about this issue.

Everyone received the classes *that* they wanted.

Everyone received the classes they wanted.

Of course, the word *that* doesn't always introduce a dependent clause. It may be a pronoun and serve as the subject or object of the sentence:

That was a long movie.

We knew *that* already.

That can also be an adjective, a descriptive word telling *which one:*

That movie always makes me laugh.

We took them to *that* park last week.

EXERCISES

Exercise 1

Each of the following sentences contains *one* independent and *one* dependent clause. Draw a broken line beneath the dependent clause in each sentence. Start at the dependent word and include all the words that go with it. Remember that dependent clauses can be in the beginning, middle, or end of a sentence.

Example: I jump whenever I hear a loud noise.

Exercise 1

1. When I was on vacation in New York City, I loved the look of the Empire State Building at night.
2. I thought that the colored lights at the top of this landmark were just decorative.
3. I did not know that their patterns also have meaning.
4. While I waited at the airport, I read a pamphlet about the patterns.
5. Some of the light combinations reveal connections that are obvious.
6. For instance, if the occasion is St. Patrick's Day, the top of the building glows with green lights.
7. When the holiday involves a celebration of America, the three levels of lights shine red, white, and blue.
8. There are other combinations that are less well known.
9. Red-black-green is a pattern that signals Martin Luther King Jr. Day.
10. Whenever I visit the city again, I'll know the meanings of the lights on the Empire State Building.

Exercises 2–5

Follow the same directions as in Exercise 1. Then, after you identify the dependent clauses, go back to both the independent and dependent clauses and mark their subjects and verbs. Draw a single underline beneath subjects and a double underline beneath verbs.

Example: I jump whenever I hear a loud noise.

Exercise 2

1. When people shop for high-priced items, they often think too much.
2. A study at the University of Amsterdam yielded results that surprised scientists.
3. If buyers thought only a little bit beforehand, they remained happy with their purchase later.

4. When they consciously considered many details about a product, they were not as satisfied with it afterward.
5. The products that researchers used in the experiments were cars and furniture.
6. For the car-buying study, they tested eighty people who were all college students.
7. The cars had many positive and negative attributes for the subjects to consider when they made their choices.
8. The subjects who took the least amount of time chose the best cars.
9. Likewise, a survey of furniture shoppers showed that quick decisions led to satisfied customers.
10. Apparently, shoppers who trust their instincts make the best decisions.

Source: Science News, February 25, 2006

Exercise 3

1. Did you know that July is National Cell Phone Courtesy Month?
2. There are few cell phone users who are courteous in public.
3. In fact, courtesy is almost impossible when someone uses a cell phone around others.
4. People who have cell phones set their ring tones on high and have loud conversations.
5. Even if they are in stores, restaurants, or libraries, cell phone users answer most of their calls.
6. The question remains about how cell phone users can be more courteous.
7. One solution is a new type of phone booth that has no phone in it.
8. It is a structure that has a cylindrical shape and a metal exterior.
9. There is a door that callers use for privacy.
10. The cell phone booth is an old-fashioned idea that makes a lot of sense.

Source: Newsweek, July 3/July 10, 2006

Exercise 4

1. I just read an article with a list of "What Doctors Wish You Knew."
2. One fact is that red and blue fruits are the healthiest.
3. Patients who have doctor's appointments after lunchtime spend less time in the waiting room.
4. Drivers who apply more sunscreen to their left sides get less skin cancer.
5. People who take ten deep breaths in the morning and evening feel less stress.
6. A clock that is visible from the bed makes insomnia worse.
7. People often suffer from weekend headaches because they get up too late.
8. They withdraw from caffeine by skipping the coffee that they usually drink on workdays.
9. Doctors suggest that people maintain weekday hours on weekends.
10. I am glad that I found this list.

Source: Good Housekeeping, November 2005

Exercise 5

1. My coworker told me about a news story that he saw on television.
2. It involved those baby turtles that hatch in the sand at night.
3. Normally, once they hatch, they run toward the comforting waves.
4. As soon as they reach the water, they begin their lives as sea turtles.
5. The story that my friend saw told of a potential danger to these motivated little animals.
6. The turtles instinctively know which direction leads to the sea.
7. The bright white foam of the waves is the trigger that lures them across the sand to their proper destination.
8. Unfortunately, on some beaches where this phenomenon occurs, the tourist business causes a big problem for the turtles.

9. Tourists who want to see the turtles gather at shoreline restaurants and dance pavilions.
10. The lights are so bright that they prompt the turtles to run in the wrong direction—up the beach away from the water.

PARAGRAPH EXERCISE

Underline the subjects once, the verbs twice, and put a broken line under the dependent clauses in this brief excerpt from *The Handy History Answer Book.*

Today experts disagree over the impact of television on our lives. Some argue that increased crime is a direct outcome of television since programs show crime as an everyday event and since advertisements make people aware of what they don't have. Critics also maintain that television stimulates aggressive behavior, reinforces ethnic stereotyping, and leads to a decrease in activity and creativity. Proponents of television counter [when they cite] increased awareness in world events, improved verbal abilities, and greater curiosity as benefits of television viewing.

SENTENCE WRITING

Write ten sentences about your own relationship with television—the patterns or routines that have developed from your choice of watching or not watching TV. Try to write sentences that have both independent and dependent clauses. Then underline your subjects once, your verbs twice, and put a broken line under your dependent clauses. Use your own paper, and save all of your sentence writing results in a folder.

Correcting Fragments

Sometimes a group of words looks like a sentence—with a capital letter at the beginning and a period at the end—but it may be missing a subject or a verb or both. Such incomplete sentence structures are called *fragments*. Here are a few examples:

Just ran around with his arms in the air. (*Who* did? There is no subject.)

Paul and his sister with the twins. (*Did* what? There is no verb.)

Nothing to do at night. (This fragment is missing a subject and a real verb. *To do* is a verbal, see p. 125.)

To change these fragments into sentences, we must make sure each has a subject and a real verb:

The lottery winner just ran around with his arms in the air. (We added a subject.)

Paul and his sister with the twins reconciled. (We added a verb.)

The jurors had nothing to do at night. (We added a subject and a real verb.)

Sometimes we can simply attach such a fragment to the previous sentence.

I want a fulfilling job. A teaching career, for example. (fragment)

I want a fulfilling job—a teaching career, for example. (correction)

Or we can add a subject or a verb to the fragment and make it a complete sentence.

I want a fulfilling job. A teaching career is one example.

Phrase Fragments

By definition, phrases are word groups without subjects and verbs, so whenever a phrase is punctuated as a sentence, it is a fragment. Look at this example of a sentence followed by a phrase fragment beginning with *hoping* (see p. 125 for more about verbal phrases):

Actors waited outside the director's office. Hoping for a chance at an audition.

We can correct this fragment by attaching it to the previous sentence.

Actors waited outside the director's office, hoping for a chance at an audition.

Or we can change it to include a subject and a real verb.

> Actors waited outside the director's office. They hoped for a chance at an audition.

Here's another example of a sentence followed by a phrase fragment:

> Philosophy classes are challenging. When taken in summer school.

Here the two have been combined into one complete sentence:

> Philosophy classes taken in summer school are challenging.

Or a better revision might be

> Philosophy classes are challenging when taken in summer school.

Sometimes, prepositional phrases are also incorrectly punctuated as sentences. Here a prepositional phrase follows a sentence, but the word group is a fragment—it has no subject and verb of its own. Therefore, it needs to be corrected.

> I live a simple life. With my family on our farm in central California.

Here is one possible correction:

> I live a simple life with my family on our farm in central California.

Or it could be corrected this way:

> My family and I live a simple life on our farm in central California.

Dependent Clause Fragments

A dependent clause punctuated as a sentence is another kind of fragment. A sentence needs a subject, a verb, *and* a complete thought. As discussed in the previous section, a dependent clause has a subject and a verb, but it begins with a word that makes its meaning incomplete, such as *after, while, because, since, although, when, if, where, who, which,* and *that.* (See p. 73 for a longer list of these words.) To correct such fragments, we need to eliminate the word that makes the clause dependent *or* add an independent clause.

Fragment

> *While* some of us wrote in our journals.

Corrected

Some of us wrote in our journals.

or

While some of us wrote in our journals, the fire alarm rang.

Fragment

Which kept me from finishing my journal entry.

Corrected

The fire alarm kept me from finishing my journal entry.

or

We responded to the fire alarm, *which* kept me from finishing my journal entry.

Are fragments ever permissible? Professional writers sometimes use fragments in advertising and other kinds of writing. But professional writers use these fragments intentionally, not in error. Until you're an experienced writer, it's best to write in complete sentences. Especially in college writing, you should avoid using fragments.

EXERCISES

Some of the following word groups are sentences, and some are fragments. The sentences include subjects and verbs and make complete statements. Write the word "correct" next to each of the sentences. Then change the fragments into sentences by making sure that each has a subject, a real verb, and a complete thought.

Exercise 1

1. I read an article about bananas for my health class in high school.
2. That bananas are in danger of extinction in the near future.
3. Due to a crop disease that infects the banana plants' leaves.
4. The disease makes the bananas get ripe too fast.
5. All of the kinds of bananas that people eat are at risk.
6. Some banana experts warning about no more bananas to eat.

7. No banana cream pies, banana splits, banana muffins, or banana bread.
8. Such an idea is new to a lot of us.
9. Most people never think about plant extinction.
10. Chocolate and coffee similar scares in the past.

Exercise 2

1. In my psychology class, we talk about gender a lot.
2. Especially ways of raising children without gender bias.
3. Meaning different expectations about boys' abilities and girls' abilities.
4. Experts have several suggestions for parents and teachers.
5. Ask girls to work in the yard and boys to do dishes sometimes.
6. Not making a big deal out of it.
7. Give both girls and boys affection as well as helpful criticism.
8. Encouraging physically challenging activities for both genders.
9. Give girls access to tools, and praise boys for kindness.
10. Most of all, value their different approaches to math and computers.

Exercise 3

Each pair contains one sentence and one phrase fragment. Correct each phrase fragment by attaching the phrase to the complete sentence before or after it.

1. A worker at the Smithsonian discovered an important historical object. On a shelf in one of the museum's storage rooms.
2. Made of cardboard and covered with short, smooth fur. It was a tall black top hat.
3. The hat didn't look like anything special. More like an old costume or prop.
4. It was special, however. Having been worn by Abraham Lincoln on the night of his assassination.
5. Once found and identified, Lincoln's hat traveled with the 150th anniversary exhibition. Called "America's Smithsonian."

6. For such a priceless object to be able to travel around the country safely. Experts needed to build a unique display case for Lincoln's top hat.
7. The design allowed visitors to view the famous stovepipe hat. Without damaging it with their breath or hands.
8. The hat traveled in a sealed box. Designed against even earthquakes.
9. Keeping the hat earthquake-proof was an important concern. Being on display in California for part of the time.
10. President Lincoln's hat is one of the most impressive. Among the millions of objects in the archives of the Smithsonian.

Source: Saving Stuff (Fireside, 2005)

Exercise 4

Each pair contains one sentence and one dependent clause fragment. Correct each dependent clause fragment by eliminating its dependent word or by attaching the dependent clause to the independent clause before or after it.

1. When Nathan King turned twelve. He had a heart-stopping experience.
2. Nathan was tossing a football against his bedroom wall. Which made the ball ricochet and land on his bed.
3. In a diving motion, Nathan fell on his bed to catch the ball. As it landed.
4. After he caught the ball. Nathan felt a strange sensation in his chest.
5. To his surprise, he looked down and saw the eraser end of a no. 2 pencil. That had pierced his chest and entered his heart.
6. Nathan immediately shouted for his mother. Who luckily was in the house at the time.
7. Because Nathan's mom is a nurse. She knew not to remove the pencil.
8. If she had pulled the pencil out of her son's chest. He would have died.
9. After Nathan was taken to a hospital equipped for open-heart surgery. He had the pencil carefully removed.
10. Fate may be partly responsible for Nathan's happy birthday story. Since it turned out to be his heart surgeon's birthday too.

Source: Time, March 20, 2000

Exercise 5

All of the following word groups are individual fragments punctuated as sentences. Make the necessary changes to turn each fragment into a sentence that makes sense to you. Your corrections will most likely differ from the sample answers at the back of the book. But by comparing your answers to ours, you'll see that there are many ways to correct a fragment.

1. One of the people sitting next to me on the train.
2. Before intermission, the movie that seemed endless.
3. Before the paint was dry in the classrooms.
4. The judge's question and the answer it received.
5. Because there were fewer students in the program this year.
6. Since his speech lasted for over an hour.
7. Whenever the teacher reminds us about the midterm exam.
8. If we move to Kentucky and stay for two years.
9. As soon as the order form reaches the warehouse.
10. Buildings with odd shapes always of interest to me.

PROOFREADING EXERCISE

Correct the five fragments in the following paragraph.

I love fireworks shows. Backyard displays or huge Fourth of July events. When the whole sky lights up with color and booms with noise. In fact, I have a dream to become a fireworks expert. If I could take a class in pyrotechnics right now, I would. Instead, I have to take general education classes. Like English, math, and psychology. Maybe an appointment with a career counselor would be a good idea. To help me find the right school. With a training program in fireworks preparation.

SENTENCE WRITING

Write ten fragments and then revise them so that they are complete sentences. Or exchange papers with another student and turn your classmate's ten fragments into sentences. Use your own paper, and keep all of your sentence writing results in a folder.

Correcting Run-on Sentences

A word group with a subject and a verb is a clause. As we have seen, the clause may be independent (making a complete statement and able to stand alone as a sentence), or it may be dependent (beginning with a dependent word and unable to stand alone as a sentence). When two *independent* clauses are written together without proper punctuation between them, the result is called a *run-on sentence.* Here are some examples:

Classical music is soothing I listen to it in the evenings.

I love the sound of piano therefore, Chopin is one of my favorites.

Run-on sentences can be corrected in one of four ways:

1. Make the two independent clauses into two sentences.

Classical music is soothing. I listen to it in the evenings.

I love the sound of piano. Therefore, Chopin is one of my favorites.

2. Connect the two independent clauses with a semicolon.

Classical music is soothing; I listen to it in the evenings.

I love the sound of piano; therefore, Chopin is one of my favorites.

When a connecting word (transition) such as

also	however	otherwise
consequently	likewise	then
finally	moreover	therefore
furthermore	nevertheless	thus

is used to join two independent clauses, the semicolon comes before the connecting word, and a comma usually comes after it.

Mobile phones are convenient; however, they are very expensive.

Earthquakes scare me; therefore, I don't live in Los Angeles.

Yasmin traveled to London; then she took the "Chunnel" to Paris.

The college recently built a large new library; thus we have more study areas.

> **NOTE**—The use of the comma after the connecting word depends on how long the connecting word is. If it is only a short word, like *then* or *thus,* the comma is not necessary.

3. Connect the two independent clauses with a comma and one of the following seven words (the first letters of which create the word *fanboys*): *for, and, nor, but, or, yet, so*.

Classical music is soothing, *so* I listen to it in the evenings.

Chopin is one of my favorites, *for* I love the sound of piano.

Each of the *fanboys* has its own meaning. For example, *so* means "as a result," and *for* means "because."

Swans are beautiful birds, *and* they mate for life.

Students may register for classes by phone, *or* they may do so in person.

I applied for financial aid, *but* I am still working.

Brian doesn't know how to use a computer, *nor* does he plan to learn.

Before you put a comma before a *fanboys,* be sure there are two independent clauses. Note that the first sentence that follows has two independent clauses. However, the second sentence contains just one clause with two verbs and therefore needs no comma.

The snow began to fall at dusk, and it continued to fall through the night.

The snow began to fall at dusk and continued to fall through the night.

4. Make one of the clauses dependent by adding a dependent word, such as *since, when, as, after, while, or because.* See p. 73 for a longer list of these words.

Since classical music is soothing, I listen to it in the evenings.

Chopin is one of my favorites *because* I love the sound of piano.

Learn these ways to join two clauses, and you'll avoid run-on sentences.

Ways to Correct Run-on Sentences

They were learning a new song. They needed to practice. (two sentences)

They were learning a new song; they needed to practice. (semicolon)

They were learning a new song; therefore, they needed to practice. (semicolon + transition)

They were learning a new song, so they needed to practice. (comma + *fanboys*)

Because they were learning a new song, they needed to practice. (dependent clause first)

They needed to practice because they were learning a new song. (dependent clause last)

EXERCISES

Exercises 1 and 2

CORRECTING RUN-ONS WITH PUNCTUATION

Some of the following sentences are run-ons. If the sentence has two independent clauses, separate them with correct punctuation. Use only a period, a semicolon, or a comma to separate the two independent clauses. Remember to capitalize after a period and to insert a comma only when the words *for, and, nor, but, or, yet,* or *so* are already used to join the two independent clauses.

Exercise 1

1. I just read an article about prehistoric rodents and I was surprised by their size.
2. Scientists recently discovered the remains of a rat-like creature called *Phoberomys* it was as big as a buffalo.
3. *Phoberomys* sat back on its large rear feet and fed itself with its smaller front feet in just the way rats and mice do now.
4. This supersized rodent lived in South America but luckily that was nearly ten million years ago.

5. At that time, South America was a separate continent it had no cows or horses to graze on its open land.
6. South America and North America were separated by the sea so there were also no large cats around to hunt and kill other large animals.
7. Scientists believe that *Phoberomys* thrived and grew large because of the lack of predators and competitors for food.
8. The *Phoberomys'* carefree lifestyle eventually disappeared for the watery separation between North and South America slowly became a land route.
9. The big carnivores of North America could travel down the new land route and the big rodents were defenseless against them.
10. The rodents who survived were the smaller ones who could escape underground and that is the reason we have no buffalo-sized rats today.

Source: Science News, September 20, 2003

Exercise 2

1. One day is hard for me every year that day is my birthday.
2. I don't mind getting older I just never enjoy the day of my birth.
3. For one thing, I was born in August but summer is my least favorite season.
4. I hate the heat and the sun so even traditional warm-weather activities get me down.
5. Sunblock spoils swimming smog spoils biking and crowds spoil the national parks.
6. To most people, the beach is a summer haven to me, the beach in the summer is bright, busy, and boring.
7. I love to walk on the beach on the cold, misty days of winter or early spring I wear a big sweater and have the whole place to myself.
8. August also brings fire season to most parts of the country therefore, even television is depressing.

9. There are no holidays to brighten up August in fact, it's like a black hole in the yearly holiday calendar—after the Fourth of July but before Halloween and the other holidays.

10. I have considered moving my birthday to February even being close to Groundhog Day would cheer me up.

Exercises 3 and 4

CORRECTING RUN-ONS WITH DEPENDENT CLAUSES

Most of the following sentences are run-ons. Correct any run-on sentences by making one or more of the clauses *dependent*. You may rephrase the sentences, but be sure to use dependent words (such as *since, when, as, after, while, because,* or the other words listed on p. 73) to begin dependent clauses. Since various words can be used to form dependent clauses, your answers might differ from those suggested at the back of the book.

Exercise 3

1. Pablo Wendel is a German student of art he feels a special connection with a particular group of ancient sculptures.

2. Pablo acted on this feeling in September of 2006 it won him his "fifteen minutes of fame."

3. He had always admired the terra cotta warriors that were discovered in the 2,200-year-old tomb of a Chinese emperor.

4. Pablo decided to see the famous army of clay soldiers first-hand and to document his trip with photographs.

5. He made a special clay-covered costume it was complete with armor and a helmet.

6. Pablo took this outfit and a pedestal with him to the museum it is located in Xian, China.

7. He planned to take a picture of himself in costume outside the museum, but his dream to stand among the soldiers was too strong.

8. He entered the excavation site, jumped into the excavation pit, and joined the terra cotta army.

9. Pablo, in disguise, stood among his fellow "soldiers" and didn't move eventually someone spotted him.

10. The museum guards confiscated Pablo's clay costume they let him go with just a warning.

Source: CNN.com, September 18, 2006

Exercise 4

1. Our town has recently installed a new rapid transit system it uses trains instead of only buses.
2. Freight trains used to run on tracks laid behind the buildings in town the new metro train tracks follow the same old route.
3. I might try this new transportation method the parking on campus has been getting worse every semester.
4. I would have to walk only a few blocks each day the stations are near my house and school.
5. Some students don't live near the train stations they have to take a bus to the train.
6. The old buses are bulky and ugly the new trains are sleek and attractive.
7. The new trains seem to be inspiring many people to be more conscious of their driving habits some people will never change.
8. I would gladly give up my car the convenience just has to match the benefits.
9. The city has plans for additional routes these routes will bring more commuters in from out of town.
10. My town is making real progress I am glad.

Exercise 5

Correct the following run-on sentences using any of the methods studied in this section: adding punctuation or using dependent words to create dependent clauses. See the chart on p. 88 if you need to review the methods.

1. White buffalos are very rare and they are extremely important in Native American folklore.
2. Many American Indian tribes feel a strong attachment to white buffalos they are viewed as omens of peace and prosperity.

3. One farm in Wisconsin is famous as a source of white buffalos three of them have been born on this farm since 1994.
4. The owners of the farm are Valerie and Dave Heider and they are as surprised as anyone about the unusual births.
5. The Heiders' first white buffalo was a female calf she was named Miracle.
6. Miracle became a local attraction visitors to the Heider farm raised tourism in the area by twenty-two percent in 1995.
7. A second white calf was born on the farm in 1996 however, it died after a few days.
8. Miracle survived until 2004 she lived for ten years.
9. In September of 2006, the Heider farm yielded a third white buffalo calf but it was a boy.
10. The odds against one white buffalo being born are high the odds against three being born in the same place are astronomical.

Sources: gazetteextra.com, September 9, 2006, and courant.com, September 15, 2006

REVIEW OF FRAGMENTS AND RUN-ON SENTENCES

If you remember that all clauses include a subject and a verb, but only independent clauses can be punctuated as sentences (since only they can stand alone), then you will avoid fragments in your writing. And if you memorize these six rules for the punctuation of clauses, you will be able to avoid most punctuation errors.

PUNCTUATING CLAUSES

I am a student. I am still learning.	(two sentences)
I am a student; I am still learning.	(two independent clauses)
I am a student; therefore, I am still learning.	(two independent clauses connected by a word such as *also, consequently, finally, furthermore, however, likewise, moreover, nevertheless, otherwise, then, therefore, thus*)
I am a student, so I am still learning.	(two independent clauses connected by *for, and, nor, but, or, yet, so*)

Because I am a student, I am still learning.	(dependent clause at beginning of sentence)
I am still learning because I am a student.	(dependent clause at end of sentence) Dependent words include *after, although, as, as if, because, before, even if, even though, ever since, how, if, since, so that, than, that, though, unless, until, what, whatever, when, whenever, where, whereas, wherever, whether, which, whichever, while, who, whom, whose,* and *why.*

It is essential that you learn the italicized words in the previous chart—which ones come between independent clauses and which ones introduce dependent clauses.

PROOFREADING EXERCISE

Rewrite the following student paragraph, making the necessary changes to eliminate fragments and run-on sentences.

Sometimes I feel like an egg. Always sitting in rows. In classrooms, the chairs are arranged in rows and at the movies the seats are connected into rows. Why can't chairs be scattered around randomly? In my classes, I usually choose a seat in the back row that way I have a view of the whole room. Luckily, I have good eyesight. Because the chalkboard or whiteboard can be hard to read at that distance. In movie theaters, the most distracting problem can come from the people behind me. I don't mind people making noise or talking but I can't stand people kicking my chair. Totally ruins my concentration. Therefore, I try to sit in the back row of the theater whenever possible.

SENTENCE WRITING

Write a sample sentence of your own to demonstrate each of the six ways to punctuate two clauses. You may model your sentences on the examples used in the review chart on page 92. Use your own paper, and keep all of your sentence writing results in a folder.

Identifying Verb Phrases

Sometimes a verb is one word, but often the whole verb includes more than one word. These are called verb phrases. Look at several of the many forms of the verb *speak,* for example. Most of them are verb phrases, made up of the main verb (*speak*) and one or more helping verbs.

speak	is speaking	had been speaking
speaks	am speaking	will have been speaking
spoke	are speaking	is spoken
will speak	was speaking	was spoken
has spoken	were speaking	will be spoken
have spoken	will be speaking	can speak
had spoken	has been speaking	must speak
will have spoken	have been speaking	should have spoken

Note that words like the following are never verbs even though they may be near a verb or in the middle of a verb phrase:

already	ever	not	really
also	finally	now	sometimes
always	just	often	usually
probably	never	only	possibly

Jason has *never* spoken to his instructor before. She *always* talks with other students.

Two forms of *speak—speaking* and *to speak*—look like verbs, but neither form can ever be the only verb in a sentence. No *ing* word by itself or *to* _______ form of a verb can be the main verb of a sentence.

Jeanine speaking French. (not a sentence because there is no complete verb phrase)

Jeanine was speaking French. (a sentence with a complete verb phrase)

And no verb with *to* in front of it can ever be the verb of a sentence.

Ted to speak in front of groups. (not a sentence because there is no real verb)

Ted likes to speak in front of groups. (a sentence with *likes* as the verb)

These two forms, *speaking* and *to speak,* may be used as subjects or other parts of a sentence.

adj

Speaking on stage is an art. *To speak* on stage is an art. Ted had a *speaking* part in that play.

E X E R C I S E S

Underline the verbs or verb phrases twice in the following sentences. The sentences may contain independent *and* dependent clauses, so there could be several verbs and verb phrases. (Remember that *ing* verbs alone and the *to* ________ forms of verbs are never real verbs in sentences.)

Exercise 1

1. Have you ever felt a craving for art?
2. Have you said to yourself, "I need a new painting, or I am going to go crazy"?
3. If you ever find yourself in this situation, you can get instant satisfaction.
4. I am referring to Art-o-Mat machines, of course.
5. These vending machines dispense small pieces of modern art.
6. You insert five dollars, pull a knob on a refurbished cigarette dispenser, and out comes an original art piece.
7. The artists themselves get fifty percent of the selling price.
8. Art-o-Mat machines can be found at locations across the country.
9. Art-o-Mats are currently dispensing tiny paintings, photographs, and sculptures in twelve states.
10. The machines have sold the works of hundreds of contemporary artists.

Source: www.artomat.org

Exercise 2

1. I am always working on my vocabulary.
2. *Lie* and *lay* can be tricky verbs to use sometimes.
3. They mean "rest" and "put," in that order.

4. Lately, I have been practicing with these two verbs.
5. I know that a sunken ship lies at the bottom of the ocean.
6. The *Titanic,* for example, has lain there for over ninety years.
7. When I left for school, my books were lying all over my desk.
8. A bricklayer is a person who lays bricks to form walls and walkways.
9. Last week, we laid a new foundation for the garage.
10. The contractors will be laying our new concrete driveway on Friday.

Exercise 3

1. I have been reading a series of books that were written by Erin McHugh.
2. These books are filled with facts about important people, places, events, and objects throughout history.
3. The series is called *The 5 W's.*
4. McHugh has included five separate books in the series: *Who?, What?, Where?, When?,* and *Why?*
5. In *Who?,* McHugh offers fun tidbits and biographical information about influential people.
6. McHugh's discussion of the faces on U.S. money is filled with surprising information.
7. All but three of the people with their pictures on U.S. bills have been presidents of the United States.
8. Alexander Hamilton and Benjamin Franklin are still shown on the ten-dollar bill and the hundred-dollar bill, respectively.
9. The U.S. Treasury does not print $10,000 bills anymore.
10. When it did print them, these big bills pictured the inventor of the nation's banking system, Salmon P. Chase.

Exercise 4

1. There have been several power outages in our neighborhood recently.
2. Last week when I was writing an essay on my computer, the power went off.

3. I had not saved my work, and I lost the last few sentences that I had written.
4. I did not enjoy the process of remembering those sentences.
5. Sometimes power outages can be fun.
6. If my whole family is at home, we light the candles on our two big candelabras and put them in the middle of the dining room table.
7. The room starts to look like the set of an old horror movie.
8. Then someone goes to the hall closet and grabs a board game to play.
9. On these special occasions, all of us can forget about school or work problems and just enjoy ourselves.
10. Maybe we should plan to spend evenings like this more often.

Exercise 5

1. Prehistoric musical instruments have been found before.
2. But the ancient flutes that were discovered in China's Henan Province included the oldest playable instrument on record.
3. The nine-thousand-year-old flute was made from the wing bone of a bird.
4. The bone was hollowed out and pierced with seven holes that produce the notes of an ancient Chinese musical scale.
5. Because one of the holes' pitches missed the mark, an additional tiny hole was added by the flute's maker.
6. The flute is played in the vertical position.
7. People who have studied ancient instruments are hoping to learn more about the culture that produced this ancient flute.
8. Other bone flutes were found at the same time and in the same location, but they were not intact or strong enough for playing.
9. Visitors to the Brookhaven National Laboratory's Web site can listen to music from the world's oldest working flute.
10. Listeners will be taken back to 7,000 years B.C.E.

Source: www.bnl.gov

REVIEW EXERCISE

To practice finding all of the sentence structures we have studied so far, mark the following paragraphs from a student essay. First, put parentheses around prepositional phrases, and then underline subjects once and verbs or verb phrases twice. Finally, put a broken line beneath dependent clauses. Begin by marking the first paragraph, and then check your answers at the back of the book before going on to the next paragraph. (Remember that *ing* verbs alone and the *to* ____ forms of verbs are never real verbs in sentences. We will learn more about them on p. 125.)

My brain feels like a computer's central processing unit. Information is continually pumping into its circuits. I organize the data, format it to my individual preferences, and lay it out in my own style. As I endlessly sculpt existing formulas, they become something of my own. When I need a solution to a problem, I access the data that I have gathered from my whole existence, even my preprogrammed DNA.

Since I am a student, teachers require that I supply them with specific information in various formats. When they assign an essay, I produce several paragraphs. If they need a summary, I scan the text, find its main ideas, and put them briefly into my own words. I know that I can accomplish whatever the teachers ask so that I can obtain a bachelor's degree and continue processing ideas to make a living.

I compare my brain to a processor because right now I feel that I must work like one. As I go further into my education, my processor will be continually updated—just like a Pentium! And with any luck, I will end up with real, not artificial, intelligence.

Using Standard English Verbs

The next two discussions are for those who need to practice using Standard English verbs. Many of us grew up doing more speaking than writing. But in college and in the business and professional worlds, knowledge of Standard Written English is essential.

The following charts show the forms of four verbs as they are used in Standard Written English. These forms might differ from the way you use these verbs when you speak. Memorize the Standard English forms of these important verbs. The first verb (*talk*) is one of the regular verbs (verbs that all end the same way according to a pattern); most verbs in English are regular. The other three verbs charted here (*have, be,* and *do*) are irregular and are important because they are used not only as main verbs but also as helping verbs in verb phrases.

Don't go on to the exercises until you have memorized the forms of these Standard English verbs.

REGULAR VERB: TALK

PRESENT TIME		PAST TIME	
I you we they	talk	I you we they he, she, it	talked
he, she, it	talks		

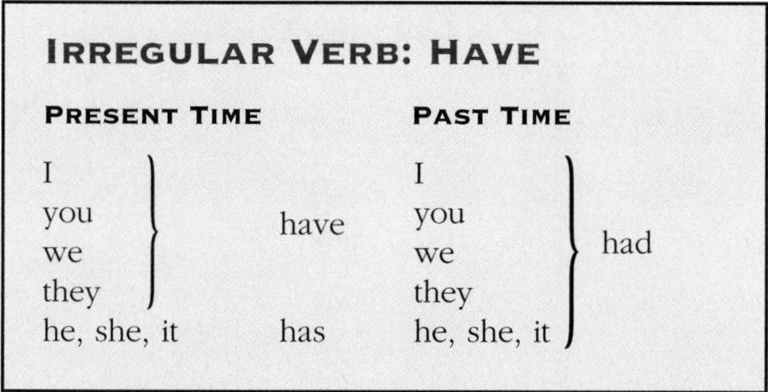

IRREGULAR VERB: HAVE

PRESENT TIME		PAST TIME	
I you we they	have	I you we they he, she, it	had
he, she, it	has		

IRREGULAR VERB: BE

PRESENT TIME		PAST TIME	
I	am	I	was
you, we, they	are	you, we, they	were
he, she, it	is	he, she, it	was

IRREGULAR VERB: DO

PRESENT TIME		PAST TIME	
I, you, we, they	do	I, you, we, they, he, she, it	did
he, she, it	does		

Sometimes you may have difficulty with the correct endings of verbs because you don't hear the words correctly. Note carefully the *s* sound and the *ed* sound at the end of words. Occasionally, the *ed* is not clearly pronounced, as in *They tried to help,* but most of the time you can hear it if you listen.

Read the following sentences aloud, making sure that you say every sound:

1. He seems satisfied with his new job.

2. She likes saving money for the future.

3. It takes strength of character to control spending.

4. Todd brings salad to every potluck he attends.

5. I used to know all of their names.

6. They supposed that they were right.

7. He recognized the suspect and excused himself from the jury.

8. The chess club sponsored Dorothy in the school's charity event.

Now read some other sentences aloud from this text, making sure that you say all the *s*'s and *ed*'s. Reading aloud and listening to others will help you use the correct verb endings automatically.

EXERCISES

In these pairs of sentences, use the *present* form of the verb in the first sentence and the *past* form in the second. All the verbs follow the pattern of the regular verb *talk* except the irregular verbs *have, be,* and *do.* Keep referring to the charts if you're not sure which form to use. Check your answers in the back of the book after each set.

Exercise 1

1. (have) My brother _____ a bad cold right now. He _____ the flu last month.

2. (do) Jennifer _____ the crossword puzzles in the newspaper. She _____ them in the *TV Guide* until we canceled our subscription.

3. (be) I _____ now the president of the chess club on campus. I _____ just a member of the club last semester.

4. (vote) Pat _____ in every election. Pat _____ with an absentee ballot in 2003.

5. (have) The twins _____ similar ideas about the environment. Last year, they _____ a fund-raiser for their local wildlife preserve.

6. (shop) He _____ for almost everything online. He _____ for groceries online last week.

7. (be) They _____ finally satisfied with their living room. They _____ embarrassed by it before the remodeling.

8. (pick) I _____ out the plants whenever we go to the nursery. Yesterday, I also _____ out the paint colors at the home improvement store.

9. (do) We _____ what we can for the birds in winter. A few years ago, we _____ our best to save a nearly frozen sparrow.

10. (end) That new movie _____ with a big surprise. It _____ before I had finished my popcorn.

Exercise 2

1. (be) They _____ rich and famous now. They _____ unknown a year ago.

2. (do) He _____ his best work in class. He _____ not do well on the take-home test.

3. (have) She _____ a new goal. She _____ an unrealistic goal before.

4. (tag) He _____ only the expensive items at his garage sales. In the past, he _____ all of the items.

5. (have) I always _____ a good time with my friends. At Disneyland, I _____ the best time of all.

6. (stuff) She _____ envelopes part time. Yesterday she _____ envelopes for five hours straight.

7. (be) Many of us _____ allergic to milk, so we _____ unable to eat the pizza at the postgame party.

8. (do) They _____ their best to help their parents. They _____ the grocery shopping and the dishes this week.

9. (dance) You _____ very well now. You _____ a little awkwardly in high school.

10. (be) At the moment, they _____ the fastest delivery people in the business. They _____ the second-fastest delivery people just six months ago.

Exercise 3

Circle the correct Standard English verb forms.

1. I recently (change, changed) my career plans; now I (want, wants) to be a teacher.
2. Last year, I (have, had) my mind set on becoming a nurse.
3. I (enroll, enrolled) in nursing classes, but they (was, were) different from what I (expect, expected).
4. The classes (was, were) often too stressful, and the teachers (was, were) very demanding.
5. We (does, did) spend part of the semester working in a clinic where we (was, were) able to observe just what a nurse (do, does).
6. The nurse that I (observe, observed) (have, had) several patients to look after.

7. I (watch, watched) him as he (cares, cared) for them and (follow, followed) the doctors' orders.
8. He (have, had) his patients, their families, and the clinic's doctors and staff to worry about all the time.
9. I never (imagine, imagined) that a nurse (have, had) so many responsibilities.
10. A teacher (need, needs) to worry about the students and the school, and those (is, are) responsibilities that I (is, am) ready to take.

Exercise 4

Circle the correct Standard English verb forms.

1. My cousin Isabel and I (has, have) a lot in common.
2. We both (play, plays) many different sports.
3. She (play, plays) soccer, softball, and basketball.
4. I (play, plays) tennis, badminton, and golf.
5. However, Isabel (practice, practices) more often than I (does, do).
6. The result (is, are) that she (win, wins) more often, too.
7. I (is, am) as skilled as she (is, am), but I (is, am) a little bit lazy.
8. Our parents (remind, reminds) us about practicing all the time.
9. Isabel really (follow, follows) their advice.
10. We both (has, have) talent, but I (is, am) not as disciplined as she (is, am).

Exercise 5

Correct any of following sentences that do not use Standard English verb forms.

1. Last semester, my drawing teacher hand us an assignment.
2. It was half of a photograph pasted onto a whole piece of paper.
3. We has to draw in the other half of the picture.
4. My picture show a woman sitting against the bottom of a tree trunk.
5. Her shoulders, hat, and umbrella was only partly there.
6. I tried to imagine what the missing parts look like.

7. The tree was easy to fill in because its shape was clear in the photo.
8. Therefore, I starts with the tree, the sky, and the ground.
9. Then I used my imagination to fill in the woman's shoulders, hat, and umbrella.
10. I receives an "A" grade for my drawing.

PROOFREADING EXERCISE

Correct any sentences in the following paragraph that do not use Standard English verb forms.

Every day, as we arrive on campus and walk to our classrooms, we see things that needs to be fixed. Many of them cause us only a little bit of trouble, so we forgets them until we face them again. Every morning, there is a long line of students in their cars waiting to enter the parking lots because the lights at all of the corners is not timed properly. The lights from the main boulevard change too slowly, and that allow too many cars to stack up on the side streets. Students who walk to school is affected, too. Many drivers don't watch where they is going and almost run over pedestrians who is walking in the driveways.

SENTENCE WRITING

Write ten sentences about a problem on your campus. Check your sentences to be sure that they use Standard English verb forms. Try exchanging papers with another student for more practice. Use your own paper, and keep all of your sentence writing results in a folder.

Using Regular and Irregular Verbs

All regular verbs end the same way in the past form and when used with helping verbs. Here is a chart showing all the forms of some *regular* verbs and the various helping verbs with which they are used.

REGULAR VERBS

BASE FORM	PRESENT	PAST	PAST PARTICIPLE	*ING* FORM
(Use after *can, may, shall, will, could, might, should, would, must, do, does, did.*)			(Use after *have, has, had.* Some can be used after *forms of be.*)	(Use after *forms of be.*)
ask	ask *(s)*	asked	asked	asking
bake	bake *(s)*	baked	baked	baking
count	count *(s)*	counted	counted	counting
dance	dance *(s)*	danced	danced	dancing
decide	decide *(s)*	decided	decided	deciding
enjoy	enjoy *(s)*	enjoyed	enjoyed	enjoying
finish	finish *(es)*	finished	finished	finishing
happen	happen *(s)*	happened	happened	happening
learn	learn *(s)*	learned	learned	learning
like	like *(s)*	liked	liked	liking
look	look *(s)*	looked	looked	looking
mend	mend *(s)*	mended	mended	mending
need	need *(s)*	needed	needed	needing
open	open *(s)*	opened	opened	opening
start	start *(s)*	started	started	starting
suppose	suppose *(s)*	supposed	supposed	supposing
tap	tap *(s)*	tapped	tapped	tapping
walk	walk *(s)*	walked	walked	walking
want	want *(s)*	wanted	wanted	wanting

NOTE—When there are several helping verbs, the last one determines which form of the main verb should be used: they *should* finish soon; they should *have* finished an hour ago.

When do you write *ask, finish, suppose, use?* And when do you write *asked, finished, supposed, used?* Here are some rules that will help you decide.

Write *ask, finish, suppose, use* (or their *s* forms) when writing about the present time, repeated actions, or facts:

He *asks* questions whenever he is confused.

They always *finish* their projects on time.

I *suppose* you want me to help you move.

Birds *use* leaves, twigs, and feathers to build their nests.

Write *asked, finished, supposed, used*

1. **When writing about the past:**

   He *asked* the teacher for another explanation.

   She *finished* her internship last year.

   They *supposed* that there were others bidding on that house.

   I *used* to study piano.

2. **When some form of *be* (other than the word *be* itself) comes before the word:**

   He was *asked* the most difficult questions.

   She is *finished* with her training now.

   They were *supposed* to sign at the bottom of the form.

   My essay was *used* as a sample of clear narration.

3. **When some form of *have* comes before the word:**

   The teacher has *asked* us that question before.

   She will have *finished* all of her exams by the end of May.

   I had *supposed* too much without any proof.

   We have *used* many models in my drawing class this semester.

All the verbs in the chart on page 105 are *regular*. That is, they're all formed in the same way—with an *ed* ending on the past form and on the past participle. But many verbs are irregular. Their past and past participle forms change spelling instead of just adding an *ed*. Here's a chart of some *irregular* verbs. Notice that the base, present, and *ing* forms end the same as regular verbs. Refer to this list when you aren't sure which verb form to use. Memorize all the forms you don't know.

Irregular Verbs

BASE FORM	PRESENT	PAST	PAST PARTICIPLE	ING FORM
(Use after *can, may, shall, will, could, might, should, would, must, do, does, did.*)			(Use after *have, has, had.* Some can be used after *forms of be.*)	(Use after *forms of be.*)
be	is, am, are	was, were	been	being
become	become *(s)*	became	become	becoming
begin	begin *(s)*	began	begun	beginning
break	break *(s)*	broke	broken	breaking
bring	bring *(s)*	brought	brought	bringing
buy	buy *(s)*	bought	bought	buying
build	build *(s)*	built	built	building
catch	catch *(es)*	caught	caught	catching
choose	choose *(s)*	chose	chosen	choosing
come	come *(s)*	came	come	coming
do	do *(es)*	did	done	doing
draw	draw *(s)*	drew	drawn	drawing
drink	drink *(s)*	drank	drunk	drinking
drive	drive *(s)*	drove	driven	driving
eat	eat *(s)*	ate	eaten	eating
fall	fall *(s)*	fell	fallen	falling
feel	feel *(s)*	felt	felt	feeling
fight	fight *(s)*	fought	fought	fighting
find	find *(s)*	found	found	finding
forget	forget *(s)*	forgot	forgotten	forgetting
forgive	forgive *(s)*	forgave	forgiven	forgiving
freeze	freeze *(s)*	froze	frozen	freezing
get	get *(s)*	got	got *or* gotten	getting
give	give *(s)*	gave	given	giving
go	go *(es)*	went	gone	going
grow	grow *(s)*	grew	grown	growing
have	have *or* has	had	had	having

IRREGULAR VERBS (CONTINUED)

BASE FORM	PRESENT	PAST	PAST PARTICIPLE	ING FORM
hear	hear *(s)*	heard	heard	hearing
hold	hold *(s)*	held	held	holding
keep	keep *(s)*	kept	kept	keeping
know	know *(s)*	knew	known	knowing
lay (to put)	lay *(s)*	laid	laid	laying
lead (like "bead")	lead *(s)*	led	led	leading
leave	leave *(s)*	left	left	leaving
lie (to rest)	lie *(s)*	lay	lain	lying
lose	lose *(s)*	lost	lost	losing
make	make *(s)*	made	made	making
meet	meet *(s)*	met	met	meeting
pay	pay *(s)*	paid	paid	paying
read	read *(s)*	read	read	reading
(pron. "reed")		(pron. "red")	(pron. "red")	
ride	ride *(s)*	rode	ridden	riding
ring	ring *(s)*	rang	rung	ringing
rise	rise *(s)*	rose	risen	rising
run	run *(s)*	ran	run	running
say	say *(s)*	said	said	saying
see	see *(s)*	saw	seen	seeing
sell	sell *(s)*	sold	sold	selling
shake	shake *(s)*	shook	shaken	shaking
shine (give light)	shine *(s)*	shone	shone	shining
shine (polish)	shine *(s)*	shined	shined	shining
sing	sing *(s)*	sang	sung	singing
sleep	sleep *(s)*	slept	slept	sleeping
speak	speak *(s)*	spoke	spoken	speaking
spend	spend *(s)*	spent	spent	spending
stand	stand *(s)*	stood	stood	standing
steal	steal *(s)*	stole	stolen	stealing
strike	strike *(s)*	struck	struck	striking
swim	swim *(s)*	swam	swum	swimming
swing	swing *(s)*	swung	swung	swinging

IRREGULAR VERBS (CONTINUED)

BASE FORM	PRESENT	PAST	PAST PARTICIPLE	ING FORM
take	take *(s)*	took	taken	taking
teach	teach *(es)*	taught	taught	teaching
tear	tear *(s)*	tore	torn	tearing
tell	tell *(s)*	told	told	telling
think	think *(s)*	thought	thought	thinking
throw	throw *(s)*	threw	thrown	throwing
wear	wear *(s)*	wore	worn	wearing
win	win *(s)*	won	won	winning
write	write *(s)*	wrote	written	writing

Sometimes verbs from the past participle column are used after some form of the verb *be* (or verbs that take the place of *be* like *appear, seem, look, feel, get, act, become*) to describe the subject or to say something in a passive, rather than an active, way.

She is contented.

You appear pleased. (You *are* pleased.)

He seems delighted. (He *is* delighted.)

She looked surprised. (She *was* surprised.)

I feel shaken. (I *am* shaken.)

They get bored easily. (They *are* bored easily.)

You acted concerned. (You *were* concerned.)

They were thrown out of the game. (Active: *The referee threw them out of the game.*)

We were disappointed by the news. (Active: *The news disappointed us.*)

Often these verb forms become words that describe the subject; at other times they still act as part of the verb in the sentence. What you call them doesn't matter. The important thing is to be sure you use the correct form from the past participle column.

EXERCISES

Write the correct form of the verbs in the blanks. Refer to the charts and explanations on the preceding pages if you aren't sure which form to use after a certain helping verb. Check your answers after each exercise.

Exercise 1

1. (live) I currently _______ with my parents.

2. (live) I have _______ with them all of my life.

3. (live) Someday I will _______ in my own apartment.

4. (live) Once I am _______ on my own, things will change for me.

5. (live) My brother has _______ in a dorm ever since he moved to Berkeley.

6. (live) In his e-mails, he describes the roommates that he _______ with.

7. (live) I am glad that I can still _______ at home while I am in college.

8. (live) My parents seem pleased that I have been _______ with them for so long.

9. (live) We know each other's habits, and we _______ with each other's quirks.

10. (live) We are all a bit sad that I will soon be _______ away from home.

Exercise 2

1. (get) A few months ago, I _______ a kitten named Samantha. She has silvery gray fur and long white whiskers. Samantha always _______ so excited when I sprinkle catnip on the rug.

2. (give) When my friend Will _______ Samantha to me, she was the sleekest, most graceful of his cat's kittens. Since then, I have _______ her almost all of my attention.

3. (be) Now I _______ a certified cat lover, and Sam _______ a great cat.

4. (think) Before I had Samantha, my parents _______ that I was too irresponsible to own a cat, but I didn't _______ so, or I wouldn't have taken her in the first place.

5. (grow) Samantha has _______ into a plump, handsome cat. And I _______ catnip plants in the backyard.

6. (leave) Before I _______ for school each day, I make sure that Sam is inside the house. Once, I _______ the kitchen window open, and I found her sitting near the street when I came home.

7. (wave) Sam loves to play with a toy that I made for her. I _______ the bunch of feathers on a string in front of her, and she _______ her paws at them and tries to eat them.

8. (know) Samantha _______ her name and will come when she hears me call. I didn't _______ that cats could do that.

9. (do) Sam _______ many cute things, and I _______ my best to keep her healthy and make her happy.

10. (be) I _______ a little nervous when I first brought Sam home, but I could not _______ happier with a pet than I _______ now.

Exercise 3

1. (take, suppose) My sister Bonnie _______ me to the movies last Tuesday afternoon even though I was _______ to be at work.

2. (be, go) It _______ the only time that Bonnie could _______ to the movies with me.

3. (call, leave, feel) So I _______ my boss and _______ a message that I didn't _______ well enough to go to work.

4. (imagine, be) I never _______ that I would get caught, but I _______ wrong.

5. (buy, drive, see) Just as Bonnie and I were _______ our tickets, my boss _______ by and _______ us.

6. (feel, know, be) I _______ such panic because I _______ that my boss would _______ mad at me.

7. (try, go) I _______ to explain myself when I _______ back to the office the next day.

8. (be, undo) The damage had ________ done, however, and nothing could ________ it.

9. (wish, take) Now I ________ that I could ________ back that day.

10. (do, be) I ________ not have much fun with Bonnie, and the movie ________ not even good.

Exercise 4

1. (use, have) Many people ________ cell phones that ________ voice-recognition capabilities.

2. (do, speak, dial) With such a system, callers ________ not have to dial phone numbers by hand. Instead, they just ________ into the phone, and the phone ________ the number.

3. (be, be) When driving a car, callers ________ then free to watch the road and steer the car without distraction. These phones ________ much safer.

4. (be, like, start) Voice dialing ________ almost always optional, but so many people ________ the system that most people have ________ to use it.

5. (do, want) My mom ________ not trust such systems; she ________ to have complete control over her own dialing.

6. (trust, be) She barely even ________ cell phones, so she ________ definitely suspicious of voice dialing.

7. (imagine, dial) I can ________ her as a teenager in the sixties. In my mind, she is ________ one of those rotary-operated princess phones.

8. (ask, tell, be) I was ________ my mom about phones the other day, and I ________ her how old-fashioned she ________.

9. (look, smile) She just ________ at me and ________.

10. (have) My mom ________ a way of saying a lot with just a smile.

Exercise 5

1. (sit, see)	I was _______ in the lobby of the haircutting place near my house when I _______ one of my old high school teachers, Mr. Blair.
2. (be, appear)	He _______ obviously waiting for a haircut too and _______ to be nervous about it.
3. (flip, turn, look)	As he _______ through a magazine, he _______ his face toward the big front window and _______ longingly in the direction of his car.
4. (be, wear, think, be)	During my high school years, Mr. Blair _______ well-liked because he _______ his hair in a pony tail, so everyone _______ that he _______ cool.
5. (pass, seem)	As the minutes _______ in the hair salon, Mr. Blair _______ to calm down.
6. (wait, cut)	I was _______ to see whether Mr. Blair would really _______ his pony tail off after all these years.
7. (call, watch, recognize)	When my name was _______, I _______ Mr. Blair's face to see whether he would _______ me.
8. (look, figure, be)	He didn't _______ up, so I _______ that he _______ too busy worrying about his own hair to notice me.
9. (get, chat, be)	I _______ my usual simple cut, and as I _______ with my haircutter, I _______ surprised to see Mr. Blair's haircutter finish his cut within just a few minutes.
10. (come, leave)	Mr. Blair had apparently just _______ in for a trim, and he _______ the lobby with the water from his long wet hair soaking into the top of his shirt.

PROGRESS TEST

This test covers everything you've studied so far. One sentence in each pair is correct. The other is incorrect. Read both sentences carefully before you decide. Then write the letter of the incorrect sentence in the blank. Try to name the error and correct it if you can.

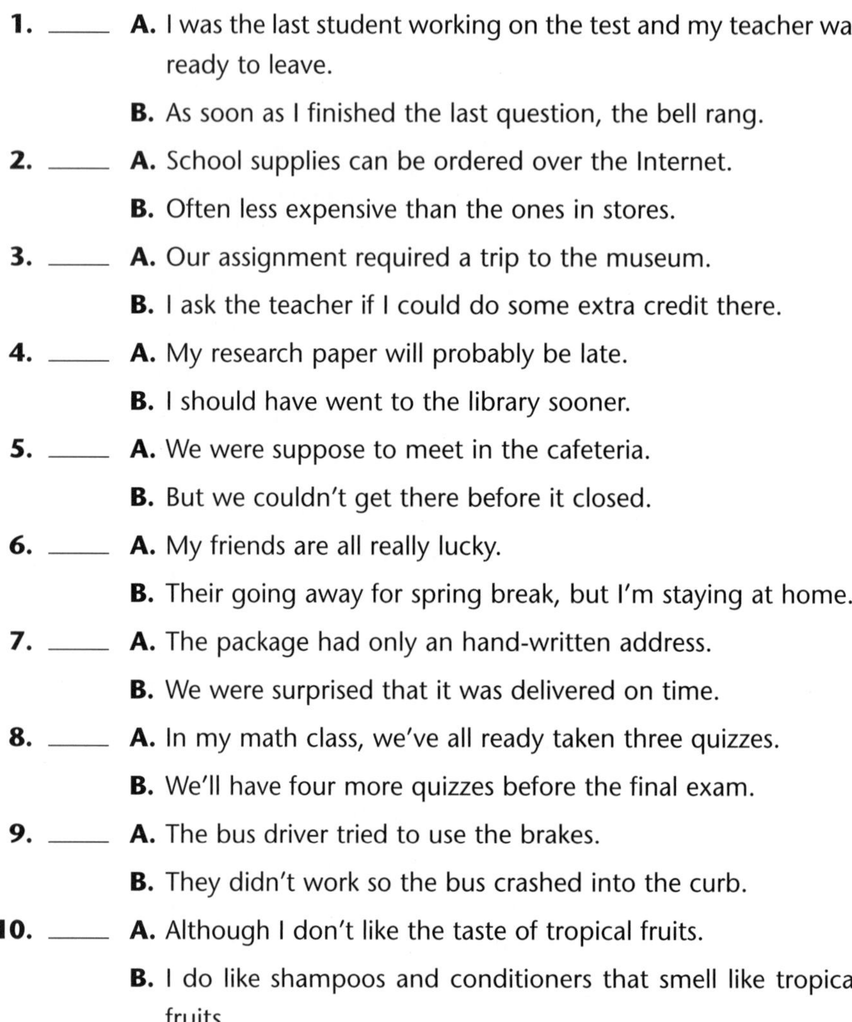

1. ______ **A.** I was the last student working on the test and my teacher was ready to leave.

B. As soon as I finished the last question, the bell rang.

2. ______ **A.** School supplies can be ordered over the Internet.

B. Often less expensive than the ones in stores.

3. ______ **A.** Our assignment required a trip to the museum.

B. I ask the teacher if I could do some extra credit there.

4. ______ **A.** My research paper will probably be late.

B. I should have went to the library sooner.

5. ______ **A.** We were suppose to meet in the cafeteria.

B. But we couldn't get there before it closed.

6. ______ **A.** My friends are all really lucky.

B. Their going away for spring break, but I'm staying at home.

7. ______ **A.** The package had only an hand-written address.

B. We were surprised that it was delivered on time.

8. ______ **A.** In my math class, we've all ready taken three quizzes.

B. We'll have four more quizzes before the final exam.

9. ______ **A.** The bus driver tried to use the brakes.

B. They didn't work so the bus crashed into the curb.

10. ______ **A.** Although I don't like the taste of tropical fruits.

B. I do like shampoos and conditioners that smell like tropical fruits.

Maintaining Subject-Verb Agreement

As we have seen, the subject and verb in a sentence work together, so they must always agree. Different subjects need different forms of verbs. When the correct verb follows a subject, we call it subject-verb agreement.

The following sentences illustrate the rule that *s* verbs follow most singular subjects but not plural subjects:

One turtle walks.	Three turtles walk.
The baby cries.	The babies cry.
A democracy listens to the people.	Democracies listen to the people.
One child plays.	Many children play.

The following sentences show how forms of the verb *be* (*is, am, are, was, were*) and helping verbs (*be, have,* and *do*) are made to agree with their subjects. We have labeled only the verbs that must agree with the subjects.

This puzzle is difficult.	These puzzles are difficult.
I am amazed.	You are amazed.
He was sleeping.	They were sleeping.
That class has been canceled.	Those classes have been canceled.
She does not want to participate.	They do not want to participate.

The following words are always singular and take an *s* verb or the irregular equivalent (*is, was, has, does*):

one	anybody	each
anyone	everybody	
everyone	nobody	
no one	somebody	
someone		

Someone feeds my dog in the morning.

Everybody was at the party.

Each does her own homework.

Remember that prepositional phrases often come between subjects and verbs. You should ignore these interrupting phrases, or you may mistake the wrong word for the subject and use a verb form that doesn't agree.

Someone from the apartments feeds my dog in the morning. (*Someone* is the subject, not *apartments*.)

Everybody on the list of celebrities was at the party. (*Everybody* is the subject, not *celebrities*.)

Each of the twins does her own homework. (*Each* is the subject, not *twins*.)

However, the words *some, any, all, none,* and *most* are exceptions to this rule of ignoring prepositional phrases. These words can be singular or plural, depending on the words that follow them in prepositional phrases. Again, we have labeled only the verbs that must agree with the subjects.

Some of the *pie* is gone.

Some of the *cookies* are gone.

Is any of the *paper* still in the supply cabinet?

Are any of the *pencils* still in the supply cabinet?

All of her *work* has been published.

All of her *poems* have been published.

None of the *jewelry* is missing.

None of the *clothes* are missing.

On July 4th, most of the *country* celebrates.

On July 4th, most of the *citizens* celebrate.

When a sentence has more than one subject joined by *and,* the subject is plural:

The teacher *and* the tutors eat lunch at noon.

A glazed doughnut *and* an onion bagel were sitting on the plate.

However, when two subjects are joined by *or,* then the subject *closest* to the verb determines the verb form:

Either the teacher *or* the *tutors* eat lunch at noon.

Either the tutors *or* the *teacher* eats lunch at noon.

A glazed doughnut *or* an onion *bagel* was sitting on the plate.

In most sentences, the subject comes before the verb. However, in some cases, the subject follows the verb, and subject-verb agreement needs special attention. Study the following examples:

Over the building flies a solitary flag. (flag flies)

Over the building fly several flags. (flags fly)

There is a good reason for my actions. (reason is)

There are good reasons for my actions. (reasons are)

EXERCISES

Circle the correct verbs in parentheses to maintain subject-verb agreement in the following sentences. Remember to ignore prepositional phrases, unless the subjects are *some*, *any*, *all*, *none*, or *most*. Check your answers ten at a time.

Exercise 1

1. I (work, works) at an insurance agency as a part-time file clerk.
2. My favorite coworkers at the office (is, are) Teresa and Jesse.
3. Teresa and I (has, have) the same shift, so we (know, knows) each other very well.
4. Our hours each day (is, are) from 3:00 to 7:00.
5. As soon as Teresa (get, gets) to the office, she (separate, separates) the files into alphabetical stacks.
6. When I (get, gets) there, I (ask, asks) the office manager if there (is, are) any special filing tasks for us.
7. If there (is, are) a special task, Teresa and I (do, does) that one first.
8. Then we (focus, focuses) on the regular filing of people's records back into their places.
9. Jesse and his managers (work, works) in the office next door to ours.
10. One of his bosses (is, are) nice, but the others (isn't, aren't) as friendly.

Exercise 2

1. There (is, are) a Web site that (rate, rates) movies based on how accurately they (portray, portrays) the laws of physics.
2. The site (is, are) called Intuitor.com.
3. Examples of bad physics in movies (include, includes) bullets that (spark, sparks) on contact, cars that (explode, explodes) in crashes, and laser beams that (is, are) visible to the naked eye.
4. The reviewers at Intuitor.com (give, gives) movies one of the following ratings: GP, PGP, PGP-13, RP, XP, and NR.
5. These labels (rank, ranks) the physics in a particular movie from good [GP] to pretty good [PGP] to totally unbelievable [XP].
6. Those movies that (get, gets) the RP rating are the ones that (is, are) so flawed in portraying the laws of physics that they (make, makes) the Intuitor reviewers "retch."
7. The NR label (is, are) reserved for the movies that (is, are) not rated because of their obvious focus on imaginative, not scientific, possibilities.
8. The recent classic films *Titanic, Speed,* and *The Da Vinci Code* (was, were) rated GP or PGP.
9. The worst rating of RP (was, were) handed out to both *The Day After Tomorrow* and *Independence Day* and to two of *The Matrix* movies.
10. Both *Spider-Man* and *The Hulk* (was, were) creative films that (was, were) given the NR label.

Exercise 3

1. In his book *Catwatching,* Desmond Morris (explain, explains) why cats (seem, seems) to be able to feel earthquakes before they (happen, happens).
2. First of all, the cat (feel, feels) sensations that we humans (doesn't, don't).

3. Earthquakes (begin, begins) with movements far under ground, and cats often (react, reacts).
4. Some of these reactions (is, are) among the reasons why cats (has, have) been thought to have magical powers.
5. Another explanation for cats' predictions (is, are) that they (sense, senses) changes in static electricity or in the earth's magnetic fields.
6. Most of us (doesn't, don't) notice such changes, but some people (get, gets) headaches before earthquakes, headaches that may be caused by the change.
7. A human being just (isn't, aren't) able to tell the difference between a pre-earthquake headache and a regular stress-related one.
8. Cats (does, do) seem to have such abilities.
9. Many people (has, have) witnessed what cats (does, do) when an earthquake (is, are) approaching.
10. Cats suddenly (look, looks) scared and (run, runs) back and forth or in and out of a house or building; research (have, has) shown that we humans should pay close attention when they (does, do).

Source: Catwatching (Three Rivers Press, 1986)

Exercise 4

1. Bulletproof windows (has, have) been used for protection for a long time.
2. Of course, they (was, were) only helpful from one direction.
3. There (was, were) no way to shoot back from inside the bulletproof glass.
4. Now there (is, are) a new kind of bulletproof window.
5. The new window (allow, allows) someone to shoot through it from inside and still be protected from bullets fired at it from outside.
6. A bullet (travel, travels) out through the new multilayered substance.

7. As the bullet (break, breaks) through on its way out, it (melt, melts) the substance and (seal, seals) it again.
8. Police departments (is, are) very interested in this new technology.
9. They (realize, realizes) how useful such a substance could be for their officers.
10. The cost of the new windows (is, are) high, but the benefits (is, are) worth it.

Source: Discover, November 2003

Exercise 5

1. An old rhyme about sneezing (give, gives) a sneeze on each day of the week special meaning.
2. The poem (sound, sounds) a lot like the one that (begin, begins) "Monday's child (is, are) full of woe."
3. This poem about sneezing also (connect, connects) Monday with a negative outcome.
4. It (say, says) that a sneeze on Monday (mean, means) "danger."
5. A Tuesday sneeze (forecast, forecasts) a meeting with a "stranger."
6. Wednesday and Thursday (is, are) days when sneezes (mean, means) we will receive a "letter" or "something better," respectively.
7. There (is, are) no TGIF celebrations for sneezes on Friday, for they (foretell, foretells) "sorrow."
8. But a sneeze on Saturday (mean, means) the visit of a loved one "tomorrow."
9. Sunday sneezes (is, are) left out of the poem altogether.
10. Such day-of-the-week rhymes from the past (seem, seems) to reveal a lot about us.

Source: Schott's Original Miscellany (Bloomsbury, 2003)

PROOFREADING EXERCISE

Find and correct the ten subject-verb agreement errors in the following paragraph.

Unfortunately, tension between members of the public are common these days. When two people at a movie theater irritates each other or have a disagreement, the whole audience suffer. Everyone who is sitting around the troublemakers want to move immediately to another section. However, if anyone get up to sit somewhere else, then everyone else start to get nervous. So most people just waits until one of two fighting people calm down. After that, the members of the audience forgets about the disturbance and enjoy the rest of the movie. The same pattern repeat itself in stadiums and ballparks, too.

SENTENCE WRITING

Write ten sentences in which you describe the classes you are taking right now. Use verbs in the present time. Then go back over your sentences—underline your subjects once, underline your verbs twice, and be sure they agree. Use your own paper, and keep all of your sentence writing results in a folder.

Avoiding Shifts in Time

People often worry about using different time frames in writing. Let common sense guide you. If you begin writing a paper in past time, don't shift back and forth to the present unnecessarily; and if you begin in the present, don't shift to the past without good reason. In the following paragraph, the writer starts in the present, shifts to the past, and then shifts again to the present:

> In the novel *To Kill a Mockingbird,* Jean Louise Finch is a little girl who lives in the South with her father, Atticus, and her brother, Jem. Everybody in town calls Jean Louise "Scout" as a nickname. When Atticus, a lawyer, chose to defend a black man against the charges of a white woman, some of their neighbors turned against him. Scout protected her father by appealing to the humanity of one member of the angry mob. In this chapter, five-year-old Scout turns out to be stronger than a group of adult men.

All the verbs should be in the present:

> In the novel *To Kill a Mockingbird,* Jean Louise Finch is a little girl who lives in the South with her father, Atticus, and her brother, Jem. Everybody in town calls Jean Louise "Scout" as a nickname. When Atticus, a lawyer, chooses to defend a black man against the charges of a white woman, some of their neighbors turn against him. Scout protects her father by appealing to the humanity of one member of the angry mob. In this chapter, five-year-old Scout turns out to be stronger than a group of adult men.

This sample paragraph discusses only the events that happen within the novel's plot, so it needs to maintain one time frame—the present, which we use to write about literature and repeated actions.

However, sometimes you will write about the present, the past, and even the future together. Then it may be necessary to use these different time frames within the same paragraph, each for its own reason. For example, if you were to give biographical information about Harper Lee, author of *To Kill a Mockingbird,* within a discussion of the novel and its influence, you might need to use all three time frames:

> Harper Lee grew up in Alabama, and she based elements in the book on experiences from her childhood. Like the character Atticus, Lee's father was a lawyer. She wrote the novel in his law offices. *To Kill a Mockingbird* is Harper Lee's most famous work, and it received the Pulitzer Prize for fiction in 1960. Lee's book turned forty years old in the year 2000. It will always remain one of the most moving and compassionate novels in American literature.

The previous paragraph uses past (*grew, based, was, wrote, received, turned*), present (*is*), and future (*will remain*) in the same paragraph without committing the error of shifting. Shifting occurs when the writer changes time frames *inconsistently* or *for no reason,* confusing the reader (as in the first example given).

PROOFREADING EXERCISES

Which of the following student paragraphs shift *unnecessarily* back and forth between time frames? In those that do, change the verbs to maintain one time frame, thus making the entire paragraph read smoothly. One of the paragraphs is correct.

1. No one knows for certain who the model for Leonardo da Vinci's *Mona Lisa* was. However, recent studies have discovered some new information. Dutch scientists used a computer program that is capable of "emotion recognition" to find out how the model felt at the time of the painting. Their results show that she was primarily happy. But her expression also registers tiny bits of anger, fear, and disgust. Another expert, Japanese forensic scientist Dr. Matsumi Suzuki, has created an actual voice for *Mona Lisa.* Using measurements of her head and hands, Dr. Suzuki has determined that she was approximately five-and-a-half feet tall and had a deep voice. A recording of what Mona Lisa might have sounded like can be heard on the Web.

Source: Renaissance Magazine, Issue #50 (2006)

2. Back in the early 1900s, Sears Roebuck sold houses through the mail. The houses are listed along with the rest of the products in Sears' famous catalog. The house kits arrived in thousands of pieces, and people will put them together themselves. Or they get a builder to help them. In 1919, one company, Standard Oil, places an order for an entire town's worth of houses as shelter for its employees. The house kits even included the paint that the homeowners use to paint the houses when they will be finished. The ability to order a whole house from the Sears catalog ended in 1940, but thousands of them are still being lived in by people across America.

Source: CBS News Sunday Morning, May 18, 2003

3. The last time I took my car in for a scheduled service, I noticed a few problems when I pick it up. I check the oil dipstick, and it has really dark oil still on it. Also, there was a screwdriver balancing on my air-filter cover. I can't believe it when I see it, but as soon as I showed the tool to the service manager, he calls the mechanic over to take my car back to the service area. After another hour, my car is ready, the dipstick has clean oil on it, and the service manager cleared the bill so that I didn't have to pay anything.

Recognizing Verbal Phrases

We know (from the discussion on p. 94) that a verb phrase is made up of a main verb and at least one helping verb. But sometimes certain forms of verbs are used not as real verbs but as some other part of a sentence. Verbs put to other uses are called *verbals.*

A verbal can be a subject:

Skiing is my favorite Olympic sport. (*Skiing* is the subject, not the verb. The verb is *is.*)

A verbal can be a descriptive word:

His *bruised* ankle healed very quickly. (*Bruised* describes the subject, ankle. *Healed* is the verb.)

A verbal can be an object:

I like *to read* during the summer. (*To read* is the object. *Like* is the verb.)

Verbals link up with other words to form *verbal phrases.* To see the difference between a real verb phrase and a verbal phrase, look at these two sentences:

I was bowling with my best friends. (*Bowling* is the main verb in a verb phrase. Along with the helping verb *was,* it shows the action of the sentence.)

I enjoyed *bowling* with my best friends. (Here the real verb is *enjoyed. Bowling* is not the verb; it is part of a verbal phrase—*bowling with my best friends*—which is what I enjoyed.)

THREE KINDS OF VERBALS

1. *ing* verbs used without helping verbs (*running, thinking, baking . . .*)
2. verb forms that often end in *ed, en,* or *t* (*tossed, spoken, burnt . . .*)
3. verbs that follow *to* ______ (*to walk, to eat, to cause . . .*)

Look at the following sentences using the previous examples in verbal phrases:

Running two miles a day is great exercise. (real verb = is)

She spent two hours *thinking of a title for her essay.* (real verb = spent)

We had such fun *baking those cherry vanilla cupcakes.* (real verb = had)

Tossed in a salad, artichoke hearts add zesty flavor. (real verb = add)

Spoken in Spanish, the dialogue sounds even more beautiful. (real verb = sounds)

The gourmet pizza, *burnt by a careless chef,* shrunk to half its normal size. (real verb = shrunk)

I like *to walk around the zoo by myself.* (real verb = like)

To eat exotic foods takes courage. (real verb = takes)

They actually wanted *to cause an argument.* (real verb = wanted)

EXERCISES

Each of the following sentences contains at least one verbal or verbal phrase. Double underline the real verbs or verb phrases, and put brackets around the verbals and verbal phrases. Remember to locate the verbals first (*running, wounded, to sleep . . .*) and include any word(s) that go with them (*running a race, wounded in the fight, to sleep all night*). Real verbs will never be inside verbal phrases. Check your answers after the first set before going on to the next.

Exercise 1

1. Philippe Halsman was a well-known portrait photographer working in the twentieth century.
2. Halsman's photographs were good enough to appear on the cover of *Life* magazine 101 times.
3. Capturing the essence of famous people on film was Halsman's specialty.
4. The list of celebrities that Halsman was asked to photograph included Marilyn Monroe, Albert Einstein, and Winston Churchill.

5. Halsman found that taking good pictures of such powerful people was not easy.

6. He often tried to find new ways to loosen them up.

7. In 1952, Halsman asked one of his elite clients to jump in the air while being photographed.

8. Halsman loved the results, and he started a series of jumping pictures.

9. Who doesn't like to see famous people like Richard Nixon jumping up like a little boy in a photograph?

10. Halsman gathered the best of the jumping photographs in a book called *Philippe Halsman's Jump Book.*

Source: *Smithsonian*, October 2006

Exercise 2

1. To paraphrase Mark Twain, golfing is just a way to ruin a good walk.

2. In fact, becoming a golfer can be dangerous.

3. Golf professionals commonly suffer a couple of injuries per year resulting from long hours of practicing their swings.

4. Amateur golfers tend to injure themselves much more often.

5. Most injuries come from the twisting, squatting, and bending involved in golfing.

6. And moving the heavy bags of clubs from cars to carts can wrench the backs of potential golfers before they even begin to play.

7. Of course, there are the unfortunate incidents of people on golf courses being struck by lightning.

8. But some of the sources of golfers' ailments may be surprising.

9. Cleaning the dirt and debris off the golf balls by licking them, for instance, may have serious repercussions.

10. After swallowing the chemicals sprayed on the turf of the golf course, players can develop liver problems.

Source: I'm Afraid, You're Afraid: 448 Things to Fear and Why (Hyperion, 2000)

Exercise 3

1. I like to listen to music at home.
2. Playing my favorite songs out loud through my speakers is my main way to relax.
3. I have tried using headphones, but they hurt my ears.
4. I also don't like to feel disconnected from everyone else.
5. Filling my house with well-chosen tunes allows me to maintain my identity.
6. We all use choices of music, fashion, and art to define ourselves.
7. Some people wear T-shirts showing pictures or slogans that they like.
8. I want everyone to hear the music that I like.
9. My neighbors have not complained about my habit of listening to music without using headphones.
10. I try to be considerate of them and turn down the volume at 10:00 every night.

Exercise 4

1. Why do plumbing emergencies always happen on the weekends?
2. Toilets, sinks, and tubs seem to know when plumbers' rates go up.
3. Some emergencies—a slow-draining sink, for instance—can be tolerated for a couple of days.
4. And a dripping shower faucet may cause annoyance, but not panic.
5. However, a backed-up sewer pipe definitely can't wait until Monday.
6. No one wants to see that water rising and overflowing the rim of the bowl.
7. At that point, the only question is which "rooter" service to call.
8. Finding the main drainage line often takes more time than clearing it.
9. Once the plumber has finished fixing the problem, he or she usually eyes future potential disasters and offers to prevent them with even more work.
10. After getting the final bill, I hope that my children will grow up to be not doctors but plumbers.

Exercise 5

1. In the past, the library was the perfect place to study or to do research or homework.
2. But lately it has become a place to meet friends.
3. Things changed when students began to access the Internet.
4. Now two or three students gather near each terminal and show each other the best sites to visit on the Web.
5. Library officials have designated certain rooms as "talking areas."
6. However, such territories are hard to enforce.
7. The old image of the librarian telling everyone to be quiet is just that—an old image.
8. So people talk to each other and giggle right there in the reading room.
9. One of the librarians told me about a plan to take the Internet-access computers out of the main study room and to put them into the "talking areas."
10. I hate to read in a noisy room, so I hope that he was right.

PARAGRAPH EXERCISE

Double underline the real verbs or verb phrases, and put brackets around the verbals and verbal phrases in the following paragraphs from the popular book *An Incomplete Education*, by Judy Jones and William Wilson.

Christo and Jeanne-Claude (1935-, 1935-)

It started as an obsession with wrapping. The Bulgarian-born artist Christo spent years swaddling bicycles, trees, storefronts, and women friends before moving on to wrap a section of the Roman Wall, part of the Australian coastline, and eventually all twelve arches, plus the parapets, sidewalks, streetlamps, vertical embankment, and esplanade, of Paris' Pont Neuf. And yes, together they did wrap the Reichstag. But Christo and his wife/manager/collaborator Jeanne-Claude are quick to insist that wrappings form only a small percentage of their total oeuvre.

There were, for instance, those twenty-four and a half miles of white nylon, eighteen feet high, they hung from a steel cable north of San Francisco; the eleven islands in Biscayne Bay, Florida, they "surrounded"—not wrapped, mind you—with pink polypropylene fabric; and the 3,100 enormous blue and yellow "umbrellas" they erected in two corresponding valleys in California and Japan. Not to mention their 2005 blockbuster, "The Gates," 7,503 sixteen-foot-tall saffron panels they suspended, to the delight of almost everybody, over twenty-three miles of footpaths in New York's Central Park.

So, what's their point? Rest assured, you're not the first to ask. And no one is more eager to tell you than the artist formerly known as Christo (now, officially, "Christo and Jeanne-Claude") whose art is nothing if not Open to the Public. In fact, taking art public—that is, taking it away from the Uptown Museum Gallery Complex by making it too big to fit in studios, museums, or galleries—was part of the original idea. Christo and Jeanne-Claude will tell you that their point is, literally, to rock your world. By temporarily disrupting one part of an environment, they hope to get you to "perceive the whole environment with new eyes and a new consciousness."

SENTENCE WRITING

Write ten sentences that contain verbal phrases. Use the ten verbals listed here to begin your verbal phrases: *thinking, folding, skiing, marking, to take, to get, to paste, to exercise, planned, given*. The last two may seem particularly difficult to use as verbals. There are sample sentences listed in the Answers section at the back of the book. But first, try to write your own so that you can compare the two. Use your own paper, and keep all of your sentence writing results in a folder.

Correcting Misplaced or Dangling Modifiers

When we modify something, we change whatever it is by adding something to it. We might modify a car, for example, by adding special tires. In English, we call words, phrases, and clauses *modifiers* when they add information to part of a sentence. As we saw on p. 28, to do its job properly, a modifier should be in the right spot—as close to the word it describes as possible. If we put new tires on the roof of the car instead of where they belong, they would be misplaced. In the following sentence, the modifier is too far away from the word it modifies to make sense. It is a misplaced modifier:

> Swinging from tree to tree, we watched the monkeys at the zoo.

Was it *we* who were swinging from tree to tree? That's what the sentence says because the modifying phrase *Swinging from tree to tree* is next to *we.* It should be next to *monkeys.*

> At the zoo, we watched the monkeys swinging from tree to tree.

The next example has no word at all for the modifier to modify:

> At the age of eight, my family finally bought a dog.

Obviously, the family was not eight when it bought a dog. Nor was the dog eight. The modifier *At the age of eight* is dangling there with no word to attach itself to, no word for it to modify. We can get rid of the dangling modifier by turning it into a dependent clause. (See p. 73 for a discussion of dependent clauses.)

> When I was eight, my family finally bought a dog.

Here the clause has its own subject and verb—*I was*—and there's no chance of misunderstanding the sentence. Here's another dangling modifier:

> After a two-hour nap, the train pulled into the station.

Did the train take a two-hour nap? Who did?

> After a two-hour nap, I awoke just as the train pulled into the station.

EXERCISES

Carefully rephrase any of the following sentences that contain misplaced or dangling modifiers. Some sentences are correct.

Exercise 1

1. Even when given by friends, people like to receive flowers.
2. She noticed a twenty-dollar bill walking down the street.
3. I have to take one of my textbooks back to the bookstore.
4. The teacher read a poem about an autumn day leaning against the chalkboard.
5. Playing poker online all night, my homework never got done.
6. On a warm piece of toast, Jan prefers butter and marmalade.
7. After making it to the airport on time, our plane departed early.
8. Biology students read about different kinds of species in their textbooks.
9. Loaded with onions, I had the best hot dog at the stadium last night.
10. I always set my phone to vibrate during class time.

Exercise 2

1. Smeared with mustard or ketchup, everyone enjoys eating corndogs.
2. Before asking for an extension, the teacher told us that we had a few extra days to finish our papers.
3. They spotted a hawk and its babies looking through their binoculars.
4. After I finished my audition, the director released everyone else.
5. I called the doctor on the roof.
6. We sat on the lawn and waited for further instructions on how to prune the roses.
7. Screeching to a stop, I got on the bus and took my seat among the rest of the passengers.
8. Without pickles, I can't eat a hamburger.
9. Given as a token of friendship, that ring means a lot to me.
10. We had to write a paragraph about the weather in our notebooks.

Exercise 3

1. Baked in an odd-shaped pan, the kids at the party still enjoyed the cake.
2. We sat quietly at our desks as we took the quiz.
3. Loaded with butter and sour cream, I looked at the baked potato and wondered how I would eat it because I am allergic to dairy products.
4. Paul contacted his travel agent through e-mail.
5. Without natural talent, the violin is almost impossible to learn.
6. Riding on a bus into town, the sunshine felt warm on my arm.
7. They were locked out of the building by accident.
8. Telling one bad joke after another, I have given up on that comedian.
9. Blue paint mixed with yellow paint usually produces green paint.
10. I loved the presents I received from my friends tied with pretty bows.

Exercise 4

1. Taken before surgery, that medicine can help your recovery.
2. Filled with the perfect amount of air, I enjoyed the way the new tires made my car handle on the road.
3. After three weeks of waiting, the textbooks that I bought online arrived just in time for the semester to begin.
4. He cooked all of his meals in his slippers.
5. The class watched the video with the door open.
6. While driving past the park, a ball bounced into the street between two parked cars.
7. Torn into tiny pieces, I didn't even want the scraps of that quiz paper near me.
8. I will take the test again tomorrow.
9. Trying to look happy, the runner-up applauded too loudly.
10. Walking in the cracks of the sidewalk, we saw tons of ants.

Exercise 5

1. Feeling the thrill of a day at the amusement park, my blisters didn't bother me.
2. Full of touching scenes, my friends and I saw the new tearjerker.
3. My classmates and I always turned our essays in on time.
4. Practicing for an hour a day, her piano has improved.
5. Gasoline prices fluctuate with politics.
6. Sitting on a bench all day, an idea came to her.
7. On the road to their cousins' house, they discovered a new outlet mall.
8. He felt the pressure of trying to get a good job from his parents.
9. I enjoy talking to new people at parties.
10. Written in chalk, the notes on the board were hard to read.

PROOFREADING EXERCISE

Find and correct any misplaced or dangling modifiers in the following paragraph.

Walking into my neighborhood polling place during the last election, a volunteer greeted me and checked my name and address. Being misspelled slightly on their printout, he couldn't find me at first. I pointed to what I thought was my name. At least upside down, I thought it was mine. But actually, it was another person's name. Once turned toward me, I could see the printout more clearly. My name was there, but it had an extra letter stuck on the end of it. The volunteer handed me a change-of-name form with a polite smile. I filled it out and punched my ballot. Stuck on my wall at home, I have my voting receipt to remind me to check my name carefully when the next election comes around.

SENTENCE WRITING

Write five sentences that contain misplaced or dangling modifiers; then revise those sentences to put the modifiers where they belong. Use the examples in the explanations as models. Keep the results in your sentence writing folder.

Following Sentence Patterns

Sentences are built according to a few basic patterns. For proof, rearrange each of the following sets of words to form a complete statement (not a question):

apples a ate raccoon the

the crashing beach were waves the on

your in am partner I lab the

been she school has to walking

you wonderful in look green

There are only one or two possible combinations for each due to English sentence patterns. Either *A raccoon ate the apples,* or *The apples ate a raccoon,* and so on. But in each case, the verb or verb phrase makes its way to the middle of the statement, and the nouns and pronouns take their places as subjects and objects.

To understand sentence patterns, you need to know that verbs can do three things. The focus is on the *double* underlined verbs below.

1. They can show actions:

The raccoon ate the apples.

The waves were crashing on the beach.

She has been walking to school.

2. They can link subjects with descriptive words:

I am your partner in the lab.

You look wonderful in green.

3. They can help other verbs form verb phrases:

The waves were crashing on the beach.

She has been walking to school.

Look at these sentences for more examples:

Mel grabbed a slice of pizza. (The verb *grabbed* shows Mel's action.)

His slice was the largest one in the box. (The verb *was* links *slice* with its description as *the largest one.*)

Mel had been craving pizza for a week. (The verbs *had* and *been* help the main verb *craving* in a verb phrase.)

Knowing what a verb does in a clause helps you gain an understanding of the three basic sentence patterns:

SUBJECT + ACTION VERB + OBJECT PATTERN

Some action verbs must be followed by an object (a person, place, thing, or idea) that receives the action.

S AV Obj
Sylvia completed the difficult math test. (*Sylvia completed* makes no sense without being followed by the object that she completed—*test.*)

SUBJECT + ACTION VERB (+ NO OBJECT) PATTERN

At other times, the action verb itself completes the meaning and needs no object after it.

S AV
She celebrated at home with her family. (*She celebrated* makes sense alone. The two prepositional phrases—*at home* and *with her family*—are not needed to understand the meaning of the clause.)

SUBJECT + LINKING VERB + DESCRIPTION PATTERN

A special kind of verb that does not show an action but links a subject with a description is called a *linking verb.* It acts like an equal sign in a clause. Learn to recognize the most common linking verbs: *is, am, are, was, were, seem, feel, appear, become, look.*

S LV Desc
Sylvia is an excellent student. (*Sylvia* equals *an excellent student.*)

S LV Desc
Sylvia has become very successful. (*Very successful* describes *Sylvia.*)

> **NOTE—**We learned on page 94 that a verb phrase includes a main verb and its helping verbs. Helping verbs can be used in any of the sentence patterns.

S AV
Sylvia is going to Seattle for a vacation. (Here the verb *is* helps the main verb *going,* which is an action verb with no object followed by two prepositional phrases—*to Seattle* and *for a vacation.*)

The following chart outlines the patterns using short sentences that you could memorize:

THREE BASIC SENTENCE PATTERNS

S + AV + Obj

Kids like candy.

S + AV

They play (with their friends) (on the playground).
not objects

S + LV + Desc

They are fourth-graders.

They look happy.

These are the basic patterns for most of the clauses used in English sentences. Knowing them can help you control your sentences and improve your use of words.

EXERCISES

First, put parentheses around any prepositional phrases. Next, underline the subjects once and the verbs or verb phrases twice. Then mark the sentence patterns above the words. Remember that the patterns never mix together. For example, unlike an action verb, a linking verb will almost never be used alone (for example, "He seems."), nor will an action verb be followed by a description of the subject (for example, "She took tall."). And if there are two clauses, each one may have a different pattern. Check your answers after the first set of ten.

Exercise 1

1. Erasto Mpemba is a big name in science.
2. In the early 1960s, he observed an odd phenomenon.
3. At the time, he was a high school student in Tanzania.
4. Mpemba made ice cream for a school project.
5. He boiled the milk and mixed it with the other ingredients.
6. Then he put the hot—not cold—mixture directly into the freezer.
7. The hot mixture froze faster.
8. Mpemba told his teachers and fellow students about his discovery.
9. They laughed at the idea.
10. Now all scientists call this phenomenon the "Mpemba effect."

Sources: *Current Science*, September 8, 2006, and physicsweb.org, April 2006

Exercise 2

1. In late September, the Stade de France in Paris hosted an unusual spectacle.
2. Hundreds of actors, stunt people, and extras reenacted the famous chariot race from the classic film *Ben-Hur*.
3. The same show included live gladiator fights and a galley ship assault.
4. Promoters also encouraged participation from the audience.
5. Many of the 60,000 audience members attended in traditional Roman costumes.
6. The stadium sold toga-like robes in advance along with the tickets.
7. Obviously, the live chariot race was the highlight of the show.
8. Participants in the dangerous race rehearsed for nine months.
9. The chariot race lasted for fifteen minutes.
10. It was the final event of the night.

Source: www.stadefrance.fr, September 2006

Exercise 3

1. Local news programs are all alike.
2. They begin with the top stories of the day.
3. These stories may be local, national, or international.
4. They might include violent crimes, traffic jams, natural disasters, and political upheavals.
5. After the top stories, one of the anchors offers a quick weather update.
6. Then a sportscaster covers the latest scores and team standings.
7. At some point, a "human interest" story lightens the mood of the broadcast.
8. And then we hear the latest entertainment news.
9. Near the end of the half hour, the weatherperson gives the full weather forecast.
10. News programs could use an update of their own.

Exercise 4

1. Some facts about coins in America might surprise you.
2. An average American handles six hundred dollars in coins every year.
3. Most Americans keep small stashes of pennies, nickels, dimes, quarters, half-dollars, and dollar coins at home.
4. The total of these unused coins may be ten billion dollars at any one time.
5. Researchers have asked people about their coin use.
6. Some people use coins in place of small tools.
7. Others perform magic with them.
8. Younger people are more careless with their coins.
9. They might toss a penny in the trash.
10. Older Americans would save the penny instead.

Source: Discover, October 2003

Exercise 5

1. Charles Osgood is a writer, editor, TV host, and radio personality.
2. He has edited a new book about letters.
3. The book's title is *Funny Letters from Famous People.*
4. In his book, Osgood shares hilarious letters from history.
5. Thomas Jefferson wrote to an acquaintance about rodents eating his wallet.
6. Benjamin Franklin penned the perfect recommendation letter.
7. Franklin did not know the recommended fellow at all.
8. Beethoven cursed his friend bitterly in a letter one day.
9. In a letter the following day, Beethoven praised the same friend excessively and asked him for a visit.
10. Osgood ends the book with a letter by Julia Child and includes her secrets for a long life.

PARAGRAPH EXERCISE

Label the sentence patterns in the following paragraphs about the history of masks from the book *Accessories of Dress*, by Katherine Lester and Bess Viola Oerke. It helps to surround prepositional phrases with parentheses and verbals with brackets first to isolate them from the main words of the sentence patterns. Then label the subjects, the verbs, and any objects after action verbs or descriptions after linking verbs (*is, am, are, was, are, become, appear, seem,* and so on).

The history of masks is one of surprising interest. Nearly every race, from the most primitive times to periods of advanced civilization, has found some use for the mask. Perhaps the painted face of a primitive warrior inspired the first mask. At any rate, many of the early tribal masks suggest the abode of a fiendish and warring spirit. In tribal and religious ceremonies, in the dance, in the drama, in peace and war, the mask has played a unique part.

One unusual use of the mask was peculiar to Rome. All families of prominence preserved waxen masks of their distinguished ancestors. These were not death masks, but portraits from life. Many families possessed large collections and looked upon them with great pride. On the occasion of a death in the family, they brought forth these masks. During the elaborate funeral ceremonies, certain men impersonated the long line of distinguished ancestors by wearing these lifelike masks.

SENTENCE WRITING

Write ten sentences describing the weather today and your feelings about it—make your sentences short and clear. Then go back and label the sentence patterns you have used. Keep the results in your sentence writing folder.

Avoiding Clichés, Awkward Phrasing, and Wordiness

Clichés

A cliché is an expression that has been used so often it has lost its originality and effectiveness. Whoever first said "light as a feather" had thought of an original way to express lightness, but today that expression is worn out. Most of us use an occasional cliché in speaking, but clichés have no place in writing. The good writer thinks up fresh new ways to express ideas.

Here are a few clichés. Add some more to the list.

the bottom line
older but wiser
last but not least
in this day and age
different as night and day
out of this world
white as a ghost
sick as a dog
tried and true
at the top of their lungs
the thrill of victory
one in a million
busy as a bee
easier said than done
better late than never

Clichés lack freshness because the reader always knows what's coming next. Can you complete these expressions?

the agony of . . .
breathe a sigh of . . .
lend a helping . . .
odds and . . .
raining cats and . . .
as American as . . .
been there . . .
worth its weight . . .

Clichés are expressions too many people use. Try to avoid them in your writing.

Awkward Phrasing

Another problem—awkward phrasing—comes from writing sentence structures that *no one* else would use because they break basic sentence patterns, omit necessary words, or use words incorrectly. Like clichés, awkward sentences might *sound* acceptable when spoken, but as polished writing, they are usually unacceptable.

Awkward

> There should be great efforts in terms of the communication between teachers and their students.

Corrected

> Teachers and their students must communicate.

Awkward

> During the experiment, the use of key principles was essential to ensure the success of it.

Corrected

> The experiment was a success. *or* We did the experiment carefully.

Awkward

> My favorite was when the guy with the ball ran the wrong way all the way across the field.

Corrected

> In my favorite part, the receiver ran across the field in the wrong direction.

Wordiness

Good writing is concise writing. Don't use ten words if you can say it better in five. "In today's society" isn't as effective as "today," and it's a cliché. "At this point in time" could be "presently" or "now."

Another kind of wordiness comes from saying something twice. There's no need to write "in the month of August" or "9 a.m. in the morning" or "my personal opinion." August *is* a month, 9 a.m. *is* morning, and anyone's opinion *is* personal. All you need to write is "in August," "9 a.m.," and "my opinion."

Still another kind of wordiness comes from using expressions that add nothing to the meaning of the sentence. "The point is that we can't afford it" says no more than "We can't afford it."

Here is a sample wordy sentence:

> The construction company actually worked on that particular building for a period of six months.

And here it is after eliminating wordiness:

> The construction company worked on that building for six months.

Wordy Writing	**Concise Writing**
advance planning	planning
an unexpected surprise	a surprise
ask a question	ask
at a later date	later
basic fundamentals	fundamentals
green in color	green
but nevertheless	but (or nevertheless)
combine together	combine
completely empty	empty
down below	below
each and every	each (or every)
end result	result
fewer in number	fewer
free gift	gift
in order to	to
in spite of the fact that	although
just exactly	exactly
large in size	large
new innovation	innovation
on a regular basis	regularly
past history	history
rectangular in shape	rectangular
refer back	refer
repeat again	repeat
serious crisis	crisis
sufficient enough	sufficient (or enough)
there in person	there
two different kinds	two kinds
very unique	unique

PROOFREADING EXERCISES

The following student paragraphs contain examples of clichés, awkward phrasing, and wordiness. Revise the paragraphs so that they are concise examples of Standard Written English. When you're done, compare your revisions with the sample answers at the back of the book.

1. In today's society, many shoppers at the supermarkets are on the lookout for organic meats, fruits, and vegetables. In fact, they don't draw the line at fresh foods; these same shoppers' eyes light up whenever they see an organic label on a box, can, or any other package. I know this for a fact since I work as an employee at the supermarket in the middle of the busiest section of town. It's not only people with a lot of money that want the foods grown without pesticides and hormones. It's just about everybody that walks in the door. I guess that what's going on is that people are taking a good long look at their lives and caring about their children's eating habits too. I do have to admit that the organic eggs I buy taste pretty good when you get right down to it. Knowing that the eggs come from happy, free-ranging chickens makes me feel good about eating them. Of course, the bottom line for some people will always be price. If organic foods cost more than traditionally grown foods, some of the shoppers are going to keep passing them by on the supermarket shelves.

2. I just saw a story on the news about an animal that didn't look like anything I'd ever seen before. It kind of looks like a teddy bear and a little monkey and a miniature dog all rolled into one. I found out that this little guy has his own Web site and in fact is quite a celebrity in his own right. The name of this odd creature is Mr. Winkle. And there's no need to go hunting around for the Web address; just head to "mrwinkle.com." On his home page, even they say they don't know what kind of animal he is. On the Web site, a bunch of questions flash across the screen while it's loading, questions like is it an "alien?" a "stuffed animal?" a "hamster with a permanent?" One thing I can say for sure is that he is pretty cute. I can see why his owner stopped her car one day when she saw the strange-looking beast walking by the side of the road and took him home with her. Since she found him that day, she has taken a whole bunch of pictures of him in quirky little costumes and even one of him running in a hamster wheel. Of course, all of these pictures are available for purchase at the click of the mouse in the form of posters and calendars, and I must say the prices are relatively reasonable.

3. I have a friend who used to be one of those struggling actors who couldn't find a steady job, but now she has become a professional house sitter, and it has really paid off in more ways than one. First of all, she joined a house sitters' organization that is supposed to find out about all of the house-sitting opportunities that are available at any one time and match house sitters up with each of them. Then she landed her first house-sitting job at a house in Malibu. You're not going to believe this, but she got paid to live in a house on the beach in Malibu and even got her meals and movie rentals for free. All she had to do to do the job she was paid for was to watch out for the house and feed one cat. The cat was even an indoor cat. Now my friend is house sitting in Sedona, watching a house for friends of the same people who own the Malibu house. Well, I'll tell you, I want a job like that and am thinking seriously about trying it out for myself.

Correcting for Parallel Structure

Your writing will be clearer and more memorable if you use parallel structure. That is, when you write two pieces of information or any kind of list, put the items in similar form. Look at this sentence, for example:

> My favorite movies are comic, romantic, or the ones about outer space.

The sentence lacks parallel structure. The third item in the list doesn't match the other two. Now look at this sentence:

> My favorite movies are comedies, love stories, and sci-fi fantasies.

Here the items are parallel; they are all plural nouns. Or you could write the following:

> I like movies that make me laugh, that make me cry, and that make me think.

Again the sentence has parallel structure because all three items in the list are dependent clauses. Here are some more examples. Note how much easier it is to read the sentences with parallel structure.

Without Parallel Structure	**With Parallel Structure**
I like to hike, to ski, and going sailing.	I like to hike, to ski, and to sail. (all "to ________" verbs)
The office has run out of pens, paper, ink cartridges, and we need more toner, too.	The office needs more pens, paper, ink cartridges, and toner. (all nouns)
They decided that they needed a change, that they could afford a new house, and wanted to move to Arizona.	They decided that they needed a change, that they could afford a new house, and that they wanted to move to Arizona. (all dependent clauses)

The parts of an outline should always be parallel. Following are two brief outlines about food irradiation. The parts of the outline on the *left* are not parallel. The first subtopic (I.) is a question; the other (II.) is just a noun. And the supporting points (A., B., C.) are written as nouns, verbs, and even clauses. The parts of the outline on the *right* are parallel. Both subtopics (I. and II.) are plural nouns, and all details (A., B., C.) are action verbs followed by objects.

Not Parallel	**Parallel**
Food Irradiation	Food Irradiation
I. How is it good?	I. Benefits
A. Longer shelf life	A. Extends shelf life
B. Using fewer pesticides	B. Requires fewer pesticides
C. Kills bacteria	C. Kills bacteria
II. Concerns	II. Concerns
A. Nutritional value	A. Lowers nutritional value
B. Consumers are worried	B. Alarms consumers
C. Workers' safety	C. Endangers workers

Using parallel structure will make your writing more effective. Note the parallelism in these well-known quotations:

> A place for everything and everything in its place.
>
> *Isabella Mary Beeton*

> Ask not what your country can do for you; ask what you can do for your country.
>
> *John F. Kennedy*

> We hold these truths to be self-evident, that all men are created equal, that they are endowed by their creator with certain unalienable rights, that among these are Life, Liberty, and the pursuit of Happiness.
>
> *Thomas Jefferson*

EXERCISES

In the following exercises, rephrase any sentences that do not contain parallel structures.

Exercise 1

1. Taking a basic grammar class last semester was fun, but I also found it challenging.
2. I was ready to learn about parts of speech, verb tenses, and using dependent clauses.
3. The teacher showed us how to identify subjects and labeling verbs.
4. We learned the differences between adjectives and adverbs and how to use them.

5. An adjective always adds information to a noun or could add to a pronoun.
6. Adverbs can modify verbs, adjectives, or they can even modify other adverbs.
7. I know that I learned a lot about grammar but needing to practice it in my writing.
8. Before I registered for the grammar class, I had to decide between taking a full load or to work part time and take only one or two classes.
9. I decided to work at my family's restaurant part time and focusing on the grammar class.
10. I waited on tables in the morning, going to class in the afternoon, and studied at night.

Exercise 2

1. The Internet is full of information about new gadgets and using the latest technology.
2. People want to have the coolest phones, the clearest photos, and travel accessories that are the best quality.
3. One of these high-tech inventions is a new kind of wedding ring.
4. The ring doesn't use technology to help people do something more easily or living more comfortably.
5. Instead, it helps people avoid doing something, and that is not to forget their anniversary.
6. The "Remember Ring" is designed for people who love gadgets, but they tend to forget special occasions.
7. It includes several hi-tech features: a perpetually charging battery, a clock run by a microchip, and a tiny element that heats up.
8. The built-in heating element activates at a preprogrammed time and reminding the wearer about an upcoming anniversary.
9. One day before the anniversary, the ring starts to heat up to 120 degrees for ten seconds once every hour.
10. The Remember Ring comes in seven styles in both white gold and the regular yellow kind.

Exercise 3

1. Going to the new car wash in my neighborhood is like a trip to paradise.
2. It has a plush lounge that offers free coffee, cookies, and there are even pretzels for those who don't like sweets.
3. The overstuffed furniture comforts weary customers as they wait for their cars to be cleaned.
4. Full plate-glass windows line the front wall of the lounge so that people can see their vehicles being dried, and sometimes they even check out the cars of the people around them.
5. For those who don't like to sit down, a full assortment of greeting cards lines the back wall of the lounge, as well as car accessories too.
6. To keep things interesting, every hour there is a drawing for a free car wash; I haven't ever won one of those though.
7. Whenever I am waiting in the luxurious setting of the car wash, I wonder about two things.
8. Why do people talk on cell phones when they could be resting, and how can you explain that some people stand up when they could be sitting on a nice leather sofa?
9. I will always love going to my neighborhood car wash.
10. It's the modern equivalent of going to the barbershop or to get a new hairdo at the beauty parlor.

Exercise 4

Rephrase the following list to improve the use of parallel structures. The list includes instructions on how to begin searching for ancestors—in other words, how to create a "family tree." Try to maintain similar phrasing at the beginning of the instructions and in any pairs or lists within them.

1. To begin, decide which person or the family you want to focus on.
2. Making a blank chart that includes spaces for all of a person's important information will help.
3. Then visit a relative who knows a lot of family history and hopefully someone who saves papers and mementos.
4. You should plan to spend a lot of time with any such valuable resource.

5. It is best to gather information from one individual at a time and about one person at a time.
6. Ask about every part of the person's life—marital status, children, believing in religion, working, and travel.
7. As you talk with your resources, thank them for providing you with valuable information.
8. Visit the attics or even going into the dusty old cupboards of anyone who has documents relating to your family.
9. Don't forget the local records office in the town where a relative grew up.
10. To make your family tree come together faster, you can purchase books that provide preprinted worksheets and family tree templates.

Exercise 5

Rephrase the following list of recommendations to improve the use of parallel structures. Try to maintain similar phrasing at the beginning of the recommendations and in any pairs or lists within them.

1. The U.S. Surgeon General makes the following recommendations for living a healthy life and to make it a happy one, too.
2. Try to eat the right amounts of fruits and vegetables, and you shouldn't forget to eat meat and dairy products (or their vegetarian equivalents).
3. Be sure to see a doctor regularly and getting all the usual tests and check-ups.
4. Of course, it is also very important to learn about any illnesses or the health conditions that run in your family.
5. Getting enough rest and to sleep for a sufficient time each night obviously helps, too.
6. Keep in touch with your friends and the members of your family.
7. Prevent injuries that can be avoided by wearing seatbelts and other safety devices, such as helmets.
8. Limit alcohol consumption and using over-the-counter drugs.
9. Try not to smoke or breathing in second-hand smoke if you can avoid it.

10. The Surgeon General's recommendations and the warnings that go with them make very good sense.

PROOFREADING EXERCISE

Proofread the following student paragraph, and revise it to correct any errors in parallel structure.

Every year in late spring, a long caravan of vehicles arrives at the park in my neighborhood. The caravan consists of a combination of trucks, campers, and vans, as well as a bunch of trailers full of folded-up kiddy rides. All of the residents and even just the people who drive by the park can tell that the fair has come to town. It isn't a big fair, but one that is small and child-friendly. Most people remember these fairs from when they were growing up. In childhood, the rides seemed huge and scary, but when you're an adult, they look almost silly in their smallness. As the fair is being set up in the park for a few days, the kids in the neighborhood can't wait to get on one of those "wild" rides. What their parents start to look forward to, of course, is the "fair food": the popcorn that comes either sweet or salty, those mouth-watering corndogs and deep-fried candy bars, and everybody loves the juicy snow cones. I can't wait until next year's fair; I'm getting hungry just thinking about it.

SENTENCE WRITING

Write ten sentences that use parallel structure. You may choose your own subject, or you may describe the process of studying for an important test. Be sure to include pairs and lists of objects, actions, locations, or ideas. Keep the results in your sentence writing folder.

Using Pronouns

Nouns name people, places, things, and ideas—such as *students, school, computers,* and *cyberspace.* Pronouns take the place of nouns to avoid repetition and to clarify meaning. Look at the following two sentences:

> Naomi's father worried that the children at the party were too loud, so Naomi's father told the children that the party would have to end if the children didn't calm down.
>
> Naomi's father worried that the children at the party were too loud, so *he* told *them* that *it* would have to end if *they* didn't calm down.

Nouns are needlessly repeated in the first sentence. The second sentence uses pronouns in their place. *He* replaces *father, they* and *them* replace *children,* and *it* takes the place of *party.*

Of the many kinds of pronouns, the following cause the most difficulty because they include two ways of identifying the same person (or people), but only one form is correct in a given situation:

Subject Group	**Object Group**
I	me
he	him
she	her
we	us
they	them

Use a pronoun from the Subject Group in two instances:

1. Before a verb as a subject:

> *He* is my cousin. (*He* is the subject of the verb *is.*)
>
> *He* is taller than *I.* (The sentence is not written out in full. It means "*He* is taller than *I* am." *I* is the subject of the verb *am.*)

Whenever you see *than* in a sentence, ask yourself whether a verb has been left off the end of the sentence. Add the verb, and then you'll automatically use the correct pronoun. In both speaking and writing, always add the verb. Instead of saying, "She's smarter than (I, me)," say, "She's smarter than I *am.*" Then you will use the correct pronoun.

2. After a linking verb (is, am, are, was, were) as a pronoun that renames the subject:

   The one who should apologize is *he.* (*He* is *the one who should apologize.* Therefore, the pronoun from the Subject Group is used.)

   The winner of the lottery was *she.* (*She* was *the winner of the lottery.* Therefore, the pronoun from the Subject Group is used.)

Modern usage allows some exceptions to this rule, however. For example, *It's me* or *It is her* (instead of the grammatically correct *It is I* and *It is she*) may be common in spoken English.

Use pronouns from the Object Group for all other purposes. In the following sentence, *me* is not the subject, nor does it rename the subject. It follows a preposition; therefore, it comes from the Object Group.

> My boss went to lunch with Jenny and *me.*

A good way to tell whether to use a pronoun from the Subject Group or the Object Group is to leave out any extra name (and the word *and*). By leaving out *Jenny and,* you will say, *My boss went to lunch with me.* You would never say, *My boss went to lunch with I.*

> My father and *I* play chess on Sundays. (*I* play chess on Sundays.)
>
> *She* and her friends rented a video. (*She* rented a video.)
>
> We saw Kevin and *them* last night. (We saw *them* last night.)
>
> The teacher gave *us* students certificates. (Teacher gave *us* certificates.)
>
> The coach asked Craig and *me* to wash the benches. (Coach asked *me* to wash the benches.)

Pronoun Agreement

Just as subjects and verbs must agree, pronouns should agree with the words they refer to. If the word referred to is singular, the pronoun should be singular. If the noun referred to is plural, the pronoun should be plural.

> Each classroom has its own chalkboard.

The pronoun *its* refers to the singular noun *classroom* and therefore is singular.

> Both classrooms have their own chalkboards.

The pronoun *their* refers to the plural noun *classrooms* and therefore is plural.

The same rules that we use to maintain the agreement of subjects and verbs also apply to pronoun agreement. For instance, ignore any prepositional phrases that come between the word and the pronoun that takes its place.

> The *box* of chocolates has lost *its* label.
>
> *Boxes* of chocolates often lose *their* labels.
>
> A *player* with the best concentration usually beats *her or his* opponent.
>
> *Players* with the best concentration usually beat *their* opponents.

When a pronoun refers to more than one word joined by *and,* the pronoun is plural:

> The *teacher* and the *tutors* eat *their* lunches at noon.
>
> The *salt* and *pepper* were in *their* usual spots on the table.

However, when a pronoun refers to more than one word joined by *or,* then the word closest to the pronoun determines its form:

> Either the teacher or the *tutors* eat *their* lunches in the classroom.
>
> Either the tutors or the *teacher* eats *her* lunch in the classroom.

Today many people try to avoid gender bias by writing sentences like the following:

> If anyone wants help with the assignment, he or she can visit me in my office.
>
> If anybody calls, tell him or her that I'll be back soon.
>
> Somebody has left his or her pager in the classroom.

But those sentences are wordy and awkward. Therefore some people, especially in conversation, turn them into sentences that are not grammatically correct.

> If anyone wants help with the assignment, they can visit me in my office.
>
> If anybody calls, tell them that I'll be back soon.
>
> Somebody has left their pager in the classroom.

Such ungrammatical sentences, however, are not necessary. It takes just a little thought to revise each sentence so that it avoids gender bias and is also grammatically correct:

> Anyone who wants help with the assignment can visit me in my office.
>
> Tell anybody who calls that I'll be back soon.
>
> Somebody has left a pager in the classroom.

Probably the best way to avoid the awkward *he or she* and *him or her* is to make the words plural. Instead of writing, "Each actor was in his or her proper place on stage," write, "All the actors were in their proper places on stage," thus avoiding gender bias and still having a grammatically correct sentence.

Pronoun Reference

A pronoun replaces a noun to avoid repetition, but sometimes the pronoun sounds as if it refers to the wrong word in a sentence, causing confusion. Be aware that when you write a sentence, *you* know what it means, but your reader may not. What does this sentence mean?

> The students tried to use the school's computers to access the Internet, but they were too slow, so they decided to go home.

Who or what was too slow, and who or what decided to go home? We don't know whether the two pronouns (both *they*) refer to the students or to the computers. One way to correct such a faulty reference is to use singular and plural nouns:

> The students tried to use a school computer to access the Internet, but it was too slow, so they decided to go home.

Here's another sentence with a faulty reference:

> Calvin told his father that he needed a haircut.

Who needed the haircut—Calvin or his father? One way to correct such a faulty reference is to use a direct quotation:

> Calvin told his father, "You need a haircut."
>
> Calvin said, "Dad, I need a haircut."

Or you could always rephrase the sentence completely:

> Calvin noticed his father's hair was sticking out in odd places, so he told his father to get a haircut.

Another kind of faulty reference is a *which* clause that appears to refer to a specific word, but it doesn't really.

> I wasn't able to finish all the problems on the exam, which makes me worried.

The word *which* seems to replace *exam,* but it isn't the exam that makes me worried. The sentence should read

> I am worried because I wasn't able to finish all the problems on the exam.

The pronoun *it* causes its own reference problems. Look at this sentence, for example:

> When replacing the ink cartridge in my printer, it broke, and I had to call the technician to come and fix it.

Did the printer or the cartridge break? Here is one possible correction:

> The new ink cartridge broke when I was putting it in my printer, and I had to call the technician for help.

EXERCISES

Exercise 1

Circle the correct pronoun. Remember the trick of leaving out the extra name to help you decide which pronoun to use. Use the correct grammatical form even though an alternate form may be acceptable in conversation.

1. My brother Martin, a few friends, and (I, me) went skiing over the holidays.

2. Martin usually enjoys skiing more than (I, me).

3. This time, however, both (he and I, him and me) challenged ourselves.

4. Since Martin is less safety conscious than (I, me), he usually doesn't want to ski with my group down the gentle slopes.

5. Every time (he and I, him and me) have been skiing before, Martin has just met my buddies and (I, me) back at the cabin at the end of the day.

6. But the one who was the most daring this time was (I, me).

7. Martin may be more of a daredevil than (I, me) most of the time, but he needed coaxing to try the steep slopes that my friends and (I, me) sailed down this time.

8. Just between (you and me, you and I), I think Martin was really scared.

9. Martin was thrilled when a ski instructor came up to (he and I, him and me) and asked, "You've been skiing for a long time, haven't you?"

10. Instead of going off on his own in the future, Martin will stay close to my friends and (I, me).

Exercise 2

Circle the pronoun that agrees with the word the pronoun replaces. If the correct answer is *his or her,* revise the sentence to eliminate the need for this awkward expression. Check your answers as you go through the exercise.

1. A good parent gives (his or her, their) children advice.
2. Most parents don't like to interfere in (his or her, their) children's lives.
3. Giving advice is not the same as interfering, however; (it's, they're) a completely different thing.
4. A child often looks to (his or her, their) parents for guidance in difficult times.
5. For instance, a child might have encountered a bully at (his or her, their) elementary school.
6. The other schoolchildren might tell the child to keep (his or her, their) mouth shut about it.
7. A parent would probably offer (his or her, their) child very different advice—to speak to the principal about the problem right away.
8. A bully can only get away with (his or her, their) activities if everyone else is too scared or too uninformed to stop (him or her, them).
9. Dealing with bullies is just one example of how parents can offer helpful advice to (his or her, their) children.
10. Most kids would rather have parents who are involved in (his or her, their) lives than parents who only think about (himself or herself, themselves).

Exercise 3

Circle the correct pronoun. Again, if the correct answer is *his or her,* revise the sentence to eliminate the need for this awkward expression.

1. No one at the zoo knows more about penguins than (she, her).
2. The visiting artist gave my classmate and (I, me) a few suggestions.
3. (You and I, You and me) are similar in many ways.
4. As we were discussing Madonna, I realized that my mother is actually younger than (she, her).

5. Each of the participants in the marathon used (his or her, their) own training methods.
6. Air conditioning companies must be very competitive in (its, their) pricing.
7. The driver mentioned in the newspaper article was (he, him).
8. Each of the art students has (his or her, their) own locker in the hallway.
9. The softball teams from each neighborhood will continue (its, their) tournament tomorrow.
10. Each citizen of a democratic country has (his or her, their) favorite candidate and can influence the election with (his or her, their) vote.

Exercises 4 and 5

Most—but not all—of the sentences in the next two sets aren't clear because we don't know what word the pronoun refers to. Revise such sentences, making the meaning clear. Since there are more ways than one to rewrite each sentence, yours may be as good as the ones at the back of the book. Just ask yourself whether the meaning is clear.

Exercise 4

1. The library issued new cards and mailed them out yesterday.
2. I finished my essay, sent it to the printer, and waited for it to print.
3. Angela told Karen that there was a cup of coffee on top of her car.
4. We hiked over several hills, which made us all tired and hungry.
5. Hank's dad let him drive his car to the bank.
6. When she placed her card in the ATM, it disappeared.
7. Ted told my brother that he didn't think that he should go on the field trip.
8. As we were talking on the phone, it fell.
9. Our teacher offers lots of suggestions about our drawings, which help us improve.
10. Carla asked her new boss why she couldn't work on weekends.

Exercise 5

1. I put the finishing touches on my painting, placed my brushes in hot water, and moved it to the drying rack.
2. When people join in community activities, they feel more involved.
3. After I filled my car with gas, it made a funny noise.
4. Whenever I see a rainbow in the sky, it makes me think of my trip to Hawaii.
5. Members of the orchestra invited the music students to sit in their seats.
6. Steve's doctor told him to put ice on his head.
7. Many students use mechanical pencils for their precision.
8. The frosting slid off the cake as it got hotter and hotter.
9. Some students are enjoying the new computer program in the lab, but it is too simple for others.
10. The teacher ordered new textbooks, and the bookstore received them within two days.

PROOFREADING EXERCISE

The following paragraph contains errors in the use of pronouns. Find and correct the errors.

Rude drivers have one thing in common: they think that they know how to drive better than anybody else. The other day, as my friends and me were driving to school, we stopped at an intersection. A very old man who used a cane to help him walk started across it in front of my friends and I just before the light was ready to change. So we waited. But while we waited for him, a male driver behind us started to honk his horn since he couldn't see him. I wondered, "Does he want us to hit him, or what?" Finally, it was clear. He pulled his car up beside ours, opened his window, and yelled at us before it sped away. The old man reached the other side safely, but he hardly noticed.

SENTENCE WRITING

Write ten sentences about a conversation between you and someone else. Then check that your pronouns are grammatically correct, that they agree with the words they replace, and that references to specific nouns are clear. Keep the results in your sentence writing folder.

Avoiding Shifts in Person

To understand what "person" means when using pronouns, imagine a conversation between two people about a third person. The first person speaks using "I, me, my . . ."; the second person would be called "you"; and when the two of them talked of a third person, they would say "he, she, they . . . ." You'll never forget the idea of "person" if you remember it as a three-part conversation.

First person—*I, me, my, we, us, our*

Second person—*you, your*

Third person—*he, him, his, she, her, hers, they, them, their, one, anyone*

You may use all three of these groups of pronouns in a paper, but don't shift from one group to another without good reason.

Wrong: Few people know how to manage *their* time. *One* need not be an efficiency expert to realize that *one* could get a lot more done if *he* budgeted *his* time. Nor do *you* need to work very hard to get more organized.

Better: *Everyone* should know how to manage *his or her* time. *One* need not be an efficiency expert to realize that *a person* could get a lot more done if *one* budgeted *one's* time. Nor does *one* need to work very hard to get more organized. (Too many *one*'s in a paragraph make it sound overly formal, and they lead to the necessity of avoiding sexism by using *s/he* or *he or she,* etc. Sentences can be revised to avoid using either *you* or *one.*)

Best: Many of *us* don't know how to manage *our* time. *We* need not be efficiency experts to realize that *we* could get a lot more done if *we* budgeted *our* time. Nor do *we* need to work very hard to get more organized.

Often students write *you* in a paper when they don't really mean *you, the reader.*

You wouldn't believe how many times I saw that movie.

Such sentences are always improved by getting rid of the *you.*

I saw that movie many times.

PROOFREADING EXERCISES

Which of the following student paragraphs shift *unnecessarily* between first-, second-, and third-person pronouns? In those that do, revise the sentences to eliminate such shifting, thus making the entire paragraph read smoothly. One of the paragraphs is correct.

1. Everyone has seen those game machines that are filled with stuffed animals, and you use a crane-like device to grab hold of one and win. Kids and adults love to play these games, but did you know that a lot of children like them so much that they try to crawl up into them? Some children are successful. A recent article in the *Chippewa Herald* tells of one seven-year-old boy who made it up into the machine. The boy's father turned his back, and before you knew it, his son was sitting inside the game with all the stuffed animals around him. It took firefighters over an hour to rescue the little boy. I wonder if he got to take home the stuffed animal that he wanted.

2. I was reading about superstitions for my psychology class, and I learned that a lot of these beliefs concern brooms and sweeping. One superstition says that, whenever you change your residence, you should get a new broom. People should not take their old brooms with them because the brooms might carry any bad luck that was swept up at the old place and bring it to the new one. Also, if you sweep dirt out an open door, make it the back door so that the bad luck will depart forever. If you sweep dirt out the front way, the same bad luck will come right back in again. Finally, I learned never to walk across a fallen broomstick unless I never want to get married, for that is the fate for anyone who steps over a broomstick. I bet most people would be surprised by how many things can go wrong when you pick up a broom.

3. Most of us in America could use more vacation time. We hear about citizens of other countries getting several weeks—and sometimes even months—off every year to rest their bodies, recharge their energies, and lift their spirits. But in the United States, we have to fight for and often forfeit our one- or two-week vacations. In fact, if we complain too loudly about needing a break, we could be the newest person on the unemployment line. It's time for all of us to stand up for our right to sit down and take a rest.

REVIEW OF SENTENCE STRUCTURE ERRORS

One sentence in each pair contains an error. Read both sentences carefully before you decide. Then write the letter of the *incorrect* sentence in the blank. Try to name the error and correct it if you can. You may find any of these errors:

awk	awkward phrasing
cliché	overused expression
dm	dangling modifier
frag	fragment
mm	misplaced modifier
pro	incorrect pronoun
pro agr	pronoun agreement error
pro ref	pronoun reference error
ro	run-on sentence
shift	shift in time or person
s-v agr	subject-verb agreement error
wordy	wordiness
//	not parallel

1. ____ **A.** The campus bookstore can be a frustrating place to shop.

B. The display of textbooks don't make it easy to find the ones I need.

2. ____ **A.** The first person to give a speech was her.

B. I listened to her speech and quickly volunteered to go next.

3. ____ **A.** The total, including food and drinks, adding up to six hundred dollars.

B. Entertaining at home is much more expensive than it used to be.

4. ____ **A.** The loud hum of the air-conditioner distracted the students in the French class.

B. Speaking very softly, the students could barely hear their professor.

5. ____ **A.** Either she or I should receive that scholarship.

B. Either she or I are going to receive that scholarship.

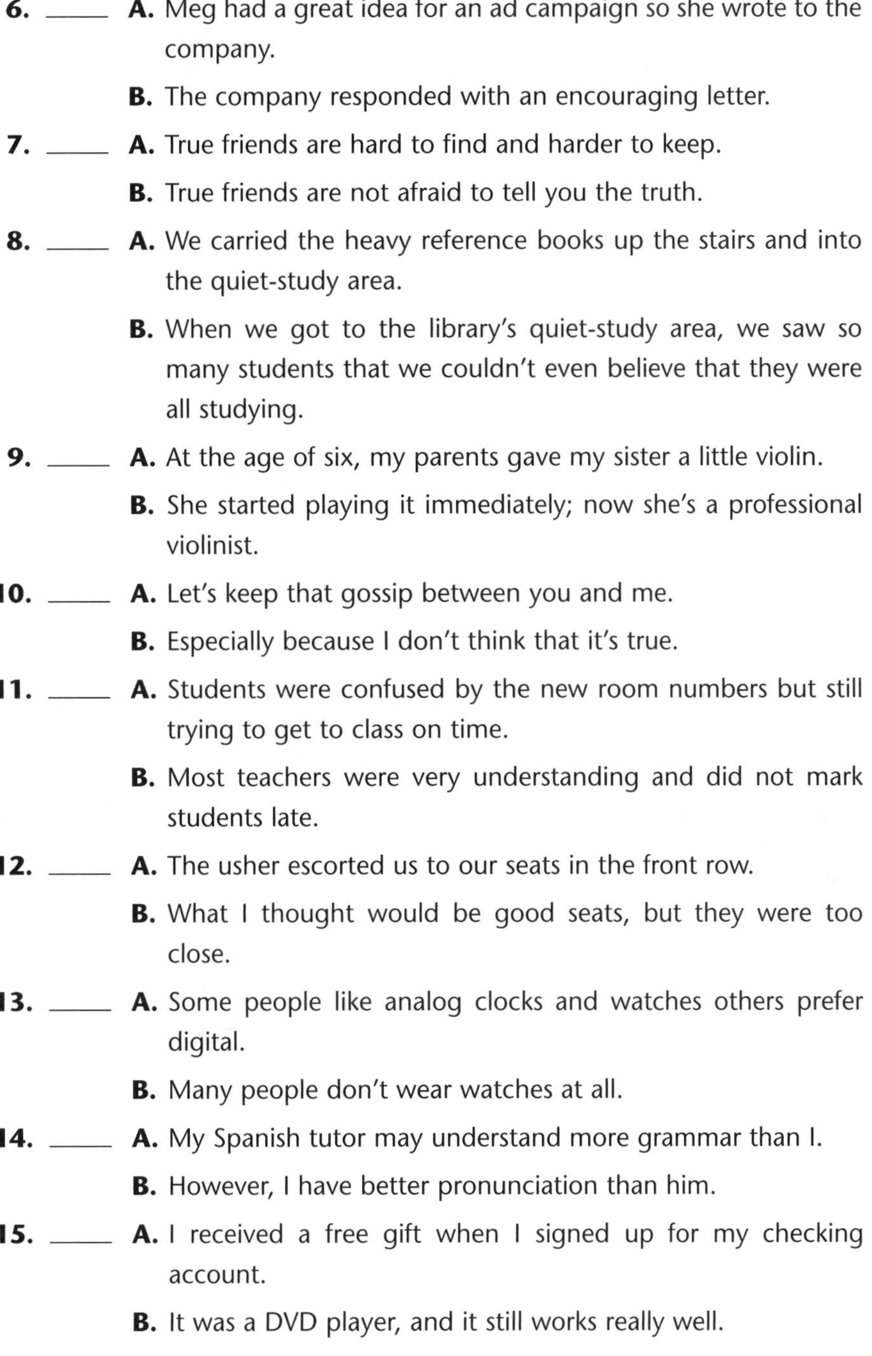

6. _____ **A.** Meg had a great idea for an ad campaign so she wrote to the company.

B. The company responded with an encouraging letter.

7. _____ **A.** True friends are hard to find and harder to keep.

B. True friends are not afraid to tell you the truth.

8. _____ **A.** We carried the heavy reference books up the stairs and into the quiet-study area.

B. When we got to the library's quiet-study area, we saw so many students that we couldn't even believe that they were all studying.

9. _____ **A.** At the age of six, my parents gave my sister a little violin.

B. She started playing it immediately; now she's a professional violinist.

10. _____ **A.** Let's keep that gossip between you and me.

B. Especially because I don't think that it's true.

11. _____ **A.** Students were confused by the new room numbers but still trying to get to class on time.

B. Most teachers were very understanding and did not mark students late.

12. _____ **A.** The usher escorted us to our seats in the front row.

B. What I thought would be good seats, but they were too close.

13. _____ **A.** Some people like analog clocks and watches others prefer digital.

B. Many people don't wear watches at all.

14. _____ **A.** My Spanish tutor may understand more grammar than I.

B. However, I have better pronunciation than him.

15. _____ **A.** I received a free gift when I signed up for my checking account.

B. It was a DVD player, and it still works really well.

PROOFREADING EXERCISE

The following is an insightful student essay. Revise it to eliminate wordiness and to correct any errors in sentence structure.

Getting Involved

Getting involved in other people's business can be a right and a wrong thing. It all depends on the relationship you have with that person and what situation that person is going through. For example, a friend of yours is having trouble in a bad relationship and you are concerned about their well-being. Getting involved not only shows that as a friend you love them, but it can help them solve their problems.

On the other hand, some people just like to be nosey. I feel that most people who do get involved in other people's business just for fun have a boring life. They need to know about others so that their lives can be more interesting. I have been in many situations where peers have tried to learn about my life and problems so that they could show and tell. All of the things they said turned into rumors.

Since I have learned from others' mistakes about not minding your own business, I would never get involved in other people's business. If it is not going to benefit them in some way. Therefore, people should better their own lives and not worry about anyone else's. This would make the world a better place.

PART 3

Punctuation and Capital Letters

Period, Question Mark, Exclamation Point, Semicolon, Colon, Dash

Every mark of punctuation should help the reader. Here are the rules for six marks of punctuation. The first three you have known for a long time and probably have no trouble with. The one about semicolons you learned when you studied independent clauses (p. 86). The ones about the colon and the dash may be less familiar.

Put a period (.) at the end of a sentence and after most abbreviations.

The students elected Ms. Daniels to represent the class.

Sept. Mon. in. sq. ft. lbs.

Put a question mark (?) after a direct question but not after an indirect one.

Will we be able to use our notes during the test? (direct)

I wonder if we will be able to use our notes during the test. (indirect)

Put an exclamation point (!) after an expression that shows strong emotion. This mark is used mostly in dialogue or informal correspondence.

I can't believe I did so well on my first exam!

Put a semicolon (;) between two independent clauses in a sentence unless they are joined by one of the connecting words *for, and, nor, but, or, yet, so*.

My mother cosigned for a loan; now I have my own car.

Some careers go in and out of fashion; however, people will always need teachers.

To be sure that you are using a semicolon correctly, see if a period and capital letter can be used in its place. If they can, you are putting the semicolon in the right spot.

My mother cosigned for a loan. Now I have my own car.

Some careers go in and out of fashion. However, people will always need teachers.

Put a colon (:) after a complete statement that introduces one of the following elements: a name, a list, a quotation, or an explanation.

The company announced its Employee-of-the-Month: Lee Jones. (The sentence before the colon introduces the name that follows it.)

That truck comes in the following colors: red, black, blue, and silver. (The complete statement before the colon introduces the list that follows it.)

That truck comes in red, black, blue, and silver. (Here the list is simply part of the sentence. There is no complete statement used to introduce the list, so it does not need a colon.)

Thoreau had this to say about time: "Time is but the stream I go a-fishin in." (The writer introduces the quotation with a complete statement. Therefore, a colon comes between them.)

Thoreau said, "Time is but the stream I go a-fishin in." (Here the writer leads directly into the quotation; therefore, no colon—just a comma—comes between them.)

Use dashes (—) to isolate inserted information, to signal an abrupt change of thought, or to emphasize what follows.

Lee Jones—March's Employee-of-the-Month—received his own special parking space.

I found out today—or was it yesterday?—that I have inherited a fortune.

We have exciting news for you—we're moving!

EXERCISES

Exercises 1 and 2

Add to these sentences the necessary end punctuation (periods, question marks, and exclamation points). The semicolons, colons, dashes, and commas used within the sentences are correct and do not need to be changed. Pay close attention to them, however, to help with further exercises.

Exercise 1

1. Have you ever had "one of those days"
2. You wake up feeling great; then you notice that your alarm didn't go off
3. You take the following steps to avoid being late to your first class: skip your shower, throw on the first clothes you see, and walk out the door without coffee or breakfast
4. You open your car door, sit in the driver's seat, and turn the key; then you discover that your car battery is dead
5. You go back inside the house and call your friend Tracy; she has a reliable car
6. Tracy's roommate—the one who doesn't like you—answers the phone out of a sound sleep
7. The roommate mumbles angrily, "She's already gone to school"
8. You try Tracy's cell phone number; you get her voice mail, as usual
9. All of your efforts to save the day have failed; there is only one option left
10. You make yourself breakfast; you sit in front of the television, and you resign yourself to a day on the couch

Exercise 2

1. What have spiders done for you lately
2. In the near future, a spider may save your life
3. Researchers in New York have discovered the healing power of one species in particular: the Chilean Rose tarantula
4. This spider's venom includes a substance that could stop a human's heart attack once it begins
5. The substance has the ability to restore the rhythm of a heart that has stopped beating
6. A scientist in Connecticut is experimenting with the killing power of another arachnid; the creature he is studying is the Australian funnel-web spider
7. Currently, pesticides that destroy insects on crops also end up killing animals accidentally

8. The funnel-web spider's venom is lethal to unwanted insects; however, it's harmless to animals
9. Scientists would have to reproduce the funnel-web spider's venom artificially in order to have enough to use in fields
10. As a result of these studies into the power of spider venom, you may live longer and enjoy pesticide-free foods

Source: Discover, September 2000

Exercises 3 and 4

Add any necessary semicolons, colons, and dashes to these sentences. The commas and end punctuation are correct and do not need to be changed.

Exercise 3

1. Chang and Eng were a famous pair of conjoined twins they lived in the 1800s.
2. They were known as the "Siamese twins" because they were born in Siam Siam is now called Thailand.
3. Chang and Eng traveled the world as celebrities of sorts and eventually made enough money to settle down.
4. They became citizens of the United States and bought farmland in North Carolina.
5. The twins enjoyed the same pastimes smoking cigars, reading books, and buying clothes.
6. Eng was known for the following having a calm disposition and playing endless games of poker.
7. Chang unlike his brother could lose his temper easily.
8. Chang and Eng married two sisters from the same family Adelaide and Sarah.
9. The two couples lived together at first then the twins divided their time between two houses one for each of their growing families.
10. The famous twins had a total 21 children their descendents are still a rich part of the Mount Airy community in North Carolina.

Source: National Geographic, June 2006

Exercise 4

1. Thunderstorms are spectacular demonstrations of nature's power.
2. Do you know where the safest places are during a thunderstorm?
3. One relatively safe place is inside a building that has plumbing pipes or electrical wires those channels can absorb the electrical energy unleashed by lightning.
4. Of course, once inside such a building, people should stay away from the end sources of plumbing and wiring faucets, hoses, phone receivers, and computer terminals.
5. Buildings without pipes or wires are not safe shelters during lightning strikes these might include pergolas, dugouts, and tents.
6. Outside, lightning can move over the ground therefore, you should be aware of a position that emergency officials call the "lightning squat."
7. This emergency position involves curling up into the smallest ball you can while balancing on the balls of your feet and covering your ears.
8. That way, there is less of you in contact with the ground if lightning strikes.
9. Lightning is electrical energy consequently, it can travel far from the actual storm clouds.
10. In fact, lightning has struck as far as twenty miles away from the storm that caused it.

Source: Current Health, October 2003

Exercise 5

Add the necessary periods, question marks, exclamation points, semicolons, colons, and dashes. Any commas in the sentences are correct and should not be changed.

1. "Am I going to get old like Grandpa"
2. This question is typical of the ones children ask their parents about aging luckily, there are books that help parents answer them
3. Lynne S. Dumas wrote the book *Talking with Your Child about a Troubled World* in it, she discusses children's concerns and suggests ways of dealing with them

4. In response to the question about getting old "like Grandpa," Dumas stresses one main point be positive

5. Too often, Dumas says, parents pass their own fears on to children parents who focus on the negative aspects of aging will probably have children who worry about growing old

6. Other subjects homelessness, for instance require special consideration for parents

7. Dumas explains that children carefully observe how parents deal with a person asking for spare change or offering to wash windshields for money

8. The unplanned nature of these encounters often catches parents off guard therefore, they should try to prepare a uniform response to such situations

9. Dumas also suggests that parents take positive action involving children in charitable donations and activities, for example in order to illustrate their compassion for the homeless

10. The most important aspect in communicating with children is honesty the second and third most important are patience and understanding

PROOFREADING EXERCISE

Can you find the punctuation errors in this student paragraph? They all involve periods, question marks, exclamation points, semicolons, colons, and dashes. Any commas used within the sentences are correct and should not be changed.

The ingredients you will need to make quick, delicious spaghetti sauce include onions, garlic, mushrooms, and canned tomato sauce meat is optional. First, at the bottom of a big heavy pot on high heat, you should sauté the onions, garlic, and mushrooms in olive oil: then put the vegetables aside and brown the meat, if any. Once the meat has browned nicely, it's time to add the tomato sauce and seasonings. You can use oregano and basil; or just salt and pepper. Actually, you can use any blend of spices: to suit your taste. Try adding a teaspoon or even a tablespoon of sugar to keep the sauce from being bitter. Next, return the sautéed vegetables to the pot. Cook the sauce mixture over medium heat until it begins to boil. Finally, lower the temperature and simmer the sauce until it achieves the perfect consistency thick and glossy. Serve the sauce on top of any kind of cooked pasta.

SENTENCE WRITING

Write ten sentences of your own that use periods, question marks, exclamation points, semicolons, colons, and dashes correctly. Imitate the examples used in the explanations if necessary. Write about an interesting assignment you have done for a class, or choose your own topic. Keep the results in your sentence writing folder.

Comma Rules 1, 2, and 3

Commas and other pieces of punctuation guide the reader through your sentence structures in the same way that signs guide drivers on the highway. Imagine what effects misplaced or incorrect road signs would have. Yet students often randomly place commas in their sentences. Try not to use a comma unless you know there is a need for it. Memorize this rhyme about comma use: *When in doubt, leave it out.*

Among all of the comma rules, six are most important. Learn these six rules, and your writing will be easier to read. You have already studied the first rule on page 87.

1. Put a comma before *for, and, nor, but, or, yet, so* (remember these seven words as the *fanboys*) when they connect two independent clauses.

The neighbors recently bought a minivan, and now they take short trips every weekend.

We wrote our paragraphs in class today, but the teacher forgot to collect them.

She was recently promoted, so she has moved to a better office.

If you use a comma alone between two independent clauses, the result is an error called a ***comma splice.***

The cake looked delicious, it tasted good too. (comma splice)

The cake looked delicious, and it tasted good too. (correct)

Before using a comma, be sure such words do connect two independent clauses. The following sentence is merely one independent clause with one subject and two verbs. Therefore, no comma should be used.

The ice cream looked delicious and tasted good too.

2. Use a comma to separate three or more items in a series.

Students in literature classes are reading short stories, poems, and plays.

Today I did my laundry, washed my car, and cleaned my room.

Occasionally, writers leave out the comma before the *and* connecting the last two items in a series, but it is more common to use it to separate all of the items equally. Some words work together and don't need commas between them even though they do make up a kind of series.

The team members wanted to wear their brand new green uniforms.

The bright white sunlight made the room glow.

To see whether a comma is needed between words in a series, ask yourself whether *and* could be used naturally between them. It would sound all right to say *short stories and poems and plays;* therefore, commas are used. But it would not sound right to say *brand and new and green uniforms* or *bright and white sunlight;* therefore, no commas are used.

If an address or date is used in a sentence, put a comma after every item, including the last.

My father was born on August 19, 1941, in Mesa, Arizona, and grew up there.

Shelby lived in St. Louis, Missouri, for two years.

When only the month and year are used in a date, no commas are needed.

My aunt graduated from Yale in May 1985.

3. Put a comma after an introductory expression (a word, a phrase, or a dependent clause) or before a comment or question tagged onto the end.

Finally, he was able to get through to his insurance company.

During her last performance, the actress fell and broke her foot.

Once I have finished my homework, I will call you.

He said he needed to ruminate, whatever that means.

The new chairs aren't very comfortable, are they?

EXERCISES

Add commas to the following sentences according to the first three comma rules. Any other punctuation already in the sentences is correct. Check your answers after the first set.

Exercise 1

Add commas according to Comma Rule 1. Put a comma before a *fanboys* when it connects two independent clauses. Some sentences may be correct.

1. Chickens are the subject of riddles, jokes, and sayings.
2. We think of funny ways to respond to the "Why did the chicken cross the road?" question and we endlessly ponder the answer to "Which came first—the chicken or the egg?"

3. A person who runs around in a hurry is often compared to "a chicken with its head cut off."
4. We try not to visualize the image of the last comparison but most people understand the reference to a fowl's final moments of frantic activity.
5. Anyone who has heard the story of Mike "the headless chicken" will consider the popular saying differently from that moment on for it will come to mean having a strong determination to live in spite of major setbacks.
6. On September 10, 1945, a farmer in Fruita, Colorado, chose one of his chickens to have for dinner that night.
7. But after having his head cut off, the rooster didn't die or seem to be in pain and it continued to act "normally."
8. In fact, Mike went on to become a national celebrity and his owner took him around the country so that people could see him for themselves.
9. Both *Time* and *Life* magazines ran feature stories complete with photos of Mike in October 1945 and the public became fascinated by the details of Mike's ability to eat drink hear and move without a head.
10. Mike lived for eighteen months after his date with a chopping block and would have lived longer but he died by accidentally choking in 1947.

Source: The Official Mike the Headless Chicken Book (Fruita Times, 2000)

Exercise 2

Add commas according to Comma Rule 2. Use a comma to separate three or more items in a series. Some sentences may not need any more commas.

1. Whenever I need to borrow some blueberries an onion or a teaspoon of ginger, I go next door to my neighbor's apartment.
2. My neighbor's name is Albert, and he is originally from Belgium.
3. Albert always has the season's best fruits the tastiest vegetables and the freshest spices.

4. Albert feels comfortable borrowing things from me, too.
5. He doesn't ask for blueberries onions or ginger, but he will ask to borrow a hammer a wrench or a Phillips-head screwdriver.
6. Albert and I have learned to offset each other's household purchases perfectly.
7. If I buy myself a new dustpan broom or rake, I buy an extra one for Albert.
8. When he visits the farmer's market on Thursdays, Albert picks up an extra basket of strawberries for me.
9. I could not have planned to have a better next-door neighbor.
10. Whatever one of us doesn't buy, the other one will.

Exercise 3

Add commas according to Comma Rule 3. Put a comma after introductory expressions or before tag comments or questions.

1. As if people didn't have enough to worry about Melinda Muse has written a book called *I'm Afraid, You're Afraid: 448 Things to Fear and Why.*
2. In her book Muse points out the dangers of common places, objects, foods, months, days, and activities.
3. If people plan a trip to Vegas they should worry because paramedics can't get to ailing gamblers due to the crowds and huge size of the buildings.
4. For another dangerous spot consider the beauty parlor, where people suffer strokes caused by leaning their heads back too far into the shampoo sink.
5. If new clothes are not washed before they are worn they may transfer dangerous chemicals to the wearers' eyes, skin, and lungs.
6. Among foods to be avoided grapefruit juice can interfere with certain medications' effectiveness, and nutmeg contains hallucinogenic substances.

7. Of all the months July ranks highest in certain kinds of accidental injuries and poisonings due to Independence Day celebrations and other summer activities.
8. Being linked with more suicides and heart attacks than any other Mondays are the most dangerous days of the week.
9. Even joining a large choir can permanently damage singers' ears.
10. After reading *I'm Afraid, You're Afraid* it's possible to be afraid of almost everything.

Exercise 4

Add commas according to the first three comma rules.

1. Speaking of worst-case scenarios there is a book about how to survive them and it's called *The Worst-Case Scenario Survival Handbook.*
2. The coauthors of this self-help book are aware that most of us will never have to overpower an alligator or make an emergency landing on an airplane yet they want us to be prepared nonetheless.
3. In the "About the Authors" section of the book readers learn that Joshua Piven is a first-time writer but he has survived encounters with robbers muggers and stalled subway trains.
4. About Piven's coauthor we discover that David Borgenicht has written two other books and has had his share of worst-case scenarios especially while traveling.
5. Although the overall tone of the book is somewhat humorous because it covers such outlandish topics the information it shares is deadly serious and could save a life.
6. There are drawings in each section of the book to help the reader picture the emergency and how to survive it.
7. One of the best examples illustrates a way to avoid being attacked by a mountain lion and that is to try to appear as large as possible so the drawing shows a man holding the sides of his jacket out wide like bat wings to scare the lion away.

8. If readers wonder whether they can trust the advice on escaping from quicksand they can just flip to the list of sources consulted for each section in this case an expert on the physics of natural phenomena at the University of Sydney Australia.
9. Wisely Piven and Borgenicht begin the book by warning readers to seek professional help whenever possible instead of trying the survival techniques themselves.
10. The authors know that if people go looking for trouble they'll probably find it.

Exercise 5

Add commas according to the first three comma rules.

1. Fish may be considered "brain food" but I've never liked it.
2. While everyone is saying how delicious a big salmon steak is or how yummy the shrimp tastes you'll find me grimacing and munching on a piece of bread and butter.
3. Part of the problem with fish is the smell but my friends who love to eat fish also love the smell of fish cooking.
4. I always thought that was strange but it makes sense doesn't it?
5. If someone hates the taste of onions that person probably also hates the smell of onions cooking.
6. Come to think of it my husband hates to eat sweets and doesn't like the smell of them either.
7. When we walk into a bakery together he practically has to hold his nose the way I would in a fish market.
8. To me that's odd but my aversion must be just as odd to someone who loves fish.
9. Our daughter loves the taste of bacon but she hates the smell of bacon frying.
10. So I guess there are exceptions to the agreement of our senses of taste and smell.

PROOFREADING EXERCISE

We have omitted the commas from the following excerpt about social behavior in the United States. It is from the book *Behave Yourself: The Essential Guide to International Etiquette* by Michael Powell. After you have added commas according to all six comma rules, check your answers at the back of the book. Remember the rule of thumb about placing any comma in a sentence: "When in doubt, leave it out."

Use a person's title and last name until you are invited to use first names which will invariably be immediately. This is not a sign of intimacy; Americans feel that the use of last names is so formal that it is uncomfortable to address others in this manner. You will find that Americans almost always introduce themselves or others using first names even in business. If you are introduced to someone by his or her first name then it is perfectly acceptable to use the first name.

Punctuality is important in business. Always phone ahead if you are going to be more than 10 minutes late. Likewise punctuality is valued for prestigious social engagements. However punctuality is considerably more flexible for casual gatherings among friends; being a few minutes late is the norm and it's not unheard of for people to trickle into a casual party among friends anywhere from 15 minutes to an hour after the designated starting time of the party.

Americans are generally very gregarious and welcoming. Frequent smiling is a cultural norm an important social custom that should not be misinterpreted as superficiality. Maintain a personal distance of at least one arm's length.

Conversation can be animated quite loud and refreshingly direct. Although in some situations political correctness obliges people to choose their words carefully so they won't offend anyone in others you will meet some of the most straightforward people in the world. The freedom to express ones opinions is highly prized in the United States.

SENTENCE WRITING

Combine the following sets of sentences in different ways using all of the first three comma rules. You may need to reorder the details and change the phrasing. Keep the results in your sentence writing folder.

The final exam was long and difficult.
Most students were unable to finish it.

The gardeners arrive at 7:00 in the morning.
They start using their lawnmowers and other loud machines.
No one in the neighborhood can sleep in anymore.

I grew up in the 1960s.
People rode in cars without seatbelts.
There were no special car seats for children.
Air bags had not been introduced yet.

Comma Rules 4, 5, and 6

The next three comma rules all involve using pairs of commas to enclose what we like to call "scoopable" elements. Scoopable elements are certain words, phrases, and clauses that can be taken out of the middle of a sentence without affecting its meaning. Notice that the comma **(,)** is shaped somewhat like the tip of an ice cream scoop? Let this similarity help you remember to use commas to enclose *scoopable* elements. Two commas are used**,** one before and one after**,** to show where scoopable elements begin and where they end.

4. Put commas around the name of a person spoken to.

Did you know, Danielle, that you left your backpack at the library?

We regret to inform you, Mr. Davis, that your policy has been canceled.

5. Put commas around expressions that interrupt the flow of the sentence (such as *however, moreover, therefore, of course, by the way, on the other hand, I believe, I think*).

I know, of course, that I have missed the deadline.

They will try, therefore, to use the rest of their time wisely.

Today's exam, I think, was only a practice test.

Read the previous examples *aloud,* and you'll hear how these expressions surrounded by commas interrupt the flow of the sentence. Sometimes such expressions flow smoothly into the sentence and don't need commas around them.

Of course he checked to see if there were any rooms available.

We therefore decided to stay out of it.

I think you made the right decision.

Remember that when a word like *however* comes between two independent clauses, that word needs a semicolon before it. It may also have a comma after it, especially if there seems to be a pause between the word and the rest of the sentence. (See p. 86.)

The bus was late; *however,* we still made it to the museum before it closed.

I am improving my study habits; *furthermore,* I am getting better grades.

She was interested in journalism; *therefore,* she took a job at a local newspaper.

I spent hours studying for the test; *finally,* I felt prepared.

Thus, you've seen a word like *however* or *therefore* used in three ways:

1. as a "scoopable" word that interrupts the flow of the sentence (needs commas around it)
2. as a word that flows into the sentence (no commas needed)
3. as a connecting word between two independent clauses (semicolon before and often a comma after)

6. Put commas around additional information that is not needed in a sentence.

Certain additional information is "scoopable" and should be surrounded by commas whenever the meaning would be clear without it. Look at the following sentence:

Maxine Taylor, who organized the fund-raiser, will introduce the candidates.

The clause *who organized the fund-raiser* is not needed in the sentence. Without it, we still know exactly who the sentence is about and what she is going to do: "Maxine Taylor will introduce the candidates." Therefore, the additional information is surrounded by commas to show that it is scoopable. Now read the following sentence:

The woman who organized the fund-raiser will introduce the candidates.

The clause *who organized the fund-raiser* is necessary in this sentence. Without it, the sentence would read as follows: "The woman will introduce the candidates." The reader would have no idea *which woman.* The clause *who organized the fund-raiser* cannot be left out because it identifies which woman. Therefore, the clause is not scoopable, and no commas are used around it. Here is another sample sentence:

Hamlet, Shakespeare's famous play, has been made into a movie many times.

The additional information *Shakespeare's famous play* is scoopable. It could be left out, and we would still understand the meaning of the sentence: "*Hamlet* has been made into a movie many times." Therefore, the commas surround the scoopable information to show that it could be taken out. Here is the same sentence with the information reversed:

Shakespeare's famous play *Hamlet* has been made into a movie many times.

Here the title of the play is necessary. Without it, the sentence would read as follows: "Shakespeare's famous play has been made into a movie many times." The reader would have no idea which of Shakespeare's famous plays has been made into a movie many times. Therefore, the title is not scoopable, and commas should not be used around it.

The trick in deciding whether additional information is scoopable or not is to remember, "If I can scoop it out and still understand the sentence, I'll put commas around it."

EXERCISES

Surround any "scoopable" elements with commas according to Comma Rules 4, 5, and 6. Any commas already in the sentences follow Comma Rules 1, 2, and 3. Some sentences may be correct. Check your answers after the first set.

Exercise 1

1. This year's graduation ceremony I believe was better than last year's.
2. I believe this year's graduation ceremony was better than last year's.
3. The valedictorian's speech however was longer than ever.
4. However the valedictorian's speech was longer than ever.
5. The person who cued the music between speeches fell asleep and missed a cue.
6. Jason Bell who cued the music between the speeches fell asleep and missed a cue.
7. The Anime Association the newest club on campus showed an inspirational short film.
8. The new Anime Association showed an inspirational short film.
9. And as usual no one felt comfortable wearing a mortarboard, so they were flying everywhere.
10. And no one as usual felt comfortable wearing a mortarboard, so they were flying everywhere.

Exercise 2

1. We hope of course that people will honor their summons for jury duty.
2. Of course we hope that people will honor their summons for jury duty.

3. People who serve as jurors every time they're called deserve our appreciation.
4. Thelma and Trevor Martin who serve as jurors every time they're called deserve our appreciation.
5. We should therefore be as understanding as we can be about the slow legal process.
6. Therefore we should be as understanding as we can be about the slow legal process.
7. A legal system that believes people are innocent until proven guilty must offer a trial-by-jury option.
8. The U.S. legal system which believes people are innocent until proven guilty offers a trial-by-jury option.
9. With that option, we hope that no one will receive an unfair trial.
10. With that option, no one we hope will receive an unfair trial.

Exercise 3

1. Bobble-head dolls those figurines with heads that bob up and down have become the souvenir of choice for many modern teams and companies.
2. The history of the bobble-head doll might go back as far as the seventeenth century when figurines with moving heads were popular in China.
3. Others say these types of ceramic nodding figures called "nodder" dolls in Europe originated there in the 1800s.
4. Much more recently in the 1960s to be exact Japan began producing what some call "bobbinheads" as souvenirs to sell at baseball parks in the United States.
5. The first four baseball nodders celebrated the careers of Roberto Clemente, Mickey Mantle, Roger Maris, and Willie Mays.
6. Two of the most famous people of the twentieth century President Kennedy and Elvis Presley were immortalized as bobble-head dolls.
7. In the year 2000, Cal Ripken's nodding doll was issued just prior to his retirement.

8. Now some cereal boxes traditionally the showplaces for athletic triumphs include tiny bobble-heads as prizes inside.
9. Even William Rehnquist Chief Justice of the U.S. Supreme Court had a bobble-head doll in his likeness.
10. The Rehnquist bobble-head a must-have for any nodding-doll collector was commissioned by a law journal to encourage people to read about legal issues.

Source: www.charleston.net, July 13, 2003

Exercise 4

1. The story of Dracula the frightening Prince Vlad Tepes has been fascinating people across the world for hundreds of years.
2. He was held as a prisoner in Bran Castle a medieval fortress in Transylvania in the 15th century.
3. Bran Castle also called Dracula's Castle has become a popular tourist attraction.
4. For the past forty years, people who traveled to Romania have been visiting the museum at Bran Castle.
5. The towers and Transylvanian charm of the castle have also made it the perfect setting for many Dracula movies.
6. The owners of Dracula's Castle have changed throughout the years.
7. It was given to Marie Queen of Romania in 1920.
8. But the political landscape changed, and the castle became national property in 1948.
9. A law that was passed in 2005 returned Bran Castle to the ancestors of the Romanian royal family.
10. Queen Marie's grandson Dominic von Habsburg now owns the castle, along with his two sisters Maria Magdalena and Elizabeth.

Source: Renaissance Magazine, Issue #51 (2006)

Exercise 5

1. One of the weirdest competitions on earth the Wife Carrying World Championships takes place in Finland once a year.
2. These load-carrying races which may have begun as training rituals for Finnish soldiers have become popular in the United States and all over the world.
3. Each pair of participants made up of one man and one "wife" has to make it through an obstacle course in the shortest time possible.
4. The "wife" half of the team has to weigh at least 49 kilos 108 pounds.
5. She does not have to be married to the man who carries her; she can indeed be someone else's wife or even unmarried.
6. The wife-carrying course includes two sections a part on land and a part in water.
7. The contest rules are few: make it to the finish line first, have fun, and don't drop the wife along the way.
8. The wife-dropping penalty which is fifteen seconds added to the pair's time is enough to disqualify most couples.
9. Contest officials allow one piece of equipment a belt that the man can wear so that the "wife" has something to hold on to during the race.
10. The winning couple wins a prize, but the coveted title Wife Carrying World Champion is reward enough for most.

Source: www.sonkajarvi.fi and *Sports Illustrated for Kids,* July 2003

PROOFREADING EXERCISE

Insert the necessary commas into this paragraph according to Comma Rules 4, 5, and 6.

There are two types of punctuation internal punctuation and end punctuation. Internal punctuation is used within the sentence, and end punctuation is used at the end of the sentence. There are six main rules for the placement of commas the most important pieces of internal punctuation. Semicolons the next most important have two main functions. Their primary function separating two independent clauses is also the most widely known. A lesser-known need for semicolons to separate items in a list already containing commas occurs rarely in college writing. Colons and dashes have special uses within sentences. And of the three pieces of end punctuation—periods, question marks, and exclamation points—one is obviously the most common. That piece is the period which signals the end of the majority of English sentences.

SENTENCE WRITING

Combine the following sets of sentences in different ways according to Comma Rules 4, 5, and 6. Try to combine each set in a way that needs commas and in a way that doesn't need commas. In other words, try to make an element "scoopable" in one sentence and not "scoopable" in another. You may reorder the details and change the phrasing as you wish. Sample responses are provided in the Answers section.

I think about the average student's life.

The average student's life is full of distractions and extraneous information from the Internet and many other forms of media.

She plans to buy herself an expensive watch.

It is sold by Tag Heuer.

Tag Heuer is her favorite brand.

Only two people were in the store when it was robbed.

One was the manager.

The other was a customer.

Review of the Comma

Six Comma Rules

1. Put a comma before *for, and, nor, but, or, yet, so* when they connect two independent clauses.
2. Put a comma between three or more items in a series.
3. Put a comma after an introductory expression or before a tag comment or question.
4. Put commas around the name of a person spoken to.
5. Put commas around words like *however* or *therefore* when they interrupt a sentence.
6. Put commas around unnecessary additional ("scoopable") information.

COMMA REVIEW EXERCISE

Add the missing commas, and identify which one of the six comma rules applies in the brackets at the end of each sentence. Each of the six sentences illustrates a different rule.

We're writing you this e-mail Lena to give you directions to the reunion this weekend. [ ] We know that you will be driving with a few others but we want to be sure that everyone knows the way. [ ] When we contacted some of our classmates over the Internet several of the messages were returned as "undeliverable." [ ] We hope therefore that this one gets through to you. [ ] We can't wait to see everyone again: Michelle Tom Olivia and Brad. [ ] Dr. Milford our favorite professor will be there to welcome all of the returning students. [ ]

SENTENCE WRITING

Write at least one sentence of your own to demonstrate each of the six comma rules. Keep the results in your sentence writing folder.

Quotation Marks and Underlining/*Italics*

Put quotation marks around a direct quotation (the exact words of a speaker) but not around an indirect quotation.

The officer said, "Please show me your driver's license." (a direct quotation)

The officer asked to see my driver's license. (an indirect quotation)

If the speaker says more than one sentence, quotation marks are used before and after the entire speech.

She said, "One of your brake lights is out. You need to take care of the problem right away."

If the quotation begins the sentence, the words telling who is speaking are set off with a comma unless the quotation ends with a question mark or an exclamation point.

"I didn't even know it was broken," I said.

"Do you have any questions?" she asked.

"You mean I can go!" I shouted.

"Yes, consider this just a warning," she said.

Notice that each of the previous quotations begins with a capital letter. But when a quotation is interrupted by an identifying phrase, the second part doesn't begin with a capital letter unless the second part is a new sentence.

"If you knew how much time I spent on the essay," the student said, "you would give me an A."

"A chef might work on a meal for days," the teacher replied. "That doesn't mean the results will taste good."

Put quotation marks around the titles of short stories, poems, songs, essays, TV program episodes, or other short works.

I couldn't sleep after I read "The Lottery," a short story by Shirley Jackson.

My favorite Woodie Guthrie song is "This Land Is Your Land."

We had to read George Orwell's essay "A Hanging" for my speech class.

Jerry Seinfeld's troubles in "The Puffy Shirt" episode are some of the funniest moments in TV history.

Underline titles of longer works such as books, newspapers, magazines, plays, record albums or CDs, movies, or the titles of TV or radio series.

The Color Purple is a novel by Alice Walker.

I read about the latest discovery of dinosaur footprints in Newsweek.

Gone with the Wind was re-released in movie theaters in 1998.

My mother listens to The Writer's Almanac on the radio every morning.

You may choose to *italicize* instead of underlining if your word processor gives you the option. Just be consistent throughout any paper in which you use underlining or italics.

The Color Purple is a novel by Alice Walker.

I read about the latest discovery of dinosaur footprints in *Newsweek*.

Gone with the Wind was re-released in movie theaters in 1998.

My mother listens to *The Writer's Almanac* on the radio every morning.

EXERCISES

Correctly punctuate quotations and titles in the following sentences by adding quotation marks or underlining (*italics*).

Exercise 1

1. I am reading a book called Don't: A Manual of Mistakes & Improprieties More or Less Prevalent in Conduct and Speech.
2. The book's contents are divided into chapters with titles such as At Table, In Public, and In General.
3. In the section about table don'ts, the book offers the following warning: Don't bend over your plate, or drop your head to get each mouthful.
4. The table advice continues by adding, Don't bite your bread. Break it off.
5. This book offers particularly comforting advice about conducting oneself in public.
6. For instance, it states, Don't brush against people, or elbow people, or in any way show disregard for others.
7. When meeting others on the street, the book advises, Don't be in a haste to introduce. Be sure that it is mutually desired before presenting one person to another.

8. In the section titled In General, there are more tips about how to get along in society, such as Don't underrate everything that others do, and overstate your own doings.
9. The Don't book has this to say about books, whether borrowed or owned: Read them, but treat them as friends that must not be abused.
10. And one can never take the following warning too much to heart: Don't make yourself in any particular way a nuisance to your neighbors or your family.

Exercise 2

1. Have you been to the bookstore yet? Monica asked.
2. No, why? I answered.
3. They've rearranged the books, she said, and now I can't find anything.
4. Are all of the books for one subject still together? I wondered.
5. Yes, they are, Monica told me, but there are no markers underneath the books to say which teacher's class they're used in, so it's really confusing.
6. Why don't we just wait until the teachers show us the books and then buy them? I replied.
7. That will be too late! Monica shouted.
8. Calm down, I told her, you are worrying for nothing.
9. I guess so, she said once she took a deep breath.
10. I sure hope I'm not wrong, I thought to myself, or Monica will really be mad at me.

Exercise 3

1. Stopping by Woods on a Snowy Evening is a poem by Robert Frost.
2. Once you finish your responses, the teacher said, bring your test papers up to my desk.
3. I subscribe to several periodicals, including Time and U.S. News & World Report.

4. Our country is the world, William Lloyd Garrison believed, our countrymen are all mankind.
5. Do you know, my teacher asked, that there are only three ways to end a sentence?
6. Edward Young warned young people to Be wise with speed. A fool at forty is a fool indeed.
7. In Shakespeare's play Romeo and Juliet, Mercutio accidentally gets stabbed and shouts, A plague on both your houses!
8. There is no such thing as a moral or an immoral book, Oscar Wilde writes in his novel The Picture of Dorian Gray; Books are either well written, or badly written.
9. Molière felt that One should eat to live, and not live to eat.
10. Did you say, I'm sleepy or I'm beeping?

Exercise 4

1. Women's Wit and Wisdom is the title of a book I found in the library.
2. The book includes many great insights that were written or spoken by women throughout history.
3. England's Queen Elizabeth I noted in the sixteenth century that A clear and innocent conscience fears nothing.
4. Nothing is so good as it seems beforehand, observed George Eliot, a female author whose real name was Mary Ann Evans.
5. Some of the women's quotations are funny; Alice Roosevelt Longworth, for instance, said, If you don't have anything good to say about anyone, come and sit by me.
6. If life is a bowl of cherries, asked Erma Bombeck, what am I doing in the pits?
7. Some of the quotations are serious, such as Gloria Steinem's statement, The future depends on what each of us does every day.
8. Maya Lin, the woman who designed Washington D.C.'s Vietnam Veterans Memorial, reminded us that, as she put it, War is not just a victory or a loss. . . . People die.

9. Emily Dickinson had this to say about truth: Truth is such a rare thing, it is delightful to tell it.
10. Finally, columnist Ann Landers advised one of her readers that The naked truth is always better than the best-dressed lie.

Exercise 5

1. In his book Who's Buried in Grant's Tomb? A Tour of Presidential Gravesites, Brian Lamb records the final words of American presidents who have passed away.
2. Some of their goodbyes were directed at their loved ones; for example, President Zachary Taylor told those around him, I regret nothing, but I am sorry that I am about to leave my friends.
3. Other presidents, such as William Henry Harrison, who died after only one month in office, addressed more political concerns; Harrison said, I wish you to understand the true principles of the government. I wish them carried out. I ask for nothing more.
4. John Tyler became president due to Harrison's sudden death; Tyler served his term, lived to be seventy-one, and said, Perhaps it is best when his time came.
5. At the age of eighty-three, Thomas Jefferson fought to live long enough to see the fiftieth anniversary of America's independence; on that day in 1826, Jefferson was one of only three (out of fifty-six) signers of the Declaration of Independence still living, and he asked repeatedly before he died, Is it the fourth?
6. John Adams, one of the other three remaining signers, died later the same day—July 4, 1826—and his last words ironically were Thomas Jefferson still survives.
7. The third president to die on the Fourth of July (1831) was James Monroe; while he was president, people within the government got along so well that his time in office was known as the era of good feelings.
8. Doctors attempted to help James Madison live until the Fourth of July, but he put off their assistance; on June 26, 1836, when a member of his family became alarmed at his condition, Madison comforted her by saying, Nothing more than a change of mind, my dear, and he passed away.

9. Grover Cleveland, who had suffered from many physical problems, was uneasy at his death; before losing consciousness, he said, I have tried so hard to do right.

10. Finally, George Washington, our first president, also suffered greatly but faced death bravely; I die hard, he told the people by his bedside, but I am not afraid to go. 'Tis well.

PARAGRAPH EXERCISE

Correctly punctuate quotations and titles in the following paragraph by adding quotation marks or <u>underlining</u> (*italics*).

We were allowed to choose a book to review in our journals last week. The teacher specified that it should be a short nonfiction book about something of interest to us. I found a great book to review. It's called Tattoo: Secrets of a Strange Art. Albert Parry breaks the contents down into chapters about tattoo legends, techniques, and purposes. A few of the chapter titles are The Art and Its Masters, The Circus, Identification, and Removal. The book also includes illustrations and photographs of tattoo designs and tattooed people and animals throughout history, including Miss Stella: The Tattooed Lady, The Famous Tattooed Cow, and Georgius Constantine. Parry describes Constantine's tattoos in the following way: the most complete, elaborate, and artistic tattooing ever witnessed in America or Europe. Parry continues, There was almost no part of his body, not a quarter-inch of the skin, free from designs. Needless to say, since I love tattoos, I loved Parry's book about them.

SENTENCE WRITING

Write ten sentences that list and discuss your favorite songs, TV shows, characters' expressions, movies, books, and so on. Be sure to punctuate quotations and titles correctly. Refer to the rules at the beginning of this section if necessary. Keep the results in your sentence writing folder.

Capital Letters

1. Capitalize the first word of every sentence.

Peaches taste best when they are cold.

A piece of fruit is an amazing object.

2. Capitalize the first word of every direct quotation.

She said, "I've never worked so hard before."

"I have finished most of my homework," she said, "but I still have a lot to do." (The *but* is not capitalized because it does not begin a new sentence.)

"I love my speech class," she said. "Maybe I'll change my major." (*Maybe* is capitalized because it begins a new sentence.)

3. Capitalize the first, last, and every important word in a title. Don't capitalize prepositions (such as *in, of, at, with*), short connecting words, the *to* in front of a verb, or *a, an,* or *the*.

I saw a copy of Darwin's *The Origin of Species* at a yard sale.

The class enjoyed the essay "How to Write a Rotten Poem with Almost No Effort."

Shakespeare in Love is a film based on Shakespeare's writing of the play *Romeo and Juliet.*

4. Capitalize specific names of people, places, languages, races, and nationalities.

English	China	Cesar Chavez
Ireland	Spanish	Japanese
Ryan White	Philadelphia	Main Street

5. Capitalize names of months, days of the week, and special days, but not the seasons.

March	Fourth of July	spring
Tuesday	Earth Day	winter
Valentine's Day	Labor Day	fall

6. Capitalize a title of relationship if it takes the place of the person's name. If *my* (or *your, her, his, our, their*) is in front of the word, a capital is not used.

I think Mom wrote to him.	*but*	I think my mom wrote to him.
We visited Aunt Sophie.	*but*	We visited our aunt.
They spoke with Grandpa.	*but*	They spoke with their grandpa.

7. Capitalize names of particular people or things, but not general terms.

I admire Professor Washborne.	*but*	I admire my professor.
We saw the famous Potomac River.	*but*	We saw the famous river.
Are you from the South?	*but*	Is your house south of the mountains?
I will take Philosophy 4 and English 100.	*but*	I will take philosophy and English.
She graduated from Sutter High School.	*but*	She graduated from high school.
They live at 119 Forest St.	*but*	They live on a beautiful street.
We enjoyed the Monterey Bay Aquarium.	*but*	We enjoyed the aquarium.

EXERCISES

Add all of the necessary capital letters to the sentences that follow. Check your answers after the first set.

Exercise 1

1. i have always wanted to learn another language besides english.
2. recently, i have been watching a lot of films from india.
3. some people call them "bollywood movies."
4. whatever they are called, i love to watch them.
5. one part of these movies that i love is their language: hindi.
6. i have to use english subtitles to understand the dialogue most of the time.

7. but sometimes i can catch what's happening without the subtitles.
8. because of my intense interest in hindi-language films, i plan to take a hindi class.
9. i have already bought a book that explains the devanagari writing system.
10. now i will enroll in a class and learn hindi as a second language.

Exercise 2

1. when people think of jazz, they think of *down beat* magazine.
2. *down beat*'s motto may be "jazz, blues & beyond," but some people think that the magazine has gone too far "beyond" by including two guitarists in the *down beat* hall of fame.
3. the two musicians in question are jimi hendrix and frank zappa.
4. jimi hendrix was inducted into the hall of fame in 1970.
5. *down beat* added frank zappa to the list in 1994.
6. since then, readers and editors have been debating whether hendrix and zappa belong in the same group as duke ellington, john coltrane, and miles davis.
7. those who play jazz guitar have some of the strongest opinions on the subject.
8. russell malone, mark elf, and john abercrombie all agree that hendrix and zappa were great guitarists but not jazz guitarists.
9. others like steve tibbetts and bill frisell don't have any problem putting hendrix on the list, but tibbetts isn't so sure about including zappa.
10. it will be interesting to see who *down beat*'s future inductees will be.

Source: Down Beat, July 1999

Exercise 3

1. i grew up watching *it's a wonderful life* once a year on tv in the winter.
2. that was before the colorized version and before every station started showing it fifteen times a week throughout the months of november and december.

3. i especially remember enjoying that holiday classic with my mother and brothers when we lived on seventh avenue.
4. "hurry up!" mom would yell, "you're going to miss the beginning!"
5. my favorite part has always been when jimmy stewart's character, george bailey, uses his own money to help the people of bedford falls and to save his father's building and loan.
6. george's disappointment turns to happiness after he and donna reed's character, mary, move into the abandoned house on their honeymoon.
7. of course, mean old mr. potter takes advantage of uncle billy's carelessness at the bank, and that starts george's breakdown.
8. in his despair, george places the petals of his daughter zuzu's flower in his pocket, leaves his house, and wants to commit suicide.
9. luckily, all of george's good deeds have added up over the years, and he is given a chance to see that thanks to a character named clarence.
10. when george feels zuzu's petals in his pocket, he knows that he's really made it home again, and the people of bedford falls come to help him.

Exercise 4

1. most people don't know the name elzie crisler segar.
2. segar was the creator of the comic character popeye.
3. segar based popeye and many of his fellow characters on residents of the town of chester, illinois, where segar was born.
4. popeye's inspiration was a chester bartender named frank "rocky" fiegel.
5. fiegel was a brawler by nature and might have even been a sailor at some point.
6. segar learned how to draw by taking a correspondence course.
7. one of segar's bosses at a chester movie house, j. william schuchert, was the prototype for wimpy.
8. segar introduced olive oyl's character in his *thimble theater* comic strip.
9. olive was based on a chester store owner, dora paskel.

10. the town of chester celebrates the work of elzie crisler segar with a yearly popeye picnic, the popeye museum, a popeye statue, and segar memorial park.

Source: Biography, November 2003

Exercise 5

1. *the new yorker* magazine has a cartoon contest every week.
2. at the back of each issue, there is a page devoted to the contest.
3. the heading at the top of the page reads "cartoon caption contest."
4. below the heading is a brief description of the rules involved in the contest.
5. it begins, "each week, we provide a cartoon in need of a caption."
6. it continues, "you, the reader, submit a caption, we choose three finalists, and you vote for your favorite."
7. then it specifies the deadline for that week's submissions.
8. at the bottom of the page are three cartoons: one is titled "the winning caption"; the second lists "the finalists," and the third shows "this week's contest."
9. winners of the caption contest are named in the magazine, and they receive a signed print of the cartoon that they helped to create.
10. any u.s. resident who is eighteen or over can enter the contest or vote.

REVIEW OF PUNCTUATION AND CAPITAL LETTERS

Punctuate these sentences. They include all the rules for punctuation and capitalization you have learned. Compare your answers carefully with those at the back of the book. Sentences may require several pieces of punctuation or capital letters.

1. the griffith park observatory is one of the most famous landmarks in hollywood
2. have you ever read langston hughes essay salvation
3. trini and tracy drove all the way from san diego to santa barbara
4. how many years of french have you taken my counselor asked
5. congratulations ms thomas on your recent promotion you deserved it
6. the person who writes the best 100-word description of that car will win it
7. i am majoring in art and my best friend lee is in the nursing program
8. due to the low number of completed loan applications in the fall the financial aid office has extended its spring deadline
9. the anime club needs volunteers to pass out flyers
10. the man who was selling T-shirts at the concert said the mens medium size is the same as the womens large size and i believed him
11. my english teacher always repeats the same little rhyme about commas when in doubt leave them out
12. jessie needs a new cell phone however she cant afford one right now
13. the road not taken is a famous poem by robert frost
14. madonnas first childrens book was called the english roses and since then she has written several other books for kids
15. the angry customer stood in front of the cash register and yelled i want my money back finally the cashier called in the manager who gave the customer a refund

COMPREHENSIVE TEST

In these sentences, you'll find all the errors that have been discussed in the entire text. Try to name the error in the blank before each sentence, and then correct the error if you can. You may find any of the following errors:

adj	incorrect adjective
adv	incorrect adverb
apos	apostrophe
awk	awkward phrasing
c	comma needed
cap	capitalization
cliché	overused expression
cs	comma splice
dm	dangling modifier
frag	fragment
mm	misplaced modifier
p	punctuation
pro	incorrect pronoun
pro agr	pronoun agreement
pro ref	pronoun reference
ro	run-on sentence
shift	shift in time or person
sp	misspelled word
s-v agr	subject-verb agreement
wordy	wordiness
ww	wrong word
//	not parallel

A perfect—or almost perfect—score will mean you've mastered the first part of the text.

1. ______ The scary scenes in the movie really effected me; I couldn't sleep that night.

2. ______ The police asked us what time the theft had occured.

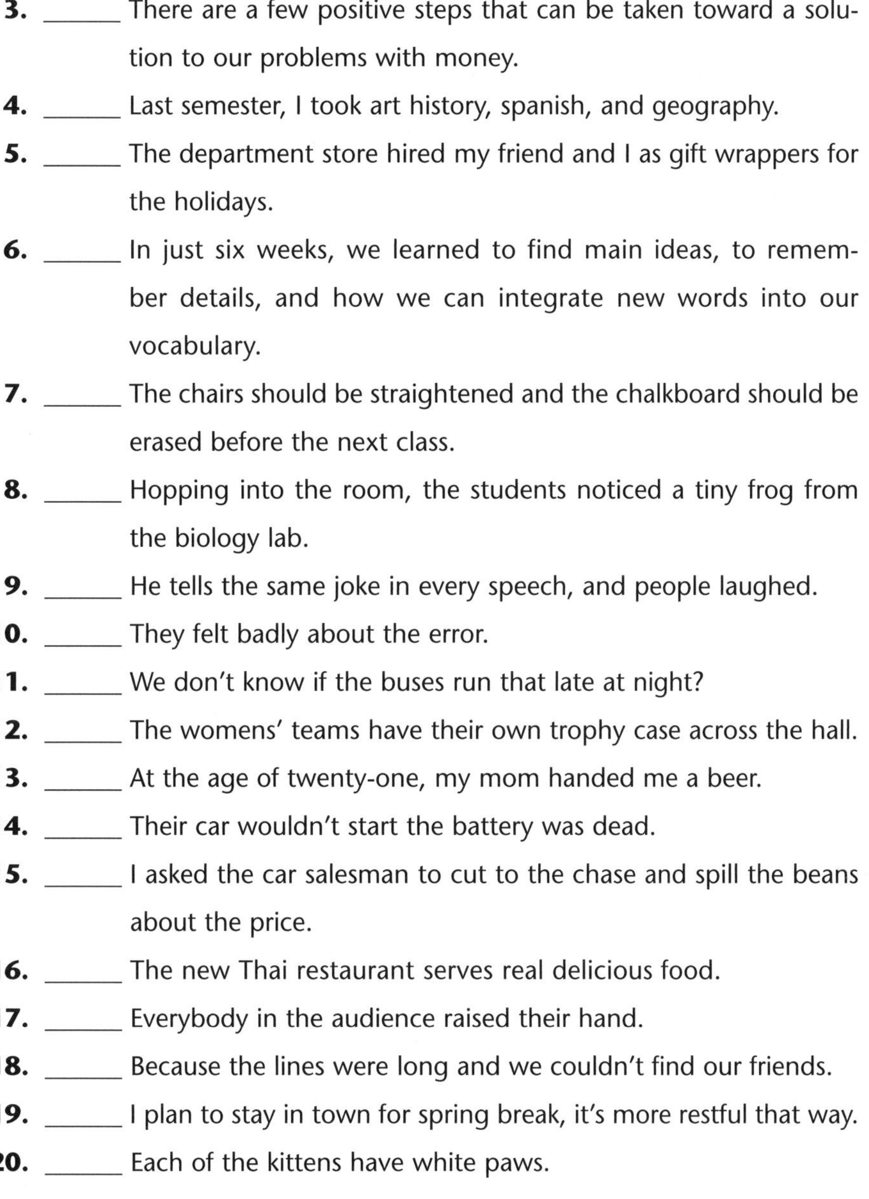

3. ______ There are a few positive steps that can be taken toward a solution to our problems with money.

4. ______ Last semester, I took art history, spanish, and geography.

5. ______ The department store hired my friend and I as gift wrappers for the holidays.

6. ______ In just six weeks, we learned to find main ideas, to remember details, and how we can integrate new words into our vocabulary.

7. ______ The chairs should be straightened and the chalkboard should be erased before the next class.

8. ______ Hopping into the room, the students noticed a tiny frog from the biology lab.

9. ______ He tells the same joke in every speech, and people laughed.

10. ______ They felt badly about the error.

11. ______ We don't know if the buses run that late at night?

12. ______ The womens' teams have their own trophy case across the hall.

13. ______ At the age of twenty-one, my mom handed me a beer.

14. ______ Their car wouldn't start the battery was dead.

15. ______ I asked the car salesman to cut to the chase and spill the beans about the price.

16. ______ The new Thai restaurant serves real delicious food.

17. ______ Everybody in the audience raised their hand.

18. ______ Because the lines were long and we couldn't find our friends.

19. ______ I plan to stay in town for spring break, it's more restful that way.

20. ______ Each of the kittens have white paws.

PART 4

Writing

Aside from the basics of word choice, spelling, sentence structure, and punctuation, what else do you need to understand to write better? Just as sentences are built according to accepted patterns, so are other "structures" of English—paragraphs and essays, for example.

Think of writing as including levels of structures, beginning small with words connecting to form phrases, clauses, and sentences. Then sentences connect to form paragraphs and essays. Each level has its own set of "blueprints." To communicate clearly in writing, words must be chosen and spelled correctly. Sentences must have a subject, a verb, and a complete thought. Paragraphs must be indented and should contain a main idea supported with sufficient detail. Essays explore a valuable topic in several coherent paragraphs, usually including an introduction, a body, and a conclusion.

Not everyone approaches writing as structure, however. It is possible to write better without thinking about structure at all. A good place to start might be to write what you care about and care about what you write. You can make an amazing amount of progress by simply being *genuine,* being who you are naturally. No one has to tell you to be yourself when you speak, but you might need encouragement to be yourself in your writing.

Writing is almost never done without a reason. The reason may come from an experience, such as receiving an unfair parking ticket, or from a requirement in a class. And when you are asked to write, you often receive guidance in the form of an assignment: tell a story to prove a point, paint a picture with your words, summarize an article, compare two subjects, share what you know about something, explain why you agree with or disagree with a statement or an idea.

Learning to write well is important, one of the most important things you will do in your education. Confidence is the key. The Writing sections will help you build confidence, whether you are expressing your own ideas or summarizing and responding to the ideas of others. Like the Sentence Structure sections, the Writing sections are best taken in order. However, each one discusses an aspect of writing that you can review on its own at any time.

What Is the Least You Should Know about Writing?

"Unlike medicine or the other sciences," William Zinsser points out, "writing has no new discoveries to spring on us. We're in no danger of reading in our morning newspaper that a breakthrough has been made in how to write [clearly]. . . . We may be given new technologies like the word processor to ease the burdens of composition, but on the whole we know what we need to know."

One thing we know is that you learn to write by *writing*—not by reading long discussions about writing. Therefore, the explanations and instructions in this section are as brief as they can be, followed by samples from student and professional writers.

Understanding the basic structures and learning the essential skills covered in this section will help you become a better writer.

BASIC STRUCTURES

I. The Paragraph
II. The Essay

WRITING SKILLS

III. Writing in Your Own Voice
IV. Finding a Topic
V. Organizing Ideas
VI. Supporting with Details
VII. Revising Your Papers
VIII. Presenting Your Work
IX. Writing about What You Read

Basic Structures

I. The Paragraph

A paragraph is unlike any other structure in English. Visually, it has its own profile: the first line is indented about five spaces, and sentences continue to fill the space between both margins until the paragraph ends (which may be in the middle of the line):

As a beginning writer, you might forget to indent your paragraphs, or you may break off in the middle of a line within a paragraph, especially when writing in class. You must remember to indent whenever you begin a new paragraph and fill the space between the margins until it ends. (*Note:* In business writing, paragraphs are not indented but double-spaced in between.)

Defining a Paragraph

A typical paragraph centers on one idea, usually phrased in a topic sentence from which all the other sentences in the paragraph radiate. The topic sentence does not need to begin the paragraph, but it most often does, and the other sentences support it with specific details. (For more on topic sentences and organizing paragraphs, see pp. 223–224.) Paragraphs usually contain several sentences, though no set number is required. A paragraph can stand alone, but more commonly paragraphs are part of a larger composition, an essay. There are different kinds of paragraphs, based on the jobs they are supposed to do.

Types of Paragraphs

Sample Paragraphs in an Essay

Introductory paragraphs begin essays. They provide background information about the essay's topic and usually include the thesis statement or main idea of the essay. (See p. 222 for information on how to write a thesis statement.) Here is the introductory paragraph of a student essay entitled "A Bit of Bad Luck":

> It's 9:45, and I'm panicking. As a student, I live a life that is almost free of misfortunes. I don't even think about bad luck. Just last week I won forty dollars in the lottery and two tickets to a concert from a radio station. So this in-class writing assignment to tell about an experience I've had with bad luck has caught me completely off guard. I don't know what to write!

In this opening paragraph, the student introduces the main idea—"I don't even think about bad luck"—and gives background information about the in-class writing assignment that has forced her to think about it.

Body paragraphs are those in the middle of essays. Each body paragraph contains a topic sentence and presents detailed information about one subtopic, stage, or idea that relates directly to the essay's thesis. (See p. 224 for more information on organizing body paragraphs.) Here are the body paragraphs of the same essay:

> I try to think of what I would call an unlucky moment. At about 9:08, we finish discussing the prompt for the assignment. "Okay," I say to myself, "this shouldn't be a problem. All I have to do is come up with a topic . . . a topic." I can feel the class ease into deep thought as I sit and scratch my head for inspiration. By 9:15, pens are flaring all over the room. The grey shirt in front of me shifts in his chair. The guy to my left has at least a paragraph already in front of him. And the girls in front of him scribble away as if they were born to write.
>
> At 9:37, I realize that I will soon run out of time. The minutes pass like seconds, and I find myself watching the class and wondering, "What's wrong with me?" while everyone else is making it look so easy. I'm thinking of high school, boyfriends, this morning's breakfast, and then I realize what is getting me all worked up—not knowing what to write. This has never happened to me before.
>
> Now I glance at my teacher, and even she's writing. How hard could it be to glide ink across a white open field? Then she gets up and tells us she'll be right back. Jennifer, to my right in blue stripes, looks at me and mouths, "Are you stuck?" I nod and add, "This has never happened to me before," cursing my bad luck. Finally, I decide to write the story of the last forty-five minutes, and it rushes easily from pen to paper.

Notice that each of the three body paragraphs discusses a single stage of her experience with bad luck in the form of writer's block.

Concluding paragraphs are the final paragraphs in essays. They bring the discussion to a close and share the writer's final thoughts on the subject. (See p. 223 for more about concluding paragraphs.) Here is the conclusion of the sample essay:

> It's about 10:05. Class is over; the teacher is waiting, and I'm still writing. Jennifer has gone, and the white shirt to my left is on his way out. Someone is rustling papers not caring who's around him. As I turn in my essay, I am disappointed in myself, knowing I could have done more. I will keep thinking about it when I get home. But in this misfortune, I still feel quite lucky knowing that I discovered my bit of bad luck, and the results could have been much, much worse.

In this concluding paragraph, the student finishes her story and shares her unwavering optimism even after her "bit of bad luck."

Sample of a Paragraph Alone

Single-paragraph writing assignments may be given in class or as homework. They test your understanding of the unique structure of a paragraph. They may ask you to answer a single question, perhaps following a reading, or to provide details about a limited topic. Look at this student paragraph, the result of a homework assignment asking students to report on a technological development in the news:

> I just read that doctors have developed a new way to cure people with certain kinds of cancer. Instead of subjecting the entire weakened patient to powerful chemicals and radiation, doctors remove the organ that contains the cancer, bombard the organ itself with customized treatments, then return the organ to the patient's body. A man in Italy was the first to undergo such a procedure to cure multiple malignant tumors in his liver. Doctors treated the man's liver outside of his body for a quarter of an hour during an operation that took nearly a day to complete. That patient, who had been given only months to live before the operation, was still free from cancer two years later. This new way to cure some types of cancer seems to make such sense. I'm glad to know that doctors are still making progress in cancer treatments.
>
> *Source: Current Science,* February 28, 2003

These shorter writing assignments help students practice presenting information within the limited structure of a paragraph.

The assignments in the upcoming Writing Skills section will sometimes ask you to write paragraphs. Remember that you may review the previous pages as often as you wish until you understand the unique structure of the paragraph.

II. The Essay

Like the paragraph, an essay has its own profile, usually including a title and several paragraphs.

Title

____

____

____

____

______________________.

____

____

____

While the paragraph is the single building block of text used in almost all forms of writing (in essays, magazine articles, letters, novels, newspaper stories, and so on), an essay is a larger, more complex structure.

The Five-Paragraph Essay and Beyond

The student essay analyzed on pages 207–208 illustrates the different kinds of paragraphs within essays. Many people like to include five paragraphs in an essay: an introductory paragraph, three body paragraphs, and a concluding paragraph. Three is a comfortable number of body paragraphs—it is not two, which makes an essay seem like a comparison even when it isn't; and it is not four, which may be too many subtopics for the beginning writer to organize clearly.

However, an essay can contain any number of paragraphs. As you become more comfortable with the flow of your ideas and gain confidence in your ability to express yourself, you are free to create essays of many different shapes and sizes. As in all things, learning about writing begins with structure and then expands to include all possibilities.

Defining an Essay

There is no such thing as a typical essay. Essays may be serious or humorous, but the best of them are thought-provoking and—of course—informative. Try looking up the word *essay* in a dictionary right now. Some words used to define an essay might need to be explained themselves:

> An essay is *prose* (meaning it is written in the ordinary language of sentences and paragraphs).
>
> An essay is *nonfiction* (meaning it deals with real people, factual information, actual opinions, and events).
>
> An essay is a *composition* (meaning it is created in parts that make up the whole, several paragraphs that explore a single topic).
>
> An essay is *personal* (meaning it shares the writer's unique perspective, even if only in the choice of topic, method of analysis, and details).
>
> An essay is *analytical* and *instructive* (meaning it examines the workings of a subject and shares the results with the reader).

A Sample Essay

For an example of a piece of writing that fits the above definition, read the following excerpt from the book *The Story of Science: Newton at the Center* by Joy Hakim. In her essay, Hakim explores the accomplishments of Alfred Nobel, the man who gave the world both dynamite and the famous peace prize.

Dynamite Man

Alfred Bernhard Nobel (1833–1896) built explosives but loved peace. A lonely millionaire bachelor, he was thought to be a "mad scientist" by his contemporaries because his wealth mostly came from weapons of destruction. Nobel, who was an idealist, actually thought his explosives would end war because they would make it too horrible. He believed his products, including the explosive nitroglycerine, had peaceful uses.

He had developed nitroglycerine on a barge in a lake so that if it exploded, few people would be hurt. (An earlier explosion in his factory had killed his brother.) He named his safe-to-handle version of nitroglycerine *dynamite*. Dynamite does have many peaceful uses and is especially valuable in construction projects. It helped open the American West by blasting rocks and mountains to make way for roads and railroad tracks. Nobel invented other things, like smokeless gunpowder and a special steel for armor plating.

Born in Stockholm, Sweden, Nobel grew up in Russia, where his father had gone to supervise an underwater mine he had designed. Educated there by private tutors, Alfred was sent to Paris to study chemistry, and in the early 1850s on to the United States to study for four years with John Ericsson, a Swedish-American inventor who would build the ironclad vessel the *Monitor*.

At his death, Nobel left a fortune to endow annual prizes honoring great achievement in five fields—peace, literature, physics, chemistry, and medicine or physiology. (A sixth prize, in economics, was established in his honor in 1969.) A money award comes with each prize, but the honor of a Nobel Prize goes way beyond money. The Nobel Foundation in Sweden was named for Alfred Nobel, and when element 102 was isolated in Berkeley, California, it was called nobelium.

Now that you have learned more about the basic structures of the paragraph and the essay, you are ready to practice the skills necessary to write them.

Writing Skills

III. Writing in Your Own Voice

All writing "speaks" on paper, and the person "listening" is the reader. Some beginning writers forget that writing and reading are two-way methods of communication, just like spoken conversations between two people. When you write, your reader listens; when you read, you also listen.

When speaking, you express a personality in your choice of phrases, your movements, your tone of voice. Family and friends probably recognize your voice messages on their answering machines without your having to identify yourself. Would they also be able to recognize your writing? They would if you extended your "voice" into your writing.

Writing should not sound like talking, necessarily, but it should have a "personality" that comes from the way you decide to approach a topic, to develop it with details, to say it your way.

The beginning of this book discusses the difference between spoken English (following looser patterns of speaking) and Standard Written English (following accepted patterns of writing). Don't think that the only way to add "voice" to your writing is to use the patterns of spoken English. Remember that Standard Written English does not have to be dull or sound "academic." Look at this example of Standard Written English that has a distinct voice, an excerpt from the book *The 5 W's: What?* by Erin McHugh:

Step Right Up, Ladies and Fleas!

Although already centuries old, the flea circus became the talk of London during the 1830s, due to L. Bertolotto, the P.T. Barnum of his time. Bertolotto had flea orchestras playing audible flea music, flea foursomes in games of flea whist, and flea waltzing, complete with dresses and frock coats. Fleas drew miniature coaches, carried guns, and fired cannons "not larger than a common pin," and fleas dressed as Napoleon and the Duke of Wellington. Bertolotto's flea circus became so popular that other impresarios developed their own flea extravaganzas, with flea circuses becoming popular fixtures in carnivals and circus sideshows throughout Europe and the United States. As late as the 1950s there was a popular flea circus near New York's Time Square. A lot has been written about the "condition" of the fleas—dead or alive—and many flea circus acts relied on dead fleas glued to their seats, to tightropes, or to other circus equipment, or on fleas manipulated by magnets hidden below a tiny flea stage. Bertolotto's playbill announced that his superior flea equipment "precludes all charges of cruelty to the fleas." Other acts, also refuting such tricks, had fleas rigged in wire

> harnesses so the fleas could move only in a particular manner. [The] following [are] some little known flea facts:
>
> - There is said to be a flea in a Kiev museum that wears horseshoes made of real gold.
> - A flea may be able to pull up to 160,000 times its own weight.
> - A flea can jump over 200 times its own height.
> - When jumping, the flea accelerates faster than the space shuttle.
> - It was popular in the 1920s to collect dead fleas dressed as wedding couples.

The above excerpt illustrates Standard Written English at its best—from its solid sentence structures to its precise use of words. But more important, the writer's clear voice speaks to us and involves us in fascinating facts about flea circuses. Students can involve us in their writing too, when they let their own voices through. Writing does not need to be about something personal to have a voice. Here is an example of a student writing about early computer hackers:

> Some mischievous hackers were only out to play a joke. One of the first examples was a group who created the famous "Cookie Monster" program at Massachusetts Institute of Technology. Several hackers programmed MIT's computer to display the word "cookie" all over the screens of its users. In order for users to clear this problem, they had to "feed" the Cookie Monster by entering the word "cookie" or lose all the data on their screens.

Notice that both the professional and the student writer tell stories (narration) and paint pictures (description) in their writing. Narration and description require practice, but once you master them, you will gain a stronger voice and will be able to add interest and clarity to even the most challenging academic writing assignments.

Narration

Narrative writing tells the reader a story, and since most of us like to tell stories, it is a good place to begin writing in your own voice. An effective narration allows readers to experience an event with the writer. Since we all see the world differently and feel unique emotions, the purpose of narration is to take readers with us through our experiences. As a result, the writer gains a better understanding of what happened, and readers get to live other lives momentarily. Listen to the "voice" of this student writer telling the story of a trip to Yosemite.

"Here Comes the Dad!"

Early one sunny summer morning in Yosemite National Park, my best friend Ashley, her Aunt Carol, her grandmother Lorna, and I were driving along a quiet road on our way to the Ahwahnee Hotel for breakfast. The sun was shining through the trees, and we could hear the birds chirping as we drove with the windows down. It was almost as if the forest was greeting us with good morning wishes as we passed through it. We never expected anything to startle or surprise us in this perfectly natural setting.

At a curve in the road, I spotted a deer alongside it. As we passed, Carol slowed the car down to walking speed so that Ashley could snap a picture of the beautiful creature. A second later, we saw another deer—only this time it was a baby fawn. She was a soft caramel-brown color with short, fuzzy fur. The movement of our car frightened her, and she jumped away from the road. Ashley said, "I have to get a picture of her. She's so cute!" We both got out of the car and slowly walked toward the fawn, being careful not to scare her again. I'll never forget how it felt when the fawn looked me in the eye for a second or two. But as soon as Ashley and I were close enough for a good picture, the fawn scurried away, this time under a tree with low branches. "Oh well," I said, "we'll see more deer later."

Ashley wasn't ready to give up on this photo opportunity. "No, I have to have a picture of *this* deer," she whined. "You stay here, and I'll follow it," she added as she crept toward the trees. Ashley was just about to duck under the thick branches for a real *National Geographic* moment when we heard Carol's voice yelling, "Here comes the dad!" I looked up, and all I saw was the silhouette of an enormous animal with antlers that seemed a hundred feet tall running toward me. In the same way that I was mesmerized by the fawn, I stood there gazing at this monster that was heading straight for me.

Then the realization hit me that a huge deer just yards away wanted to hurt me for potentially harming its baby. "Ahhh!" I started running as fast as I could. Ashley made it to the car, but the deer was gaining on me. Every stomp of its hooves sounded like the beginning of a earthquake. Faster and faster I ran. The car seemed to be miles away. Branches slammed into my body as I passed because I had no time to dodge them. I put the rest of my energy into those last few frightening steps and jumped into the car. The deer, who had obviously chased many forest visitors back to their vehicles, gave us a final look, turned, and leapt heavily back to the protection of the trees.

As I caught my breath in the back seat, tears started rolling down my cheeks as I cried with relief, but after a few moments, the four of us looked at each other and started to laugh so hard that we all started crying. We had taken our trip to Yosemite to get closer to nature, and we definitely had succeeded. We knew it was a story that we would be telling for years to come.

Description

Descriptive writing paints word pictures with details that appeal to the reader's five senses—sight, sound, touch, taste, and smell. The writer of description often uses comparisons to help readers picture one thing by imagining something else, just as the writer of "Here Comes the Dad!" compares the forest to a person "greeting us with good morning wishes as we passed through it." In the following paragraph, a student uses vivid details to bring the place she loves best to life:

> Fort Baker is located across the bay from San Francisco, almost under the Golden Gate Bridge. When I lived there as a child, nature was all I saw. Deer came onto our porch and nibbled the plants; raccoons dumped the trash cans over; skunks sprayed my brother because he poked them with a stick, and little field mice jumped out of the bread drawer at my sister when she opened

> it. Behind the house was a small forest of strong green trees; the dirt actually felt soft, and tall grassy plants with bright yellow flowers grew all around. I don't know the plants' real name, but my friend and I called it "sour grass." When we chewed the stems, we got a mouth full of sour juice that made our faces crinkle and our eyes water.

Here is another example, the description of the first meeting of Coretta Scott and her future husband Martin Luther King, Jr. The following is an excerpt from the book *Marry Me! Courtship and Proposals of Legendary Couples,* by Wendy Goldberg and Betty Goodwin. It all started on a blind date arranged by mutual friends. As we read Goldberg and Goodwin's description, we can see, hear, and feel along with these two famous people.

> As soon as Martin picked up Coretta for their first date, lunch at Sharaf's Restaurant, he liked what he saw. She was a pretty woman with long hair and bangs. The first thing Coretta noticed about Martin was that he was short and not terribly handsome. However, when he started talking, she began to find him extremely appealing and magnetic. Coretta liked his focus and self-confidence, but nothing could have prepared her for what came next.
>
> After lunch, Martin drove her back to [the New England Conservatory of Music, where Coretta was a student] and said, "Do you know something?"
>
> "What is that?"
>
> "You have everything I have ever wanted in a wife. There are four things, and you have them all."
>
> "I don't see how you can say that. You don't even know me."
>
> "Yes, I can tell," he said. "The four things that I look for in a wife are character, intelligence, personality and beauty. And you have them all. I want to see you again. When can I?"
>
> "I don't know," said Coretta. "I'll have to check my schedule. You may call me later."
>
> This was all happening much too quickly. Coretta was intent on pursuing her career and wasn't even thinking about getting married now. Besides, as genuine as Martin seemed, his sudden proposal aroused her suspicions. . . .
>
> Soon, Coretta learned that Martin was thoughtful and polite. They continued to see each other that winter, frequently discussing philosophy, religion and the condition of black Americans. . . .
>
> On June 18, 1953, Daddy King [Martin's father] married Martin and Coretta in the garden of her parents' home in Marion. . . . Daddy King agreed to delete the section of the bride's vows about promising to obey.

You may have noticed that many of the examples in this section use both narration and description. In fact, most effective writing—even a good résumé or biology lab report—calls for clear storytelling and the creation of vivid word pictures for the reader.

Writing Assignments

The following two assignments will help you develop your voice as a writer. For now, don't worry about topic sentences or thesis statements or any of the things we'll consider later. Narration and description have their own logical structures. A story has a beginning, a middle, and an end. And we describe things from top to bottom, side to side, and so on.

Assignment 1

NARRATION: FAMOUS SAYINGS

The following is a list of well-known expressions. No doubt you have had an experience that proves at least one of these to be true. Write a short essay that tells a story from your own life that relates to one of these sayings. You might want to identify the expression you have chosen in your introductory paragraph. Then tell the beginning, middle, and end of the story. Be sure to use vivid details to bring the story to life. Finish with a brief concluding paragraph in which you share your final thoughts on the experience.

When in Rome, do as the Romans do.

Good things come to those who wait.

While the cat's away, the mice will play.

Actions speak louder than words.

Enough is as good as a feast.

Assignment 2

DESCRIPTION: TOY CHOICES

Children have varied taste in toys. Some play with character dolls, action figures, and electronic games, while others go for the more generic building blocks and craft supplies. Think back to your childhood and write a description of a few of your favorite toys. Did your choice of toys have any impact on your goals as an adult? Try to use details and comparisons that appeal to the reader's senses in some way. Your goal is to make the reader visualize your toys of choice and understand their effect on you.

IV. Finding a Topic

You will most often be given a topic to write about, perhaps based on a reading assignment. However, when the assignment of a paper calls for you to choose your own topic without any further assistance, try to go immediately to your interests.

Look to Your Interests

If the topic of your paper is something you know about and—more important—something you *care* about, then the whole process of writing will be smoother and more enjoyable for you. If you ski, if you are a musician, or even if you just enjoy watching a lot of television, bring that knowledge and enthusiasm into your papers.

Take a moment to think about and jot down a few of your interests now (no matter how unrelated to school they may seem), and then save the list for use later when deciding what to write about. One student's list of interests might look like this:

buying and selling on eBay
playing games with friends
surfing in summer
collecting baseball cards

Another student's list might be very different:

playing the violin
going to concerts
watching "Bollywood" movies
drawing pictures of my friends

While still another student might list the following interests:

going to the horse races
reading for my book club
traveling in the summer
buying lottery tickets

These students have listed several worthy topics for papers. And because they are personal interests, the students have the details needed to support them. With a general topic to start with, you can use several ways to gather the details you will need to support it in a paragraph or an essay.

Focused Free Writing (or Brainstorming)

Free writing is a good way to begin. When you are assigned a paper, try writing for ten minutes by putting down all your thoughts on one subject—drawing pictures of my friends, for example. Don't stop to think about organization, sentence structures, capitalization, or spelling—just let details flow onto the page. Free writing will help you see what material you have and will help you figure out what aspects of the subject to write about.

Here is an example:

I like to draw pictures of my friends but sometimes they don't like it when I draw them. The nose is to big they think or the hair isn't just right. Once in awhile I get it perfect, but not that often. I like to style my drawings like cartoons kind of. Its almost like you'll see little baloons like in a cartoon strip with little sayings in them. I'm not a big talker myself, so I can express myself with my friends thru my drawings of them. Again, some of them like it and some of them don't.

Now the result of this free writing session is certainly not ready to be typed and turned in as a paragraph. But what did become clear in it was that the student could probably compare the two types of friends—those who like to be drawn and those who don't.

Clustering

Clustering is another way of putting ideas on paper before you begin to write an actual draft. A cluster is more visual than free writing. You could cluster the topic of "book clubs," for instance, by putting it in a circle in the center of a piece of paper and then drawing lines to new circles as ideas or details occur to you. The idea is to free your mind from the limits of sentences and paragraphs to generate pure details and ideas. When you are finished clustering, you can see where you want to go with a topic.

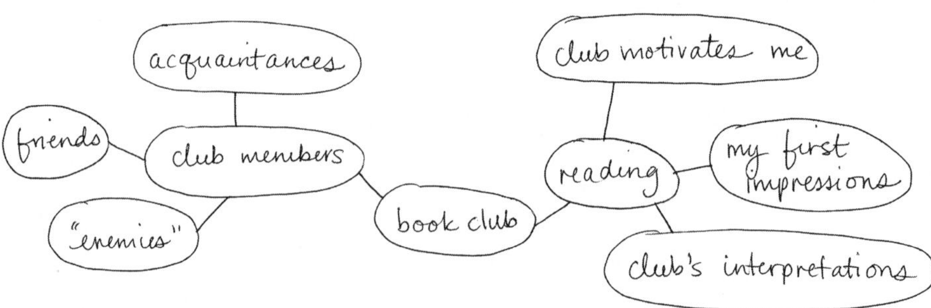

This cluster shows that the student has found two aspects of her book club that she could write about. This cluster might lead to another where the student chooses one subcategory—club members, for instance—and thinks of more details about them.

Talking with Other Students

It may help to talk to others when deciding on a topic. Many teachers break their classes up into groups at the beginning of an assignment. Talking with other students helps you realize that you see things just a little differently. Value the difference—it will help your written voice that we discussed earlier emerge.

Assignment 3

LIST YOUR INTERESTS

Make a list of four or five of your own interests. Be sure that they are as specific as the examples listed on p. 219. Keep the list for later assignments.

Assignment 4

DO SOME FREE WRITING

Choose one of your interests, and do some focused free writing about it. Write for ten minutes with that topic in mind but without stopping. Don't worry about anything such as spelling or sentence structures while you are free writing. The results are meant to help you find out what you have to say about the topic *before* you start to write a paper about it. Save the results for a later assignment.

Assignment 5

TRY CLUSTERING IDEAS

Choose another of your interests. Put it in the center of a piece of paper, and draw a cluster of details and ideas relating to it following the sample shown earlier. Take the cluster as far as it will go. Then choose one aspect to cluster again on its own. This way you will arrive at specific, interesting details and ideas—not just the first ones that come to mind. Save the results of all your efforts.

V. Organizing Ideas

Most important to keep in mind, no matter what you are writing, is the idea you want to get across to the reader. Whether you are writing a paragraph or an essay, you must have in mind a single idea that you want to express. In a paragraph, such an idea is called a *topic sentence;* in an essay it's called a *thesis statement,* but they mean the same thing—an idea you want to get across. We will begin with a discussion of thesis statements.

Thesis Statements

Let's choose one of the students' interests listed on p. 219 as a general topic. "Buying and selling on eBay" by itself doesn't make any point. What about it? What does it do for you? What point about buying and selling on eBay would you like to present to your reader? You might write

> Buying and selling on eBay is fun and educational.

But this is a vague statement, not worth developing. You might move into more specific territory and write

> I have learned about business and geography by buying and selling items on eBay.

Now you have said something specific. *When you write in one sentence the point you want to present to your reader, you have written a thesis statement.*

Most good writers have a thesis in mind when they begin to write, or the thesis may well evolve as they write. Whether they are writing essays, novels, poems, or plays, they eventually have in mind an idea they want to present to the reader. They may develop it in various ways, but behind whatever they write is their ruling thought, their reason for writing, their thesis.

For any writing assignment, after you have done some free writing or clustering to explore your topic, the next step is to write a thesis statement. As you write your thesis statement, keep two things in mind:

1. A thesis statement must be a sentence *with a subject and a verb* (not merely a topic).
2. A thesis statement must be *an idea that you can explain or defend* (not simply a statement of fact).

Exercise 1

THESIS OR FACT?

Which of the following are merely topics or facts, and which are thesis statements that you could explain or defend? In front of each one that could be a thesis statement, write THESIS. In front of each one that is just a fact, write FACT. Check your answers with those at the back of the book.

1. _____ Gasoline prices are rising again.

2. _____ Some animals seem to be able to predict earthquakes.

3. _____ On July 20, 1969, Neil Armstrong planted an American flag on the moon.

4. _____ After I became a music major, many job opportunities opened up for me.

5. _____ Computer-generated movie characters can affect us in the same ways as "real-life" characters.

6. _____ Voice-recognition software is improving all the time.

7. _____ Home schooling has both advantages and disadvantages.

8. _____ Tiger Woods is an amazing golfer.

9. _____ Traveling to different countries makes people more open-minded.

10. _____ Vegetarians can suffer from health problems related to their diets.

Assignment 6

WRITE A THESIS STATEMENT

Use your free-writing or clustering results from Assignments 4 and 5 (p. 221) and write at least one thesis statement based on one of your interests. Be sure that the thesis you write is phrased as a complete thought that can be defended or explained in an essay.

Organizing an Essay

Once you have written a good thesis and explored your topic through discussion with others or by free writing and clustering, you are ready to organize your essay.

First, you need an introductory paragraph. It should catch your reader's interest, provide necessary background information, and either include or suggest your thesis statement. (See p. 207 and p. 216 for two examples of student writers' introductory paragraphs.) In your introductory paragraph, you may also list supporting points, but a more effective way is to let them unfold paragraph by paragraph rather than to give them all away in the beginning of the essay. Even if your supporting points don't appear in your introduction, your reader will easily spot them later if your paper is clearly organized.

Your second paragraph will present your *first* supporting point—everything about it and nothing more.

Your next paragraph will be about your *second* supporting point—all about it and nothing more.

Each additional paragraph will develop *another* supporting point.

Finally, you'll need a concluding paragraph. In a short paper, it isn't necessary to restate your points. Your conclusion may be brief; even a single sentence to round out the paper may do the job. Remember that the main purpose of a concluding paragraph is to bring the paper to a close by sharing your final thoughts on the subject. (See p. 208 and p. 217 for two examples of concluding paragraphs.)

Learning to write a brief organized essay of this kind will help you to distinguish between the parts of an essay. Then when you're ready to write a longer paper, you'll be able to organize it clearly and elaborate on its design and content.

Topic Sentences

A topic sentence does for a paragraph what a thesis statement does for an essay—it states the main idea. Like thesis statements, topic sentences must be phrased as complete thoughts to be proven or developed through the presentation of details. But the topic sentence introduces an idea or subtopic that is the right size to cover in a paragraph. The topic sentence doesn't have to be the first sentence in a paragraph. It may come at the end or even in the middle, but putting it first is most common.

Each body paragraph should contain only one main idea, and no detail or example should be in a paragraph if it doesn't support the topic sentence or help to transition from one paragraph to another. (See p. 208, p. 214, and pp. 215–216 for more examples of effective body paragraphs within essays and of paragraphs alone.)

Organizing Body Paragraphs (or Single Paragraphs)

A single paragraph or a body paragraph within an essay is organized in the same way as an entire essay only on a smaller scale. Here's the way you learned to organize an essay:

Thesis: stated or suggested in introductory paragraph
First supporting paragraph
Second supporting paragraph
Additional supporting paragraphs
Concluding paragraph

And here's the way to organize a paragraph:

Topic sentence
First supporting detail or example
Second supporting detail or example
Additional supporting details or examples
Concluding or transitional sentence

You should have several details to support each topic sentence. If you find that you have little to say after writing the topic sentence, ask yourself what details or examples will make your reader believe that the topic sentence is true for you.

Transitional Expressions

Transitional expressions within a paragraph and between paragraphs in an essay help the reader move from one detail or example to the next and from one supporting point to the next. When first learning to organize an essay, you might start each supporting paragraph in a paper with a transitional expression. Later, if they sound too repetitious, take these expressions out and replace them with more detailed prepositional phrases or dependent clauses, thereby improving your sentence variety.

Here are some transitions that show sequence:

First	Next	One (example, point, step, etc. . . .)
Second	Then	Another (example, point, step, etc. . . .)
Third . . .	Finally	In conclusion

Here are a few to show addition:

Also
Furthermore
In addition

Here are several that show comparison or contrast:

Similarly	In the same way	In comparison
However	On the other hand	In contrast

Here are those that show consequence:

Therefore	Consequently
As a result	In other words

Exercise 2

ADDING TRANSITIONAL EXPRESSIONS

Place appropriate transitional expressions from the lists above into the blanks in the following paragraph to make it read smoothly. Compare your answers with those in the back of the book.

This year, my family and I decided to celebrate the Fourth of July in a whole new way. ________, we always attended a fireworks show at the sports stadium near our house. The firework shows got better every year; ________, we were getting tired of the crowds and the noise. ________, we were starting to feel bad about our own lack of creativity. The goal this time was to have each family member think of a craft project, recipe, or game related to the Fourth. The result was a day full of fun activities and good things to eat—all created by us! ________, my sister Helen taught us to make seltzer rockets from an idea she found on the Internet. We used the fireless "firecrackers" as table decorations until late afternoon when we set them off. ________, we ate dinner. Mom and Dad's contribution was "Fourth of July Franks," which were hot dogs topped with ketchup, onions, and a sprinkling of blue-corn chips. For dessert, my brother Leon assembled tall parfaits made with layers of red and blue Jell-O cubes divided by ridges of whipped cream. ________, we played a game of charades in which all of the answers had something to do with the American flag, the Declaration of Independence, Paul Revere's ride, and other such topics. We all enjoyed the Fourth so much that the events will probably become our new tradition.

Assignment 7

ORGANIZE THIS!

To practice using transitions, write a paragraph about the steps you would take to reorganize an area at home or at work. It could be a small task, such as reorganizing your CDs or DVDs at home, or a larger task, such as reorganizing your desk or area at work. What would you organize in a different way if you could? What materials would you need? How would you proceed? Report the steps in order, one by one, using transitional expressions from the list on p. 225 wherever you see fit. Sometimes it's helpful to add humor to a "how-to" paragraph or essay to avoid sounding like an instruction manual.

VI. Supporting with Details

Now you're ready to support your main ideas with subtopics and specific details. That is, you'll think of ways to convince your reader that what you say in your thesis is true. How could you convince your reader that buying and selling on eBay has taught you about business and geography? You might write

> I have learned a great deal about business and geography by buying and selling items on eBay. (because)

1. I must be honest in my dealings with other buyers and sellers.
2. I have to keep good records and be very organized.
3. I learn about places I have never heard of before by shipping packages all over the world.

NOTE—Sometimes if you imagine a *because* at the end of your thesis statement, it will help you write your reasons or subtopics clearly and in parallel form.

Types of Support

The subtopics developing a thesis and the details presented in a paragraph are not always *reasons*. Supporting points may take many forms based on the purpose of the essay or paragraph. They may be

examples (in an illustration)
steps (in a how-to or process paper)
types or kinds (in a classification)
meanings (in a definition)
similarities and/or differences (in a comparison/contrast)
causes or effects (in a cause-and-effect analysis)

Whatever they are, supporting points should develop the main idea expressed in the thesis or topic sentence and prove it to be true.

Here is the final draft of a student essay about an embarrassing experience. Notice how the body paragraphs follow the stages of the experience. And all of the details within the body paragraphs bring the experience to life.

Super Salad?

About a year ago, I had a really embarrassing experience. It happened at a restaurant in Arcadia. I had moved to California three days before, so everything was new to me. Since I didn't have any relatives or friends in California, I had to move, unpack, and explore the neighborhood on my own. That day, I decided to treat myself to dinner as a reward, but I needed some courage because I had never dined out alone before.

As I opened the door of the restaurant, everybody looked at me, and the attention made me nervous. The manager greeted me with several menus in his hands and asked how many people were in my party. I said, "Just me." He led me over to a square table right in the middle of the restaurant. It had four chairs around it and was set with four sets of napkins and silverware. The manager pulled out one of the chairs for me, and a busboy cleared away the three extra place settings.

A waitress arrived to take my order, and I tried to keep it simple. I asked for steak and a baked potato. Truthfully speaking, before I went to the restaurant, I had practiced ordering, but as she was speaking to me, I got flustered. She said, "Super salad?" as if it were a specialty of the house, so I said, "Okay, that sounds good." Suddenly, her eyebrows went up, and she asked again, "Super salad?" And again I answered, "Yes." Her face turned the color of a red leaf in fall. "You wanna a super salad?" she asked in a louder voice this time, and I answered with certainty, "Yes, that will be fine." From her reaction, I knew that something was wrong.

When the waitress returned, she had the manager with her. He asked, "Do you want soup or a salad? You can't have both." I finally realized the stupid mistake I had been making. But the way the waitress had said "Soup or salad?" sounded just like "Super salad?" to my flustered ears. I clarified that I wanted a salad and eventually finished my meal without incident. I don't remember how the steak tasted or whether I had sour cream on my potato. I just kept going over my moment of confusion in my head while trying to look like a normal person eating dinner.

At the time, I felt embarrassed and ashamed. Going out for a meal isn't usually such a traumatic experience. Of course, whenever I tell the story, instead of sympathy, I get uncontrollable laughter as a response. I guess it is pretty funny. Now whenever I order a meal alone, I use a drive-thru. That way I can blame any misunderstandings on the microphones in the drive-thru lane.

(*Note:* See pp. 230–231 for a rough draft of the preceding essay, before its final revisions.)

Learning to support your main ideas with vivid details is perhaps the most important goal you can accomplish in this course. Many writing problems are not really *writing* problems but *thinking* problems. Whether you're writing a term paper or merely an answer to a test question, if you take enough time to think, you'll be able to write a clear thesis statement and support it with paragraphs full of meaningful details.

Assignment 8

WRITE AN ESSAY ON ONE OF YOUR INTERESTS

Return to the thesis statement you wrote about one of your interests for Assignment 6 on p. 223. Now write a short essay to support it. You can explain the allure of your interest, its drawbacks, or its benefits (such as the one about the Internet improving the student's reading and writing skills). Don't forget to use any free writing or clustering you may have done on the topic beforehand and to use transitional expressions.

Assignment 9

AN EMBARRASSING EXPERIENCE

Like the student writer of "Super Salad?" (pp. 227–228), we have all had embarrassing moments in our lives. Write an essay about a mildly embarrassing experience that you have had or one that you witnessed someone else have. Be sure to include the details that contributed to the embarrassment. For instance, the student writer showed how being in the restaurant alone made it worse. Had he been there with friends or family members, misunderstanding the waitress might have just been humorous, not embarrassing.

VII. Revising Your Papers

Great writers don't just sit down and write a final draft. They write and revise. You may have heard the expression "Easy writing makes hard reading." True, it is *easier* to turn in a piece of writing the first time it lands on paper. But you and your reader will be disappointed by the results. Try to think of revision as an opportunity instead of a chore, as a necessity instead of a choice.

Whenever possible, write the paper several days before the first draft is due. Let it sit for a while. When you reread it, you'll see ways to improve the organization or to add more details to a weak paragraph. After revising the paper, put it away for another day and try again to improve it. Save all of your drafts along the way to see the progress that you've made or possibly to return to an area left out in later drafts but that fits in again after revision.

Don't call any paper finished until you have worked it through several times. Revising is one of the best ways to improve your writing.

Take a look at an early draft of the student essay you read on pages 227–228. Notice that the student has revised his rough draft by crossing out some parts, correcting word forms, and adding new phrasing or reminders for later improvement.

Super Salad?

~~An Embarrassing Experience~~

About a year ago, ~~Once~~. I had a really embarrassing experience. It happened ~~a year ago~~ (*move over) at a restaurant in Arcadia. I had moved to California three days before ~~that day~~, so everything was new to me. Since ~~As~~ I didn't have any relatives ~~relations~~ or friends in California, I had to (take care of everything by myself.) (*add details) That day, I decided to treat myself ~~go out~~ to dinner ~~by myself~~ as a reward ~~treat~~, but I needed some courage because I had never dined out ~~been in a restaurant all~~ alone before.

As ~~When~~ I opened the door of the restaurant, I (gathered everybody's attention, and it made me a little nervous.) (*clarify and correct) ~~Eating in a restaurant alone was very new to me~~. The (*add details) manager asked me how many people were in my party. ~~and~~ I said, "Just me." He led ~~walked~~ me over to a square table right in the middle ~~part~~ of the restaurant. (It had four chairs pulled up to it, and he pulled out one for me to sit down.) *add details

A ~~The~~ waitress arrived ~~came~~ to take my order, and I tried to keep it simple. I asked for steak and a baked potato. Truthfully ~~Frankly~~ speaking, before I went to the restaurant, I had practiced ordering, but as ~~by the time~~ she was speaking to me, I got ~~all~~ flustered. ~~and embarrassed.~~ ~~I thought~~ She said, "Super salad?" as if that were a specialty of the restaurant, so I said, "Okay, that sounds good." Suddenly, her eyebrows went up, and she asked again, "Super salad?" and again I answered, "Yes." Her face turned the color of a red leaf in fall. "You wanna a super salad?", she asked, in a louder voice this time, and I answered, with certainty, "Yes, that will be fine." From her reaction, I ~~thought~~ knew that something was wrong.

~~The next time~~ When the waitress returned, she had the manager ~~of the restaurant~~ with her. He asked, "Do you want *soup* or *a salad?* You can't have both." I finally realized ~~what a~~ the stupid mistake I had been making. But I swear the way the waitress had said "Soup or salad?" sounded just like "Super salad?" to my flustered ears. ~~as if that were a specialty of the restaurant.~~ * add end of meal details * move up

At the time, I was ~~really~~ embarrassed and ashamed ~~of myself~~. * add more But whenever I tell ~~anybody~~ the story, (they laugh so hard that I can't get anyone to feel sorry for me.) * clarify and correct Now I hardly ever eat alone at restaurants after my first disaster. I if do, I make it a drive-thru. That way I can always blame a misunderstanding on the microphones in the drive-thru lane.

combine and clarify

Can you see why each change was made? Analyzing the reasons for the changes will help you improve your own revision skills.

Assignment 10

FIRST IMPRESSIONS

On page 217, you read about Coretta Scott and Martin Luther King's first date and the different first impressions that they made on each other. Note that these impressions went *far* beyond the way they looked. Write about meeting someone that you know now for the first time. What were your first impressions of that person? Did they turn out to be accurate? Discuss the effect that your first impressions had on the relationship.

Write a rough draft of the paper and then set it aside. When you finish writing, reread your paper to see what improvements you can make to your rough draft. Use the Revision Checklist on the next page to help guide you through this or any other revision.

Revision Checklist

Here's a checklist of revision questions. If the answer to any of these questions is no, revise that part of your paper until you're satisfied that the answer is yes.

1. Does the introductory paragraph introduce the topic clearly and suggest or include a thesis statement that the paper will explain or defend?
2. Does each of the other paragraphs support the thesis statement?
3. Does each body paragraph contain a clear topic sentence and focus on only one supporting point?
4. Do the body paragraphs contain enough details, and are transitional expressions well used?
5. Do the final thoughts expressed in the concluding paragraph bring the paper to a smooth close?
6. Does your (the writer's) voice come through?
7. Do the sentences read smoothly and appear to be correct?
8. Are words well-chosen, and are spelling and punctuation consistent and correct?

Exchanging Papers

The Revision Checklist could also be used when you exchange papers with another student in your class. Since you both have written a response to the same assignment, you will understand what the other writer went through and learn from the differences between the two papers.

Proofreading Aloud

Finally, read your finished paper *aloud.* If you read it silently, you will see what you *think* is there, but you are sure to miss some errors. Read your paper aloud slowly, pointing to each word as you read it to catch omissions and errors in spelling and punctuation. Reading a paper to yourself this way may take fifteen minutes to half an hour, but it will be time well spent. There are even programs that will "speak" your text in a computer's voice. Using your computer to read your paper to you can be fun as well as helpful. If you don't like the way something sounds, don't be afraid to change it! Make it a rule to read each of your papers *aloud* before handing it in.

Here are four additional writing assignments to help you practice the skills of writing and revising.

Assignment 11

ARE YOU AN OPTIMIST OR A PESSIMIST?

The old test of optimism and pessimism is to look at a glass filled with water to the midpoint. An optimist, or positive thinker, would say it was "half *full.*" But a pessimist, or negative thinker, would say it was "half *empty.*" Which are you—an optimist or a pessimist? Organize your thoughts into the structure of a brief essay.

Assignment 12

ARE THERE DIFFERENT WAYS TO BE SMART?

No word has just one meaning. Take, for example, the word *smart.* The common definition usually involves retaining a lot of knowledge and taking tests well. If that were the only meaning, then why do we call someone "street smart"? Think about the different ways a person can be "smart," and write a long paragraph or short essay about the ways in which people in general and you in particular are smart.

Assignment 13

THE BEST (OR WORST) DECISION

What was one of the best (or worst) decisions you ever made? Choose one that you feel comfortable sharing with others. When and why did you make the decision, and what effects has it had on your life? Organize the answers to these questions into the structure of a brief essay.

Assignment 14

I WOULD IF I COULD

If you could travel anywhere right now, where would you go? Write a short essay about a trip that you would take if you suddenly had the time, money, and ability necessary to do it. Be sure to state what your destination would be, and use plenty of details for the reader to understand your reasons and what's involved in getting there.

VIII. Presenting Your Work

Part of the success of a paper could depend on how it looks. The same paper written sloppily or typed neatly might even receive different grades. It is human nature to respond positively when a paper has been presented with care. Here are some general guidelines to follow.

Paper Formats

Your paper should be typed or written on a computer, double-spaced, or copied neatly in ink on 8 1/2-by-11-inch paper on one side only. A one-inch margin should be left around the text on all sides for your instructor's comments. The beginning of each paragraph should be indented five spaces.

Most instructors have a particular format for presenting your name and the course material on your papers. Always follow such instructions carefully.

Titles

Finally, spend some time thinking of a good title. Just as you're more likely to read a magazine article with an interesting title, so your readers will be more eager to read your paper if you give it a good title. Which of these titles from student papers would make you want to read further?

A Sad Experience

Falling into "The Gap"

Hunting: The Best Sport of All?

Of Mice and Me

Buying Clothes Can Be Depressing

Got Elk?

Remember these three rules about titles:

1. Only the first letter of the important words in a title should be capitalized.

A Night at the Races

2. Don't put quotation marks around your own titles unless they include a quotation or title of an article, short story, or poem within them.

"To Be or Not to Be" Is Not for Me

3. Don't underline (or *italicize*) your own titles unless they include the title of a book, play, movie, or magazine within them.

Still Stuck on *Titanic*

A wise person once said, "Haste is the assassin of elegance." Instead of rushing to finish a paper and turn it in, take the time to give your writing the polish it deserves.

IX. Writing about What You Read

Reading and writing are related skills. The more you read, the better you will write. When you are asked to prepare for a writing assignment by reading a newspaper story, a magazine article, a professional essay, or part of a book, there are many ways to respond in writing. Among them, you may be asked to write your reaction to a reading assignment or a summary of a reading assignment.

Writing a Reaction

Reading assignments become writing assignments when your teacher asks you to share your opinion about the subject matter or to relate the topic to your own experiences. In a paragraph, you would have enough space to offer only the most immediate impressions about the topic. However, in an essay you could share your personal reactions, as well as your opinions on the value of the writer's ideas and support. Of course, the first step is always to read the selection carefully, looking up unfamiliar words in a dictionary.

Sample Reaction Paragraph

Here is a sample paragraph-length response following the class's reading of an essay called "What Is Intelligence?" by Isaac Asimov. In the essay, Asimov explains that there are other kinds of intelligence besides just knowledge of theories and facts. This student shares Asimov's ideas about intelligence, and she uses her own experiences to support her statements.

> I totally agree with Isaac Asimov. Intelligence doesn't only belong to Nobel Prize winners. I define "intelligence" as being able to value that special skill that a person has been born with. Not everyone is a math genius or a brain surgeon. For example, ask a brain surgeon to rotate the engine in your car. It isn't going to happen. To be able to take that certain skill that you've inherited and push it to its farthest limits I would call "intelligence." Isaac Asimov's definition is similar to mine. He believes that academic questions are only correctly answered by academicians. He gives the example of a farmer. A farming test would only be correctly answered by a farmer. Not everyone has the same talent; we are all different. When I attend my math classes, I must always pay attention. If I don't, I end up struggling with what I missed. On the other hand, when I'm in my singing class, I really do not have to struggle because the musical notes come to me with ease. This is just one example of how skills and talents differ from each other. I would rather sing a song than do math any day. We are all made differently. Some people are athletic, and some people are brainy. Some people can sing, and some can cook. It really doesn't matter what other people can do. If they have a talent—that's a form of intelligence.

If this had been an essay-length response, the student would have included more details about her own and other people's types of intelligence. And she may have wanted to quote and discuss Asimov's most important points.

Assignment 15

WRITE A REACTION PARAGRAPH

The following is an excerpt from *I'm Afraid, You're Afraid: 448 Things to Fear and Why* by Melinda Muse, in which she discusses the surprising effects our initials might have on our lives. Write a paragraph in which you respond thoughtfully to Muse's information, discuss the details she uses to support it, and perhaps share your thoughts about your own initials.

Bad Initials

BUMs and RATs don't live as long as VIPs and GODs, according to a University of California study that examined twenty-seven years worth of men's death certificates. Dr. Nicholas Christenfeld categorized the names of 5 million dead guys according to their initials. He then assigned the words that the initials spelled with the qualities of "good," "bad," or "neutral." The psychologist determined that people with good monograms like JOY, WOW, and LOV lived more than 4.5 years longer than those in the neutral-monogram (WDW and JAY) category. Gents with bad tags, the DUDs and ASSes, died an average of almost 3 years earlier than the more neutrally initialed. SAD also is that people in the bad group—the APEs and PIGs—were more apt to commit suicide or die in an accident.

Dr. Christenfeld asserts that having "bad initials" is a lifelong negative psychological factor. It's a bummer to be called PIG but an ego boost to be recognized as ACE or WOW. The doctor says if a person holds the notion that "accidents aren't really accidents," then the lack of self-esteem might lead to self-destructive behavior.

He could be DED right.

Before starting your reaction paragraph, *read the selection again carefully.* Be sure to use a dictionary to look up any words you don't know. You can also use the free writing and clustering techniques explained on pages 219–220. Or your instructor may want you to discuss the reading in groups.

Coming to Your Own Conclusions

Often you will be asked to come to your own conclusions based on a reading that requires interpretation. In other words, you will have to think about and write about what it might mean based only on the details that the writer provides. Such a reading might be a poem, a short story, or even an advertisement.

Here is a poem by Philip F. Deaver in which he describes a dream that he has had many times. In this poem, Deaver brings us into his dream so that we can see what he sees.

Flying

I have a flying dream,
have since I was a kid.
In it, I remember suddenly
how to fly, something
for some reason I've forgotten;
by getting to a certain place
in my mind, I'm able simply to rise.

I go up only about sixty or seventy feet,
but that's high enough to look down on
my house, the one I grew up in,
in Tuscola, look down on it
and the trees of the neighborhood;
it's high enough to watch my father
from above as he leaves for work,
to see my mother as she gathers grapes
from the backyard arbor,
to see my sister in her pretty dress,
pulling all her friends in our wagon
down the long, new sidewalks,
to see our many dogs over the years—
high enough to see the blur of childhood,
to put my quiet shadow over all of us
early on. In the dream it's a summer's day
and I might sometimes also
be the one looking up, squinting hard
and seeing way high above
birds moving, black spots against the blue.

Source: "Flying," by Philip F. Deaver, from *How Men Pray.* © Anhinga Press. Reprinted with permission.

Assignment 16

COMING TO YOUR OWN CONCLUSIONS

Consider the poem "Flying" on pages 236–237. Be sure to read the poem aloud at least once, and listen to it closely. Then write a page that shares your conclusions about Deaver's poem. Explain how he seems to feel about the people and places in his life. Why do you think he has chosen to include himself as one of the people he sometime sees in his dream? What does he mean by phrases like "the blur of childhood" and "to put my quiet shadow over all of us early on"?

Here are two tips for reading and writing about poetry: first, have fun with it; and second, look for words and phrases that might hint at more than one meaning.

As an alternative or additional assignment, write a page that shares what your *own* dream about flying over the important people and places in your life might be like. It could be about the present (or even the future) instead of the past. Be creative, and use short, descriptive steps, as Deaver does, to help the reader picture the "dream" and understand its significance. If you choose to imitate the structure of Deaver's poem, remember not to copy his exact phrasing, but to write your own version of "Flying."

Writing 100-Word Summaries

One of the best ways to learn to read carefully and to write concisely is to write 100-word summaries. Writing 100 words sounds easy, but actually it isn't. Writing 200- or 300- or 500-word summaries isn't too difficult, but condensing all the main ideas of an essay or article into 100 words is a time-consuming task—not to be undertaken in the last hour before class.

A summary presents only the main ideas of a reading, *without including any reactions to it.* A summary tests your ability to read, understand, and *rephrase* the ideas contained in an essay, article, or book.

If you work at writing summaries conscientiously, you'll improve both your reading and your writing. You'll improve your reading by learning to spot main ideas and your writing by learning to construct a concise, clear, smooth paragraph. Furthermore, your skills will carry over into your reading and writing for other courses.

Sample 100-Word Summary

First, read the following excerpt from the book *The True History of Chocolate,* by Sophie D. Coe and Michael D. Coe. It is followed by a student's 100-word summary.

Milton Hershey and the "Good Old Hershey Bar"

Milton Snavely Hershey (1857–1945) has been aptly characterized as "the Henry Ford of Chocolate Makers." . . . [B]y the time he was 19, he had established his own candy business, . . . producing mainly caramel confections. . . . But after a trip to the chocolate centers of Europe, he sold the caramel business for one million dollars (a huge sum in those days), bought a farm in Derry Township, Pennsylvania, and built his chocolate factory on it. . . .

"Hershey, The Chocolate Town" . . . was dominated by Milton Hershey's imposing private mansion . . . [from which] the great man would sally forth each day to survey the vast domain he had built: the milk chocolate and cocoa factory, . . . the industrial school for orphan boys, . . . The Hershey Department Store, the Hershey Bank, men's and women's clubs, five churches, the free library, the Volunteer Fire Department, two schools, Hershey Park with its fine gardens, zoo, and rollercoaster, the Hershey Hotel, and a golf course. . . . [Y]et this triumph of paternalistic capitalism was a town in name only: it had no mayor nor any form of elected municipal government—it existed only at the whim of its benevolent dictator, Milton S. Hershey. . . .

There is no doubt that Hershey was a marketing genius. . . . Hershey and his chocolate bars soon commanded the American market. Everything was mechanized, with machines and conveyor belts organized into a true assembly-line operation. Hershey's best-selling bar contained almonds imported from southern Europe. . . . But even more popular than these were "Hershey's Kisses." . . . Small wonder that the streetlights of "The Chocolate Town" are the shape of Kisses.

Milton Hershey died peacefully at the age of 85, in his own hospital. His paternalistic empire lives on. . . . So many tourists flock to the wonders of Hershey, Pennsylvania, that the company no longer offers tours of its chocolate factory.

Here is a student's 100-word summary of the article:

> Milton Hershey is a big name in the history of chocolate. He was an early achiever, but he wasn't satisfied with just making money selling caramels. Once he saw the way chocolate was made overseas, he decided to become the best chocolate maker in America. The result of his passion for chocolate was a community that he designed himself and named after himself: Hershey, Pennsylvania. It was a complete community, but it wasn't a democracy. Hershey made all the decisions there. Hershey's chocolate was and still is extremely popular due to Milton Hershey's technological advances and devoted interest in chocolate.

Assignment 17

WRITE A 100-WORD SUMMARY

Your aim in writing your summary should be to give someone who has not read a piece of writing a clear idea of its content. First, read the following excerpt from the introduction to the book *Catwatching,* by Desmond Morris. Then follow the instructions given after it.

Cat Lovers vs. Dog Lovers

Because of this difference between domestic cats and domestic dogs, cat lovers tend to be rather different from dog lovers. As a rule they have a stronger personality bias toward independent thought and action. Artists like cats; soldiers like dogs. The much-lauded "group loyalty" phenomenon is alien to both cats and cat lovers. . . . The ambitious Yuppie, the aspiring politician, the professional athlete, these are not typical cat owners. It is hard to picture a football player with a cat in his lap—much easier to envisage him taking his dog for a walk.

Those who have studied cat owners and dog owners as two distinct groups report that there is also a gender bias. Cat lovers show a greater tendency to be female. This is not surprising in view of the division of labor that developed during human evolution. Prehistoric males became specialized as group hunters, while the females concentrated on food-gathering and childrearing. This difference led to a human male "pack mentality" that is far less marked in females. . . . [S]o the modern dog has much more in common with the human male than with the human female. . . .

The argument will always go on—feline self-sufficiency and individualism versus canine camaraderie and good-fellowship. But it is important to stress that in making a valid point I have caricatured the two positions. In reality there are many people who enjoy equally the company of both cats and dogs. All of us, or nearly all of us, have both feline and canine elements in our personalities. We have moods when we want to be alone and thoughtful, and other times when we wish to be in the center of a crowded, noisy room.

A good way to begin the summary is to figure out the thesis statement, the main idea the author wants to get across to the reader. Write that idea down now *before reading further.*

How honest are you with yourself? Did you write that thesis statement? If you didn't, *write it now* before you read further.

You probably wrote something like this:

Certain characteristics make people prefer either cats or dogs as pets.

Using that main idea as your first sentence, summarize the article by choosing the most important points. *Be sure to put them in your own words.* Your rough draft may be 150 words or more.

Now cut it down by including only essential points and by getting rid of wordiness. Keep within the 100-word limit. You may have a few words less but not one word more. (And every word counts—even *a, and,* and *the.*) By forcing yourself to keep within 100 words, you'll get to the kernel of the author's thought and understand the article better.

When you have written the best summary you can, then and only then compare it with the summary on page 319. If you look at the model sooner, you'll cheat yourself of the opportunity to learn to write summaries because, once you read the model, it will be almost impossible not to make yours similar. So do your own thinking and writing, and then compare.

SUMMARY CHECKLIST

Even though your summary is different from the model, it may be just as good. If you're not sure how yours compares, answer these questions:

1. Did you include the same main ideas *without* adding your own reactions or opinions?
2. Did you leave out all unnecessary words and examples?
3. Did you rephrase the writer's ideas, not just recopy them?
4. Does the summary read smoothly?
5. Would someone who had not read the article get a clear idea of it from your summary?

Assignment 18

WRITE A REACTION OR A 100-WORD SUMMARY

Respond to the following reading in any of the three ways we've discussed—in a reaction paragraph, a reaction essay, or a 100-word summary. The reading is an excerpt from Fuad Omar's book *Bollywood: An Insider's Guide. Bollywood* is a word that combines "Bombay" (now known as Mumbai) and "Hollywood," and it is often used to describe Indian cinema. If you plan to respond to Omar's excerpt with an essay, briefly summarize his main ideas in your introductory paragraph. Then explore and support your reactions to his ideas in your body paragraphs. Save your final thoughts for your concluding paragraph.

Notice that Fuad Omar punctuates his sentences very lightly, creating a conversational tone that fits his purpose to provide "An Insider's Guide" to Bollywood.

Bollywood: Behind the Glamour

Bollywood is the name given to the Indian film industry and I literally have loathed that word from day one. It's too camp and similar to Hollywood in sound, in fact, it's a direct derivation of the term. It implies the Indian film industry is a cheap imitation or wannabe second rate version of Hollywood, which is not the case. In fact, historically speaking India was making films way before its American counterparts and so we should say they're copying us! But enough of the banter, I put up with the term and moved on. Bollywood is a completely different world from the place we live in. There are characters, genuine people, hopefuls, technically brilliant minded individuals and amazing families. There are also a lot of parties, many fake people (read as having to be courteous) and hours that come from within other hours of the day. The Indian film industry is anything but glamorous. It looks great on-screen, but to create that perfect image takes a lot of people, a lot of time, and a whole lot of effort and retakes. Yes every heroine looks beautiful and every man looks idealistic, but that's what the industry is there to do: sell dreams.

Even in the photos everyone looks perfect, carrying off the most absurd costumes with panache and style and without a morsel of regret, and you think these people have it easy. I've heard it many times: people come up to you and say how easy it is to be an actor in Indian cinema and how all you have to do is have makeup put on, perform a few really easy lines, and dance with beautiful girls. You wish. It's extremely tough and the hours are gruelling, the pressure immense, and it's true when they say "every Friday holds someone's fortune" because when a film that's taken years to complete finally makes it onto the big screen, it only takes three shows in the first day to decide it and its stars' fates.

An actress I know very well was shooting for two films one weekend and leaving for shows the following day. [Actors in Indian films perform in stage shows regularly.] She woke up and was on set by 5 am, makeup took two hours almost, she began the shot not before midday and wrapped up only two scenes by 6 pm, was scurried by car to another location and walked into another film set, knackered as can be, and began mouthing dialogues of a completely different character within seconds as she was being made up for a different film. She finished at 3 am, went home to finish packing for the shows she's meant to depart for in less than six hours and, while she was packing and instructing friends what would need to be taken in which suitcase, a dress designer came round (yep at 4 am) and began a costume fitting which needed to be done for a shoot when she came back. 24 hours after her day began she was still working, having only napped in the car. On landing at the destination wearing dark glasses and smiling for everyone (because dare I say no one would understand an actress being cranky in public, after all she's not allowed to, right, whatever the conditions). Greeted by hoards of fans that cause a security issue, she plods through to TV cameras who want to know how it is to be on this tour and catch her while they can. She smiles and delivers an impeccably perfect two-minute interview before being whisked away in a limo to the hotel where she has three hours to catch up on some sleep before a press conference to promote the very show she's on. Still sound glamorous?

The only glamorous part is what you see on screen, what you don't see is the hard work that goes into making that one song look as it does. All the different costumes and locations may be made fun of at times, but each location was a plane trip away, every costume took hours to get into, forward planning and the right lighting and even then all you see are edited shots composed together from hours of footage to make it look like a wondrous song. It aint all song and dance though. Rehearsals for shows, in between script-readings, story narrations, photo-shoots, interviews and, of course, shooting, there's very little time left when you're in this mad, bad world of Bollywood.

So that's partly what some of it is like, but what about the fame, money and glory? Well it's not a secure industry because one flop and you're written off courtesy of certain journalists, so you really better make good while you're here. You can make lots of money but only with the right filmmakers and deals, and if you work with the best production houses, working with them is reward enough to cause a dent in your pay packet, so what do you choose—moolah or good films? The only guarantee you have is that there is no guarantee. If you keep your head down, work hard and round the clock for a few years, you may get enough bank to support your wife and kids, who you might not get to see all that much, because did I mention you're working all hours and all across the world?

But that's what the industry is: a dream factory. It produces and sells dreams to the public, and they take it as escapism or entertainment that takes them away from reality or gives them hope that a better life is within reach. It's a dream factory because once you enter the industry, your eyes are full of hope and dreams and you can live out every role you wanted to as a kid everyday and have a lot of fun. Just don't think it's not hard work.

Don't get me wrong though, everyone (well almost everyone) loves it here. You think an eighteen hour shoot is a long time, but when you get there and don the greasepaint, crack a laugh with your co-stars and the technicians, you actually enjoy it and make the atmosphere as pleasant as possible and time can go fast. I've yet to come across a miserable actor who regrets being in the industry; it's a great job and you can live out amazing experiences every day. I'm just saying it isn't the glamour industry many perceive it to be. So what's it like being the guy who is neither of this world nor that, but sits on the fence that is the celluloid 70mm screen and listens to the audience to report back to those behind the screen and vice versa? I'll tell you another day. But for now, Welcome to Bollywood! It's mad, it's fun and it's full of dreams, just don't give anyone a hard time because you think it's an easy job.

Source: *Bollywood: An Insider's Guide* by Fuad Omar. Reprinted with permission of the author.

Answers

WORD CHOICE AND SPELLING

WORDS OFTEN CONFUSED, SET 1 (PP. 8–12)

EXERCISE 1

1. new
2. It's, due
3. choose, an
4. a, its
5. already
6. complement
7. choose
8. It's, know, accept
9. hear
10. an, it's

EXERCISE 2

1. It's, new
2. have, accepted
3. feel, an
4. chose
5. already, fourth
6. fill, except, have
7. hear, an, advice
8. are
9. course, effects
10. complemented

EXERCISE 3

1. clothes, an
2. Due, a
3. accept
4. course, are, all ready
5. coarse, new
6. conscious
7. an
8. break, feel
9. have, already
10. It's, no

EXERCISE 4

1. already
2. clothes
3. its, brakes
4. choose, advice
5. desert
6. affected, coarse
7. here, conscious
8. It's, feel, our
9. know, have
10. forth, accept

Exercise 5

1. are
2. our
3. accept
4. It's
5. New, forth
6. effects
7. know, fill
8. It's, feel
9. effect
10. fill, an

Proofreading Exercise

In the middle of a debate in my speech class last week, I suddenly became very self-~~conscience~~ *conscious.* My heart started beating faster, and I didn't ~~no~~ *know* what to ~~due~~ *do.* I looked around to see if my show of nerves was having ~~a~~ *an* ~~affect~~ *effect* on the audience. Of ~~coarse~~ *course,* they could ~~here~~ *hear* my voice trembling. The topic that we were debating involved whether it would be best to eliminate letter grades in college, and everyone else was doing so well. But for some reason, my face turned red, and I would ~~of~~ *have* left the room if the door had been closer. After the debate, my classmates tried to give me ~~complements~~ *compliments,* but I ~~new~~ *knew* that they were just trying to make me feel better.

WORDS OFTEN CONFUSED, SET 2 (PP. 17–21)

Exercise 1

1. There
2. through
3. to
4. They're
5. personnel
6. past, lose
7. there
8. led, through, were
9. than
10. whether

Exercise 2

1. lose
2. where
3. quiet, write
4. personnel
5. there, two, right
6. principal
7. who's
8. principal
9. whether, quiet, past
10. than

Exercise 3

1. You're, where
2. Whether, you're, woman, wear
3. too, loose, too
4. They're, quite, right

5. who's, than
6. personal
7. your, you're, who's, wear
8. passed, right
9. whose
10. woman, weather

Exercise 4

1. quite
2. There, two, women
3. principal
4. they're, their
5. whose
6. to, woman
7. right
8. who's, than
9. too
10. to, to

Exercise 5

1. your
2. you're, than
3. whether
4. piece, women
5. They're, their
6. principle
7. to, than
8. principal, their
9. to, then
10. they're, through

Proofreading Exercise

Sometimes it's hard to find the ~~write~~ *right* place to study on campus. The library used ~~too~~ *to* be the ~~principle~~ *principal* location for students to do ~~they're~~ *their* difficult course work, ~~weather~~ *whether* it was preparing research papers or writing critical essays. But now most library resources are available online, ~~two~~ *too.* This change has ~~lead~~ *led* students to use campus computer labs and cafés as study halls. There, students can go online, get up-to-date sources, write their reports, and have peace and ~~quite~~ *quiet* without the stuffy atmosphere of the library. The only problem with doing research online is that it's easier to ~~loose~~ *lose* a piece of information on the computer ~~then~~ *than* it is to lose a hard copy in the library.

THE EIGHT PARTS OF SPEECH (PP. 24–27)

Exercise 1

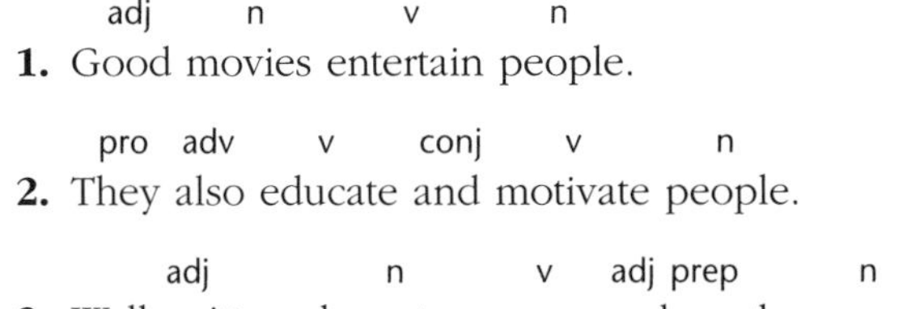

adj n conj n v adj n prep n
4. Their downfalls or successes have lasting effects on the audience.

n v n prep adj n prep pro
5. A person sees a movie with a wild character in it.

pro conj pro v prep n
6. She or he learns about wildness.

adv n v prep n
7. Often, the story revolves around a secret.

pro v n conj v pro prep n
8. Someone discovers the secret and reveals it in the end.

n adv v adv conj adj n v
9. The story usually moves ahead when the main character changes.

adj n v adv adv adj
10. Such changes are not always positive.

Exercise 2

n v adj n n prep n
1. Clyde Tombaugh discovered the ninth "planet," Pluto, in 1930.

n v prep n prep n prep n
2. Tombaugh died in 1997 at the age of 90.

n v adj n prep n adj n pro v
3. Scientists loaded Tombaugh's ashes onto New Horizons, a space probe that was

v prep n prep n
launched in January of 2006. (Note: *That* is a relative pronoun standing for "probe.")

n v v prep n prep n
4. New Horizons will arrive near Pluto in 2015.

prep n prep n n v n prep n prep adj
5. After the launch of New Horizons, astronomers deleted Pluto from the list of real

n
planets.

pro v conj adj n v v adj adj n
6. They determined that real planets must control their own orbits. (Note: *That* is a conjunction joining two clauses.)

n v adj n prep n prep adj n
7. Pluto is an icy ball under the influence of Neptune's orbit.

n v n prep adj n
8. Astronomers put Pluto into a new category.

adv adj n prep n v v
9. Therefore, the official number of planets has changed.

interj pro v adj n
10. Wow! That is an amazing development.

Exercise 3

adj n v adj n
1. Mechanical pencils are delicate instruments.

pro v adj n prep pro
2. I see other students with them.

adv pro v pro
3. Then I buy one.

pro v n
4. I open the package.

pro v n prep adj n prep n
5. I load the pencil with the tiny shaft of lead.

conj pro v adj n adv prep n n v adv
6. As I put the pencil tip down on the paper, the lead snaps off.

v pro adj n
7. Am I an unrefined clod?

pro v conj pro v
8. I believe that I am.

adv pro v adj n
9. Now I know my limitations.

adj n conj adj n v adj adj n prep pro
10. Ballpoint pens and wooden pencils are the only writing tools for me.

Exercise 4

adj adj n adv v n adv
1. The following old sayings still have meaning today.

n adj v n adj
2. A penny saved is a penny earned.

n prep n v n adj n
3. A stitch in time saves nine (or nine stitches).

n v n
4. Haste makes waste.

v pro v adj n

5. Love me, love my dog.

n v adj adj n

6. A picture is worth a thousand words.

pro conj pro pro v v adj

7. He or she who hesitates is lost.

n v conj pro v v n

8. Time flies when you are having fun.

n v adv adj prep adj n prep n

9. The grass is always greener on the other side of the fence.

n prep adj adj n v prep adj n

10. The truth of many old sayings lies beneath their surfaces.

Exercise 5

adj n v adj n conj adj n

1. Some people collect rare coins and paper money.

adj adj n v adv adj

2. The Del Monte twenty-dollar bill is very famous.

n v v conj pro v adj n

3. The mint made a mistake when it printed this bill.

n prep n adv v pro prep n prep adj n

4. A sticker from a banana accidentally attached itself to the paper during the printing process.

adj adj conj adj n v n prep n

5. The round green and red sticker became a part of the bill.

adj n adv v prep adj n

6. Such mistakes usually lead to a bill's destruction.

adj adj n adv v n prep adj n

7. This flawed note, however, left the mint with the normal twenties.

n adv v adj adj n

8. Experts immediately authenticated its rare status.

n adv v prep n prep n

9. The bill first sold on eBay for $10,000.

adv n prep n v n prep adj adj n

10. Eventually, a couple from Texas paid $25,000 for this one-of-a-kind note.

Paragraph Exercise

pro prep adj adj adj n v adv prep adj n pro v
Some of the richest American street names live only in people's minds. They are

adj conj pro v adv prep n conj adv v v v prep pro
permanent because they are not on the map and therefore cannot be stricken from it.

n n n n n n conj
Hell's Kitchen, Back Bay, The Gas House District, The Loop, Harlem, Chinatown, and

n prep pro v v adv adv conj n v v n adv
thousands of others will live on long after the place has changed character entirely.

prep adj n prep n adj n v adv conj pro adj v v
Like the great men of the past, their names remain long after all else has vanished.

ADJECTIVES AND ADVERBS (PP. 31–34)

Exercise 1

1. adjective adding to the noun *buildings*
2. adverb adding to the adjective *pretty*
3. adjective adding to the noun *letters*
4. adjective adding to the noun *walls*
5. adverb adding to the verb *constructed*
6. adjective adding to the noun *pride*
7. adjective adding to the noun *afternoon*
8. adverb adding to the verb *falls*
9. adverb adding to the adjective *happy*
10. adverb adding to the verb *be*

Exercise 2

1. adjective adding to the noun *textbook*
2. adverb adding to the adjective *one*
3. adjective adding to the pronoun *I*
4. adverb adding to the adjective *used*
5. adverb adding to the adjective *new*
6. adjective adding to the pronoun *one*

7. adjective adding to the noun *students*
8. adverb adding to the adverb and adjective *heavily marked*
9. adjective adding to the noun *fraction*
10. adjective adding to the pronoun *one*

Exercise 3

1. close
2. closely
3. close
4. badly
5. bad
6. badly
7. very happily
8. very happy
9. good
10. well

Exercise 4

1. the smallest
2. a small
3. smaller
4. the newest
5. newer
6. newer
7. better
8. the best
9. better
10. more important

Exercise 5

adv adj adj
1. I took a very unusual acting class over the summer.

adj adj
2. The title of the summer seminar was "Clowning and Physical Acting."

adj adj
3. It was a special class for students majoring in theater arts.

adv adj
4. We usually started with warm-up exercises.

adv adj adj
5. Then we experimented with unique movements and crazy combinations.

adv adj adj
6. Sometimes, we would combine "happy knees" with "curious elbows."

adv adj adj adj
7. Next, we added costume elements, such as padded leggings or strange hats.

adv adj
8. Some of us transformed into totally unrecognizable characters.

adv adj
9. I was very happy with my progress as a clown.

adj adj adj adj adj
10. We learned many valuable skills during our first clown seminar.

Proofreading Exercise

I didn't do very ~~good~~ *well* during my first semester at community college. I feel ~~badly~~ *bad* whenever I think of it. I skipped classes and turned in sloppy work. My counselor warned me about my negative attitude, but I was ~~real~~ *really* stubborn. I dropped out for a year and a half. Now that I have come back to college, I am even ~~stubborner~~ *more stubborn* than before. I go to every class and do my best. Now, a college degree is ~~only~~ my *only* goal.

CONTRACTIONS (PP. 36–40)

Exercise 1

1. you've, hadn't
2. that's
3. It's
4. no contractions
5. no contractions
6. couldn't
7. no contractions
8. There's
9. It's
10. Lets, don't

Exercise 2

1. wasn't
2. I'll
3. isn't
4. It's, It's, I'm
5. you've
6. don't, don't
7. there's
8. you'll
9. haven't
10. we'd

Exercise 3

1. There's, that's
2. wasn't
3. don't, it's
4. hasn't
5. don't
6. aren't
7. They're
8. haven't
9. They've
10. they're, don't

Exercise 4

1. aren't
2. They're, isn't
3. we're
4. doesn't
5. don't, weren't
6. That's
7. don't, won't
8. there'll
9. shouldn't
10. Let's, it's

Exercise 5

1. I'm, she's
2. We've, we've
3. aren't
4. they're
5. they're
6. that's
7. We've, can't, doesn't
8. we'd
9. that's, it's, they're
10. isn't

Proofreading Exercise

Jokes affect people differently based on their content and the way ~~theyre~~ *they're* told. No two individuals tell jokes in the same way or react to them in the same way. ~~Thats~~ *That's* why using humor at work or with people we ~~dont~~ *don't* know ~~isnt~~ *isn't* usually a good idea. I have an Irish friend, Grace, ~~whos~~ *who's* very good at making people laugh. It ~~isnt~~ *isn't* that her jokes are so funny; ~~its~~ *it's* the way she tells them. For instance, ~~shell~~ *she'll* ask someone, "What comes from Ireland and stays outside all night?" While ~~shes~~ *she's* waiting for the person to answer, ~~shell~~ *she'll* tilt her head and look at the person with a twinkle in her eye. Just as the person is about to take a guess, Grace will blurt out, "Patio furniture! Get it? Patty O'Furniture?" The expression on Grace's face after she tells the joke is often funnier than its punch line.

POSSESSIVES (PP. 45–46)

Exercise 4

1. bat's, animal's
2. patient's
3. person's
4. condition's
5. bat's
6. no possessives
7. patients', bat's
8. enzyme's
9. DSPA's
10. bat's

Exercise 5

1. pencil's
2. England's
3. valley's
4. world's
5. artist's, writer's
6. pencils'
7. Conte's
8. pencil's
9. pencil's (Note: The word *its* is a possessive pronoun that needs no apostrophe.)
10. students'

Proofreading Exercise

I have a cat named Shelby who always keeps me company when I do my homework. ~~Shelbys'~~ *Shelby's* favorite spot to lie down is right in the middle of my desk. Whenever she can, she makes herself comfortable on top of my actual homework. All of my ~~books~~ *books'* pages have ~~Shelbys~~ *Shelby's* fur on them. Many people are allergic to ~~cat's~~ *cats'* fur, so I wipe off my assignment sheets before I turn them in to my ~~teachers'~~ *teachers.* Shelby's purring noise helps me relax when I'm working on a difficult math problem or starting a new writing assignment.

REVIEW OF CONTRACTIONS AND POSSESSIVES (PP. 47–48)

1. isn't
2. cloud's, it's
3. aren't
4. They're
5. Sloane's, clouds'
6. shouldn't
7. They're, they're
8. artist's
9. mustn't
10. It's, cloudscape's

A Journal of My Own

I've been keeping a journal ever since I was in high school. I *don't* write it for my *teachers'* sake. I *wouldn't* turn it in even if they asked me to. *It's* mine, and it helps me remember all of the changes *I've* gone through so far in my life. The way I see it, a *diary's* purpose *isn't* just to record the facts; *it's* to capture my true feelings.

When I record the *day's* events in my journal, they *aren't* written in minute-by-minute details. Instead, if *I've* been staying at a *friend's* house for the weekend, *I'll* write something like this: "*Sharon's* the only friend I have who listens to my whole sentence before starting hers. *She's* never in a hurry to end a good conversation. Today we talked for an hour or so about the pets *we'd* had when we were kids. We agreed that *we're* both 'dog people.' We *can't* imagine our lives without dogs. Her favorites are Pomeranians, and mine are golden retrievers." *That's* the kind of an entry *I'd* make in my journal. It *doesn't* mean much to anyone but me, and *that's* the way it should be.

I know that another *person's* diary would be different from mine and that most people *don't* even keep one. *I'm* glad that writing comes easily to me. I *don't* think *I'll* ever stop writing in my journal because it helps me believe in myself and value *others'* beliefs as well.

RULE FOR DOUBLING A FINAL LETTER (PP. 50–51)

Exercise 1

1. betting
2. quitting
3. waiting
4. parking
5. skimming
6. admitting
7. slapping
8. thinking
9. tapping
10. hitting

Exercise 2

1. towing
2. ripping
3. peeling
4. referring
5. investing
6. ordering
7. profiting
8. screaming
9. slipping
10. predicting

Exercise 3

1. boxing
2. munching
3. rolling
4. mopping
5. flavoring
6. cashing
7. beeping
8. talking
9. traveling
10. playing

Exercise 4

1. painting
2. rowing
3. shivering
4. defending
5. trimming
6. pressing
7. dealing
8. knitting
9. blundering
10. chugging

Exercise 5

1. shouting
2. deploying
3. referring
4. equaling
5. digging
6. mixing
7. dripping
8. sending
9. hemming
10. taxing

PROGRESS TEST (P. 52)

1. B. They should *have* practiced more.
2. A. Kyle bought a *new* cell phone with his first paycheck.
3. A. My teacher *complimented* me on my attendance.
4. B. I feel *bad* whenever I hurt someone's feelings.
5. A. The tutors didn't know *where* the extra handouts were.
6. B. *It's* fun to shift gears.
7. A. Our new computer has *already* broken down several times.
8. B. I'm learning more from one of them *than* the other.
9. A. Eating a snack before an exam can have positive *effects.*
10. A. I always *accept* my best friend's advice.

SENTENCE STRUCTURE

FINDING SUBJECTS AND VERBS (PP. 63–66)

Exercise 1

1. The summer heat causes many problems for people.
2. Food spoils more quickly in the summer.

3. Insects and other pests seek shelter inside.
4. There are power outages due to excessive use of air conditioners and fans.
5. In some areas, smog levels increase dramatically in the summer.
6. Schoolchildren suffer in overheated classrooms.
7. On the worst days, everyone searches for a swimming pool or drives to the beach.
8. Sleeping comfortably becomes impossible.
9. No activity seems worth the effort.
10. But the heat of summer fades in our minds at the first real break in the weather.

Exercise 2

1. I got an actual letter in the mail last month.
2. It came from my aunt Leone in England.
3. She used real stationery and wrote her thoughts with an ink pen.
4. I read the letter several times and really enjoyed its one-of-a-kind qualities.
5. My aunt's personality and voice came through her letter.
6. She crossed out her mistakes and added little notes and drawings in the margins.
7. It felt like an original artwork in my hands.
8. Until recently, I wrote only e-mails or sent only preprinted cards to my friends and relatives.
9. Aunt Leone's letter changed my habits.
10. Nothing captures an artistic personality better than paper and pen.

Exercise 3

1. Katharine M. Rogers recently published her biography of L. Frank Baum.
2. Most people know Baum's work but not his name.
3. L. Frank Baum wrote *The Wonderful Wizard of Oz* and many other children's books and stories.
4. Of course, filmmakers used Baum's tale of the Wizard of Oz in the classic movie of the same name.
5. Baum's memorable character of the Scarecrow has an interesting story behind him.
6. During Baum's childhood, his father bought some farmland.

7. Baum saw scarecrows in the fields and found them fascinating.
8. Unfortunately, his keen imagination led to bad dreams about a scarecrow.
9. The scarecrow in his dreams ran after him but always fell into a heap of straw just in time.
10. As a writer, Baum brought the Scarecrow to life in his Oz stories and made him less of a nightmare and more of a friend.

Exercise 4

1. In 1940, four teenagers took a walk and discovered something marvelous.
2. They entered an underground cavern in Lascaux, France, and found vivid images of animals on its walls.
3. There were horses, deer, bulls, cats, and oxen.
4. The prehistoric artists also left tracings of their handprints on the walls.
5. Scientists dated the paintings and engravings at approximately 17,000 years old.
6. After its discovery, the Lascaux cave became a popular tourist attraction.
7. Twelve hundred people visited the site daily.
8. These visitors had a negative impact on the cave's prehistoric artwork.
9. They breathed carbon dioxide into the cave and increased its humidity.
10. French officials closed the Lascaux cave to the public in 1963.

Exercise 5

1. Movies and television programs often include real dogs as actors.
2. Disney's live-action *101 Dalmatians* is just one example.
3. *Snow Dogs*, *Eight Below*, and *The Shaggy Dog* are three other dog-friendly films.
4. According to experts, dogs in films both help and hurt certain dog breeds.
5. For instance, sales and adoptions of Dalmatians rose dramatically after the Disney movie's popularity.
6. The other films caused the same effect for Siberian huskies and bearded collies.
7. However, these breeds are not good choices for everyone.
8. Many people become unhappy with them and put them up for adoption.
9. Disney now attaches warning labels to their DVDs of dog-related films.
10. The labels caution the public about the choice of dogs based on their movie roles.

Paragraph Exercise

I was on the volleyball team in high school, so my high school gym was a special place for me. It was an ordinary gym with bleachers on both sides. There were basketball court lines on the floors and the school's mascot in the center. We stretched a net across the middle for our volleyball games. The pale wooden floors sparkled, sometimes with sweat and sometimes with tears. The gym had a distinct stuffy smell of grimy socks, stale potato chips, and sticky sodas. I liked the smell and remember it fondly. Songs from dances and screams and cheers from games echoed throughout the big old building. In the gym during those high school years, I felt a sense of privacy and community.

LOCATING PREPOSITIONAL PHRASES (PP. 69–72)

Exercise 1

1. Everyone worries (about identity theft).
2. Thieves search (for certain pieces) (of information).
3. These facts are names, addresses, dates (of birth), and social security numbers.
4. (With these facts), thieves attempt access (to people's accounts).
5. There are some new forms (of protection) (on the Internet).
6. One program checks the Web (for groupings) (of people's most valuable information).
7. The name (of the program) is Identity Angel.
8. Carnegie Mellon University (in Pittsburgh) created the program.
9. Identity Angel sends e-mail warnings (to vulnerable people).
10. It warns them (about possible identity theft).

Exercise 2

1. One fact (about William Shakespeare and his work) always surprises people.
2. There are no copies (of his original manuscripts).
3. No museum or library has even one page (from a Shakespeare play) (in Shakespeare's own handwriting).
4. Museums and libraries have copies (of the First Folio) instead.

5. (After Shakespeare's death) (in 1616), actors (from his company) gathered the texts (of his plays) and published them (as one book), the First Folio, (in 1623).
6. They printed approximately 750 copies (at the time).
7. Currently, there are 230 known copies (of the First Folio) (in the world).
8. Many owners (of the Folio) remain anonymous (by choice).
9. One woman inherited her copy (of the Folio) (from a distant relative).
10. Another copy (of the First Folio) recently sold (for five million dollars).

EXERCISE 3

1. Twiggy the Squirrel is a star (in the world) (of trained animals).
2. Twiggy performs (on a pair) (of tiny water skis) and delights crowds (at boat shows and other events).
3. (Like many other famous animal entertainers), the current Twiggy is not the original.
4. The Twiggy (of today) is fifth (in the line) (of Twiggys).
5. Lou Ann Best is Twiggy's trainer and continues the work begun (by her husband Chuck) (during the 1970s). [*Begun* is a verbal.]
6. (In his time), Chuck Best convinced many types (of animals) to ride (on water skis). [*To ride* is a verbal.]
7. He had success (with everything) (from a dog) (to a frog).
8. But Twiggy the Squirrel was a hit (with crowds) (from the beginning).
9. All (of the Twiggys) seemed happy (with their show-biz lifestyles).
10. (In fact), the Bests received four (of the Twiggys) (from the Humane Society).

EXERCISE 4

1. (At 2 A.M.) (on the second Sunday) (in March), something happens (to nearly everyone) (in America): Daylight Saving Time.
2. But few people are awake (at two) (in the morning).
3. So we set the hands or digits (of our clocks) ahead one hour (on Saturday night) (in preparation) (for it).
4. And (before bed) (on the first Saturday) (in November), we turn them back again.
5. (For days) (after both events), I have trouble (with my sleep patterns and my mood).

6. (In spring), the feeling is one (of loss).
7. That Saturday-night sleep (into Sunday) is one hour shorter than usual.
8. But (in fall), I gain a false sense (of security) (about time).
9. That endless Sunday morning quickly melts (into the start) (of a hectic week) (like the other fifty-one) (in the year).
10. All (of this upheaval) is due (to the Uniform Time Act) (of 1966).

Exercise 5

1. I saw a news story (about an art exhibit) (with a unique focus and message).
2. All (of the pieces) (in the art show) started (with the same basic materials).
3. The materials were all (of the parts) (of a huge English oak tree).
4. Most (of a tree) usually becomes waste (except the large trunk section).
5. But (in the case) (of this tree), artists took every last bit and made "art" (with it) (as a tribute) (to the tree).
6. One artist even made clothes (from some) (of the smallest pieces)—tiny branches, sawdust, and leaves.
7. Another artist used thousands (of bits) (of the tree) (in a kind) (of mosaic painting).
8. Still another turned one hunk (of the tree's timber) (into a pig sculpture).
9. Other chunks, branches, and even the roots became abstract pieces (of art).
10. The tree lives on (as art) and (as a new tree) (with the sprouting) (of an acorn) (in its old location).

Paragraph Exercise

A whole collection (of clay toys) was discovered (during the nineteenth century) (in Strasbourgh), (in the workshop) (of a thirteenth-century potter). (Since then), we know more (about medieval children's games): bird-shaped whistles, miniature tiles and pitchers, tiny moneyboxes, little dolls, and diminutive horses (with riders) (on their backs). Children fought battles (with wooden swords), competed (in play tournaments), played games (with balls and wooden sticks) (in a remote precursor) (to modern field hockey).

(In families) (with more means), there were "educational toys," such as an alphabet wheel (in gesso) (from the fourteenth century) or a covered pewter cup decorated (with the entire alphabet). The letter A, the first the child would pronounce, is (on the knob). We find out (about the instruction) (of children) primarily (from images) (of family life).

UNDERSTANDING DEPENDENT CLAUSES (PP. 75–79)

EXERCISE 1

1. When I was on vacation in New York City, I loved the look of the Empire State Building at night.
2. I thought that the colored lights at the top of this landmark were just decorative.
3. I did not know that their patterns also have meaning.
4. While I waited at the airport, I read a pamphlet about the patterns.
5. Some of the light combinations reveal connections that are obvious.
6. For instance, if the occasion is St. Patrick's Day, the top of the building glows with green lights.
7. When the holiday involves a celebration of America, the three levels of lights shine red, white, and blue.
8. There are other combinations that are less well known.
9. Red-black-green is a pattern that signals Martin Luther King, Jr. Day.
10. Whenever I visit the city again, I'll know the meanings of the lights on the Empire State Building.

EXERCISE 2

1. When people shop for high-price items, they often think too much.
2. A study at the University of Amsterdam yielded results that surprised scientists.
3. If buyers thought only a little bit beforehand, they remained happy with their purchase later.
4. When they consciously considered many details about a product, they were not as satisfied with it afterward.
5. The products that researchers used in the experiments were cars and furniture.
6. For the car-buying study, they tested eighty people who were all college students.

7. The cars had many positive and negative attributes for the subjects to consider when they made their choices.

8. The subjects who took the least amount of time chose the best cars.

9. Likewise, a survey of furniture shoppers showed that quick decisions led to satisfied customers.

10. Apparently, shoppers who trust their instincts make the best decisions.

EXERCISE 3

1. Did you know that July is National Cell Phone Courtesy Month?

2. There are few cell phone users who are courteous in public.

3. In fact, courtesy is almost impossible when someone uses a cell phone around others.

4. People who have cell phones set their ring tones on high and have loud conversations.

5. Even if they are in stores, restaurants, or libraries, cell phone users answer most of their calls.

6. The question remains about how cell phone users can be more courteous.

7. One solution is a new type of phone booth that has no phone in it.

8. It is a structure that has a cylindrical shape and a metal exterior.

9. There is a door that callers use for privacy.

10. The cell phone booth is an old-fashioned idea that makes a lot of sense.

EXERCISE 4

1. I just read an article with a list of "What Doctors Wish [that] You Knew."

2. One fact is that red and blue fruits are the healthiest.

3. Patients who have doctor's appointments after lunchtime spend less time in the waiting room.

4. Drivers who apply more sunscreen to their left sides get less skin cancer.
5. People who take ten deep breaths in the morning and evening feel less stress.
6. A clock that is visible from the bed makes insomnia worse.
7. People often suffer from weekend headaches because they get up too late.
8. They withdraw from caffeine by skipping the coffee that they usually drink on workdays.
9. Doctors suggest that people maintain weekday hours on weekends.
10. I am glad that I found this list.

Exercise 5

1. My coworker told me about a news story that he saw on television.
2. It involved those baby turtles that hatch in the sand at night.
3. Normally, once they hatch, they run toward the comforting waves.
4. As soon as they reach the water, they begin their lives as sea turtles.
5. The story that my friend saw told of a potential danger to these motivated little animals.
6. The turtles instinctively know which direction leads to the sea.
7. The bright white foam of the waves is the trigger that lures them across the sand to their proper destination.
8. Unfortunately, on some beaches where this phenomenon occurs, the tourist business causes a big problem for the turtles.
9. Tourists who want to see the turtles gather at shoreline restaurants and dance pavilions.
10. The lights are so bright that they prompt the turtles to run in the wrong direction—up the beach away from the water.

Paragraph Exercise

Today experts disagree over the impact of television on our lives. Some argue that increased crime is a direct outcome of television since programs show crime as an everyday event and since advertisements make people aware of what they don't have. Critics also maintain that television stimulates aggressive behavior, reinforces ethnic stereotyping, and leads to a decrease in activity and creativity. Proponents of television counter [when they cite] increased awareness in world events, improved verbal abilities, and greater curiosity as benefits of television viewing.

CORRECTING FRAGMENTS (PP. 82–85)

Exercise 1

Changes used to make the fragments into sentences are *italicized.*

1. Correct
2. *The article said that* bananas are in danger of extinction in the near future.
3. *The danger comes from* a crop disease that infects the banana plants' leaves.
4. Correct
5. Correct
6. Some banana experts *are warning* about no more bananas to eat.
7. *That would mean* no banana cream pies, banana splits, banana muffins, or banana bread.
8. Correct
9. Correct
10. Chocolate and coffee *have been threatened by* similar scares in the past.

Exercise 2

Changes used to make the fragments into sentences are *italicized.*

1. Correct
2. *We discuss* ways of raising children without gender bias.

3. *Gender bias means having* different expectations about boys' abilities and girls' abilities.
4. Correct
5. Correct (In numbers 5–10, the subject is an understood *You.*)
6. *Do not make* a big deal out of it.
7. Correct
8. *Encourage* physically challenging activities for both genders.
9. Correct
10. Correct

EXERCISE 3

Answers may vary, but here are some possible revisions.

1. A worker at the Smithsonian discovered an important historical object on a shelf in one of the museum's storage rooms.
2. Made of cardboard and covered with short, smooth fur, it was a tall black top hat.
3. The hat didn't look like anything special—more like an old costume or prop.
4. It was special, however, having been worn by Abraham Lincoln on the night of his assassination.
5. Once found and identified, Lincoln's hat traveled with the 150th anniversary exhibition, called "America's Smithsonian."
6. For such a priceless object to be able to travel around the country safely, experts needed to build a unique display case for Lincoln's top hat.
7. The design allowed visitors to view the famous stovepipe hat without damaging it with their breath or hands.
8. The hat traveled in a sealed box that was designed against even earthquakes.
9. Keeping the hat earthquake-proof was an important concern because it would be on display in California for part of the time.
10. Among the millions of objects in the archives of the Smithsonian, President Lincoln's hat is one of the most impressive.

EXERCISE 4

Answers may vary, but here are some possible revisions.

1. When Nathan King turned twelve, he had a heart-stopping experience.
2. Nathan was tossing a football against his bedroom wall, which made the ball ricochet and land on his bed.

3. In a diving motion, Nathan fell on his bed to catch the ball as it landed.
4. After he caught the ball, Nathan felt a strange sensation in his chest.
5. To his surprise, he looked down and saw the eraser end of a no. 2 pencil that had pierced his chest and entered his heart.
6. Nathan immediately shouted for his mother, who luckily was in the house at the time.
7. Because Nathan's mom is a nurse, she knew not to remove the pencil.
8. If she had pulled the pencil out of her son's chest, he would have died.
9. After Nathan was taken to a hospital equipped for open-heart surgery, he had the pencil carefully removed.
10. Fate may be partly responsible for Nathan's happy birthday story since it turned out to be his heart surgeon's birthday too.

Exercise 5

Answers may vary, but here are some possible revisions. (Changes and additions are in *italics.*)

1. One of the people sitting next to me on the train *sneezed four times in a row.*
2. Before intermission, the movie seemed endless.
3. Before the paint was dry in the classrooms, *the new semester began.*
4. The judge's question and the answer it received *surprised everyone.*
5. Because there were fewer students in the program this year, *it ran smoothly.*
6. *His speech lasted* for over an hour.
7. Whenever the teacher reminds us about the midterm exam, *we get nervous.*
8. If we move to Kentucky and stay for two years, *we will save money.*
9. *Please notify us* as soon as the order form reaches the warehouse.
10. Buildings with odd shapes always interest me.

Proofreading Exercise

Answers may vary, but here are some possible revisions. (Changes are in *italics.*)

I love fireworks shows. *They can be* backyard displays or huge Fourth of July events. *The whole sky lights up* with color and booms with noise. In fact, I have a dream to become a fireworks expert. If I could take a class in pyrotechnics right now, I would. Instead, I have to take general education *classes like English, math, and psychology.* Maybe an appointment with a career counselor would be a good idea. *The counselor could* help me find the right *school—one with a training program* in fireworks preparation.

CORRECTING RUN-ON SENTENCES (PP. 88–92)

EXERCISE 1

Your answers may differ depending on how you chose to separate the two clauses.

1. I just read an article about prehistoric rodents, and I was surprised by their size.
2. Scientists recently discovered the remains of a rat-like creature called *Phoberomys;* it was as big as a buffalo.
3. *Phoberomys* sat back on its large rear feet and fed itself with its smaller front feet in just the way rats and mice do now.
4. This supersized rodent lived in South America, but luckily that was nearly ten million years ago.
5. At that time, South America was a separate continent; it had no cows or horses to graze on its open land.
6. South America and North America were separated by the sea, so there were also no large cats around to hunt and kill other large animals.
7. Scientists believe that *Phoberomys* thrived and grew large because of the lack of predators and competitors for food.
8. The *Phoberomys'* carefree lifestyle eventually disappeared, for the watery separation between North and South America slowly became a land route.
9. The big carnivores of North America could travel down the new land route, and the big rodents were defenseless against them.
10. The rodents who survived were the smaller ones who could escape underground, and that is the reason we have no buffalo-sized rats today.

EXERCISE 2

Your answers may differ depending on how you chose to separate the two clauses.

1. One day is hard for me every year. That day is my birthday.
2. I don't mind getting older; I just never enjoy the day of my birth.
3. For one thing, I was born in August, but summer is my least favorite season.
4. I hate the heat and the sun, so even traditional warm-weather activities get me down.
5. Sunblock spoils swimming; smog spoils biking; and crowds spoil the national parks.
6. To most people, the beach is a summer haven. To me, the beach in the summer is bright, busy, and boring.

7. I love to walk on the beach on the cold, misty days of winter or early spring. I wear a big sweater and have the whole place to myself.

8. August also brings fire season to most parts of the country; therefore, even television is depressing.

9. There are no holidays to brighten up August. In fact, it's like a black hole in the yearly holiday calendar—after the Fourth of July but before Halloween and the other holidays.

10. I have considered moving my birthday to February. Even being close to Groundhog Day would cheer me up.

Exercise 3

Your answers may differ since various words can be used to begin dependent clauses.

1. Pablo Wendel is a German student of art who feels a special connection with a particular group of ancient sculptures.

2. When Pablo acted on this feeling in September of 2006, he won his "fifteen minutes of fame."

3. The sentence is correct.

4. The sentence is correct.

5. He made a special clay-covered costume that was complete with armor and a helmet.

6. Pablo took this outfit and a pedestal with him to the museum, which is located in Xian, China.

7. The sentence is correct.

8. The sentence is correct.

9. Pablo, in disguise, stood among his fellow "soldiers" and didn't move until eventually someone spotted him.

10. Although the museum guards confiscated Pablo's clay costume, they let him go with just a warning.

Exercise 4

Your answers may differ since various words can be used to begin dependent clauses.

1. Our town has recently installed a new rapid transit system that uses trains instead of only buses.

2. The new metro train tracks follow the same old route that freight trains used to run on behind the buildings in town.

3. I might try this new transportation method since the parking on campus has been getting worse every semester.

4. Because the stations are near my house and school, I would have to walk only a few blocks each day.

5. Students who don't live near the train stations would have to take a bus to the train.

6. Whereas the old buses are bulky and ugly, the new trains are sleek and attractive.

7. Although the new trains seem to be inspiring many people to be more conscious of their driving habits, some people will never change.

8. I would gladly give up my car if the convenience matched the benefits.

9. The city has plans for additional routes that will bring more commuters in from out of town.

10. I am glad that my town is making progress.

EXERCISE 5

Your answers may differ depending on how you chose to separate the clauses.

1. White buffalos are very rare, and they are extremely important in Native American folklore.

2. Many American Indian tribes feel a strong attachment to white buffalos because they are viewed as omens of peace and prosperity.

3. One farm in Wisconsin is famous as a source of white buffalos. Three of them have been born on this farm since 1994.

4. The owners of the farm are Valerie and Dave Heider, and they are as surprised as anyone about the unusual births.

5. The Heiders' first white buffalo was a female calf who was named Miracle.

6. After Miracle became a local attraction, visitors to the Heider farm raised tourism in the area by twenty-two percent in 1995.

7. A second white calf was born on the farm in 1996; however, it died after a few days.

8. Miracle survived until 2004; she lived for ten years.

9. In September of 2006, the Heider farm yielded a third white buffalo calf, but it was a boy.

10. The odds against one white buffalo being born are high; the odds against three being born in the same place are astronomical.

REVIEW OF FRAGMENTS AND RUN-ON SENTENCES (P. 93)

Your revisions may differ depending on how you chose to correct the errors.

Sometimes I feel like an egg—always sitting in rows. In classrooms, the chairs are arranged in rows, and at the movies the seats are connected into rows. Why can't chairs be scattered around randomly? In my classes, I usually choose a seat in the back row; that way I have a view of the whole room. Luckily, I have good eyesight because the chalkboard or whiteboard can be hard to read at that distance. In movie theaters, the most distracting problem can come from the people behind me. I don't mind people making noise or talking, but I can't stand people kicking my chair. It totally ruins my concentration. Therefore, I try to sit in the back row of the theater whenever possible.

IDENTIFYING VERB PHRASES (PP. 95–98)

Exercise 1

1. Have you ever felt a craving for art?
2. Have you said to yourself, "I need a new painting, or I am going to go crazy"?
3. If you ever find yourself in this situation, you can get instant satisfaction.
4. I am referring to Art-o-Mat machines, of course.
5. These vending machines dispense small pieces of modern art.
6. You insert five dollars, pull a knob on a refurbished cigarette dispenser, and out comes an original art piece.
7. The artists themselves get fifty percent of the selling price.
8. Art-o-Mat machines can be found at locations across the country.
9. Art-o-Mats are currently dispensing tiny paintings, photographs, and sculptures in twelve states.
10. The machines have sold the works of hundreds of contemporary artists.

Exercise 2

1. I am always working on my vocabulary.
2. *Lie* and *lay* can be tricky verbs to use sometimes.
3. They mean "rest" and "put," in that order.
4. Lately, I have been practicing with these two verbs.
5. I know that a sunken ship lies at the bottom of the ocean.

6. The *Titanic,* for example, has lain there for over ninety years.
7. When I left for school, my books were lying all over my desk.
8. A bricklayer is a person who lays bricks to form walls and walkways.
9. Last week, we laid a new foundation for the garage.
10. The contractors will be laying our new concrete driveway on Friday.

Exercise 3

1. I have been reading a series of books that were written by Erin McHugh.
2. These books are filled with facts about important people, places, events, and objects throughout history.
3. The series is called *The 5 W's.*
4. McHugh has included five separate books in the series: *Who?, What?, Where?, When?,* and *Why?*
5. In *Who?,* McHugh offers fun tidbits and biographical information about influential people.
6. McHugh's discussion of the faces on U.S. money is filled with surprising information.
7. All but three of the people with their pictures on U.S. bills have been presidents of the United States.
8. Alexander Hamilton and Benjamin Franklin are still shown on the ten-dollar bill and the hundred-dollar bill, respectively.
9. The U.S. Treasury does not print $10,000 bills anymore.
10. When it did print them, these big bills pictured the inventor of the nation's banking system, Salmon P. Chase.

Exercise 4

1. There have been several power outages in our neighborhood recently.
2. Last week when I was writing an essay on my computer, the power went off.
3. I had not saved my work, and I lost the last few sentences that I had written.
4. I did not enjoy the process of remembering those sentences.
5. Sometimes power outages can be fun.
6. If my whole family is at home, we light the candles on our two big candelabras and put them in the middle of the dining room table.

7. The room starts to look like the set of an old horror movie.
8. Then someone goes to the hall closet and grabs a board game to play.
9. On these special occasions, all of us can forget about school or work problems and just enjoy ourselves.
10. Maybe we should plan to spend evenings like this more often.

Exercise 5

1. Prehistoric musical instruments have been found before.
2. But the ancient flutes that were discovered in China's Henan Province included the oldest playable instrument on record.
3. The nine-thousand-year-old flute was made from the wing bone of a bird.
4. The bone was hollowed out and pierced with seven holes that produce the notes of an ancient Chinese musical scale.
5. Because one of the holes' pitches missed the mark, an additional tiny hole was added by the flute's maker.
6. The flute is played in the vertical position.
7. People who have studied ancient instruments are hoping to learn more about the culture that produced this ancient flute.
8. Other bone flutes were found at the same time and in the same location, but they were not intact or strong enough (for playing).
9. Visitors to the Brookhaven National Laboratory's Web site can listen to music from the world's oldest working flute.
10. Listeners will be taken back to 7,000 years B.C.E.

Review Exercise (p. 98)

My brain feels (like a computer's central processing unit). Information is continually pumping (into its circuits). I organize the data, format it (to my individual preferences), and lay it out (in my own style). As I endlessly sculpt existing formulas, they become something (of my own). When I need a solution (to a problem), I access the data that I have gathered (from my whole existence), even my preprogrammed DNA.

Since I am a student, teachers require that I supply them (with specific information) (in various formats). When they assign an essay, I produce several paragraphs. If they need a summary, I scan the text, find its main ideas, and put them briefly (into my own words). I know that I can accomplish whatever the teachers ask so that I can obtain a bachelor's degree and continue processing ideas to make a living.

I compare my brain (to a processor) because right now I feel that I must work (like one). As I go further (into my education), my processor will be continually updated—just (like a Pentium)! And (with any luck), I will end up (with real, not artificial, intelligence).

USING STANDARD ENGLISH VERBS (PP. 101–104)

Exercise 1

1. has, had
2. does, did
3. am, was
4. votes, voted
5. have, had
6. shops, shopped
7. are, was
8. pick, picked
9. do, did
10. ends, ended

Exercise 2

1. are, were
2. does, did
3. has, had
4. tags, tagged
5. have, had
6. stuffs, stuffed
7. are, were
8. do, did
9. dance, danced
10. are, were

Exercise 3

1. changed, want
2. had
3. enrolled, were, expected
4. were, were
5. did, were, does
6. observed, had
7. watched, cared, followed
8. had
9. imagined, had
10. needs, are, am

Exercise 4

1. have
2. play
3. plays
4. play
5. practices, do
6. is, wins
7. am, is, am
8. remind
9. follows
10. have, am, is

Exercise 5

1. Last semester, my drawing teacher *handed* us an assignment.
2. The sentence is correct.
3. *We had* to draw in the other half of the picture.
4. My picture *showed* a woman sitting against the bottom of a tree trunk.
5. Her shoulders, hat, and umbrella *were* only partly there.
6. I tried to imagine what the missing parts *looked* like.
7. The sentence is correct.
8. Therefore, I *started* with the tree, the sky, and the ground.
9. The sentence is correct.
10. I *received* an "A" grade for my drawing.

Proofreading Exercise

Every day, as we arrive on campus and walk to our classrooms, we see things that ~~needs~~ *need* to be fixed. Many of them cause us only a little bit of trouble, so we ~~forgets~~ *forget* them until we face them again. Every morning, there is a long line of students in their cars waiting to enter the parking lots because the lights at all of the corners ~~is~~ *are* not timed properly. The lights from the main boulevard change too slowly, and that ~~allow~~ *allows* too many cars to stack up on the side streets. Students who walk to school ~~is~~ *are* affected, too. Many drivers don't watch where they ~~is~~ *are* going and almost run over pedestrians who ~~is~~ *are* walking in the driveways.

USING REGULAR AND IRREGULAR VERBS (PP. 109–113)

Exercise 1

1. live
2. lived
3. live
4. living
5. lived
6. lives
7. live
8. living
9. live
10. living

Exercise 2

1. got, gets
2. gave, given
3. am, is
4. thought, think
5. grown, grow
6. leave, left
7. wave, waves
8. knows, know
9. does, do
10. was, be, am

Exercise 3

1. took, supposed
2. was, go
3. called, left, feel
4. imagined, was
5. buying, drove, saw
6. felt, knew, be
7. tried, went (or got)
8. been, undo
9. wish, take
10. did, was

Exercise 4

1. use, have
2. do, speak, dials
3. are, are
4. is, like, started
5. does, wants
6. trusts, is
7. imagine, dialing
8. asking, told, is
9. looked, smiled
10. has

Exercise 5

1. sitting, saw
2. was, appeared
3. flipped, turned, looked
4. was, wore, thought, was
5. passed, seemed
6. waiting, cut
7. called, watched, recognize
8. look, figured, was
9. got, chatted, was
10. come, left

PROGRESS TEST (P. 114)

1. A. run-on sentence (*Needs a comma:* I was the last student working on the test, and my teacher was ready to leave.)
2. B. fragment (*They are* often less expensive than the ones in stores.)
3. B. incorrect verb form (I *asked* the teacher if I could do some extra credit there.)
4. B. incorrect verb form (I should have *gone* to the library sooner.)
5. A. incorrect verb form (We were *supposed* to meet in the cafeteria.)
6. B. wrong word (*They're* going away for spring break, but I'm staying at home.)
7. A. wrong word (The package had only *a* handwritten address.)
8. A. wrong word (In my math class, we've *already* taken three quizzes.)
9. B. run-on sentence (*Needs a comma:* They didn't work, so the bus crashed into the curb.)
10. A. fragment (*Combine A and B:* Although I don't like the taste of tropical fruits, I do like shampoos and conditioners that smell like tropical fruits.)

MAINTAINING SUBJECT-VERB AGREEMENT (PP. 117–121)

Exercise 1

1. work
2. are
3. have, know
4. are
5. gets, separates
6. get, ask, are
7. is, do
8. focus
9. work
10. is, aren't

Exercise 2

1. is, rates, portray
2. is
3. include, spark, explode, are
4. give
5. rank
6. get, are, make
7. is, are
8. were
9. was
10. were, were

Exercise 3

1. explains, seem, happen
2. feels, don't
3. begin, react
4. are, have
5. is, sense
6. don't, get
7. isn't
8. do
9. have, do, is
10. look, run, has, do

Exercise 4

1. have
2. were
3. was
4. is
5. allows
6. travels
7. breaks, melts
8. are
9. realize
10. is, are

Exercise 5

1. gives
2. sounds, is
3. connects
4. says, means
5. forecasts
6. are, mean
7. are, foretell
8. means
9. are
10. seem

Proofreading Exercise

Unfortunately, tension between members of the public ~~are~~ *is* common these days. When two people at a movie theater ~~irritates~~ *irritate* each other or have a disagreement, the whole audience ~~suffer~~ *suffers.* Everyone who is sitting around the troublemakers ~~want~~ *wants* to move immediately to another section. However, if anyone ~~get~~ *gets* up to sit somewhere else, then everyone else ~~start~~ *starts* to get nervous. So most people just ~~waits~~ *wait* until one of two fighting people ~~calm~~ *calms* down. After that, the members of the audience ~~forgets~~ *forget* about the disturbance and enjoy the rest of the movie. The same pattern ~~repeat~~ *repeats* itself in stadiums and ballparks, too.

AVOIDING SHIFTS IN TIME (PP. 123–124)

1. The paragraph is correct.
2. Back in the early 1900s, Sears Roebuck sold houses through the mail. The houses *were* listed along with the rest of the products in Sears' famous catalog. The house kits arrived in thousands of pieces, and people *would* put them

together themselves. Or they *got* a builder to help them. In 1919, one company, Standard Oil, *placed* an order for an entire town's worth of houses as shelter for their employees. The house kits even included the paint that the homeowners *used* to paint the houses when they *were* finished. The ability to order a whole house from the Sears catalog ended in 1940, but thousands of them are still being lived in by people across America.

3. The last time I took my car in for a scheduled service, I noticed a few problems when I *picked* it up. I *checked* the oil dipstick, and it *had* really dark oil still on it. Also, there was a screwdriver balancing on my air-filter cover. I *couldn't* believe it when I *saw* it, but as soon as I showed the tool to the service manager, he *called* the mechanic over to take my car back to the service area. After another hour, my car *was* ready, the dipstick *had* clean oil on it, and the service manager cleared the bill so that I didn't have to pay anything.

RECOGNIZING VERBAL PHRASES (PP. 126–130)

Exercise 1

1. Philippe Halsman was a well-[known] portrait photographer [working in the twentieth century].
2. Halsman's photographs were good enough [to appear on the cover of *Life* magazine 101 times].
3. [Capturing the essence of famous people on film] was Halsman's specialty.
4. The list of celebrities that Halsman was asked [to photograph] included Marilyn Monroe, Albert Einstein, and Winston Churchill.
5. Halsman found that [taking good pictures of such powerful people was not easy].
6. He often tried [to find new ways] [to loosen them up].
7. In 1952, Halsman asked one of his elite clients [to jump in the air] while [being photographed].
8. Halsman loved the results, and he started a series of [jumping] pictures.
9. Who doesn't like [to see famous people like Richard Nixon] [jumping up like a little boy] in a photograph?
10. Halsman gathered the best of the [jumping] photographs in a book [called *Philippe Halsman's Jump Book*].

Exercise 2

1. [To paraphrase Mark Twain], [golfing] is just a way [to ruin a good walk].
2. In fact, [becoming a golfer] can be dangerous.

3. Golf professionals commonly suffer a couple of injuries per year [resulting from long hours] of [practicing their swings].
4. Amateur golfers tend [to injure themselves] much more often.
5. Most injuries come from the [twisting], [squatting], and [bending] [involved in [golfing]].
6. And [moving the heavy bags of clubs] from cars to carts can wrench the backs of potential golfers before they even begin [to play].
7. Of course, there are the unfortunate incidents of people on golf courses [being struck by lightning].
8. But some of the sources of golfers' ailments may be [surprising].
9. [Cleaning the dirt and debris off the golf balls] by [licking them], for instance, may have serious repercussions.
10. After [swallowing the chemicals] [sprayed on the turf] of the golf course, players can develop liver problems.

Exercise 3

1. I like [to listen to music at home].
2. [Playing my favorite songs out loud through my speakers] is my main way [to relax].
3. I have tried [using headphones], but they hurt my ears.
4. I also don't like [to feel disconnected from everyone else].
5. [Filling my house with well-chosen tunes] allows me [to maintain my identity].
6. We all use choices of music, fashion, and art [to define ourselves].
7. Some people wear T-shirts [showing pictures or slogans that they like].
8. I want everyone [to hear the music that I like].
9. My neighbors have not complained about my habit of [listening to music] without [using headphones].
10. I try [to be considerate of them] and turn the volume down at 10:00 every night.

Exercise 4

1. Why do [plumbing] emergencies always happen on the weekends?
2. Toilets, sinks, and tubs seem [to know when plumbers' rates go up].
3. Some emergencies—a slow-[draining] sink, for instance—can be tolerated for a couple of days.

4. And a [dripping] shower faucet may cause annoyance, but not panic.
5. However, a [backed]-up sewer pipe definitely can't wait until Monday.
6. No one wants [to see that water [rising] and [overflowing] the rim of the bowl].
7. At that point, the only question is which "rooter" service [to call].
8. [Finding the main drainage line] often takes more time than [clearing it].
9. Once the plumber has finished [fixing the problem], he or she usually eyes future potential disasters and offers [to prevent them with even more work].
10. After [getting the final bill], I hope that my children will grow up [to be not doctors but plumbers].

Exercise 5

1. In the past, the library was the perfect place [to study] or [to do research or homework].
2. But lately it has become a place [to meet friends].
3. Things changed when students began [to access the Internet].
4. Now two or three students gather near each terminal and show each other the best sites [to visit on the Web].
5. Library officials have designated certain rooms as ["talking areas"].
6. However, such territories are hard [to enforce].
7. The old image of the librarian [telling everyone [to be quiet]] is just that—an old image.
8. So people talk to each other and giggle right there in the [reading] room.
9. One of the librarians told me about a plan [to take the Internet-access computers out of the main study room] and [to put them into the "[talking] areas"].
10. I hate [to read in a noisy room], so I hope that he was right.

Paragraph Exercise

Christo and Jeanne-Claude (1935-, 1935-)

It started as an obsession with [wrapping]. The Bulgarian-[born] artist Christo spent years [swaddling bicycles, trees, storefronts, and women friends] before [moving on] [to wrap a section of the Roman Wall, part of the Australian coastline, and eventually all twelve arches, plus the parapets, sidewalks, streetlamps, vertical embankment, and esplanade, of Paris' Pont Neuf]. And yes, together they did wrap the Reichstag. But Christo and his wife/manager/collaborator Jeanne-Claude are quick [to insist] that [wrappings] form only a small percentage of their total oeuvre. There were, for instance, those twenty-four and a half miles of white nylon, eighteen feet high, they hung from a steel cable north of San Francisco; the eleven islands in Biscayne Bay, Florida, they "surrounded"—not wrapped, mind you—with pink polypropylene fabric; and the 3,100 enormous blue and yellow "umbrellas" they erected in two [corresponding] valleys in California and Japan. Not [to mention] their 2005 blockbuster, "The Gates," 7,503 sixteen-foot-tall saffron panels they suspended, to the delight of almost everybody, over twenty-three miles of footpaths in New York's Central Park.

So, what's their point? Rest assured, you're not the first [to ask]. And no one is more eager [to tell you] than the artist formerly [known] as Christo (now, officially, "Christo and Jeanne-Claude") whose art is nothing if not Open to the Public. In fact, [taking art public]—that is, [taking it away from the Uptown Museum Gallery Complex] by [making it too big] [to fit in studios, museums, or galleries]—was part of the original idea. Christo and Jeanne-Claude will tell you that their point is, literally, [to rock your world.] By temporarily [disrupting one part of an environment], they hope [to get you] [to "perceive the whole environment with new eyes and a new consciousness."]

Sentence Writing

Your sentences may vary, but make sure that your verbals are not actually the main verbs of your clauses. You should be able to double underline your real verbs, as we have done here.

1. [Thinking of a good title] takes time.
2. We spent the morning [folding laundry].
3. I enjoy [skiing in spring] even though the snow is better in winter.
4. I was taught that [marking up a book] is wrong.

5. I would love [to take you to school].

6. I need [to get a good grade on the next quiz].

7. Yesterday, I started [to paste my old photos in a scrapbook].

8. He doesn't have the desire [to exercise regularly].

9. The school canceled the [planned] parking lot next to the library.

10. [Given the opportunity], my dog will escape from our yard.

CORRECTING MISPLACED OR DANGLING MODIFIERS (PP. 131–134)

Answers may vary. Corrections are in *italics.*

EXERCISE 1

1. People like to receive flowers, *even when given by friends.*
2. *Walking down the street,* she noticed a twenty-dollar bill.
3. The sentence is correct.
4. *Leaning against the chalkboard,* the teacher read a poem about an autumn day.
5. *Because I was playing poker online all night,* my homework never got done.
6. *Jan prefers butter and marmalade on her toast.*
7. *After we made it to the airport on time,* our plane departed early.
8. The sentence is correct.
9. I had the best hot dog at the stadium last night; *it was loaded with onions.*
10. The sentence is correct.

EXERCISE 2

1. Everyone enjoys eating corndogs *smeared with mustard or ketchup.*
2. *Before we asked for an extension,* the teacher told us that we had a few extra days to finish our papers.
3. *Looking through their binoculars,* they spotted a hawk and its babies.
4. The sentence is correct.
5. I called the doctor *while I was on the roof.*
6. The sentence is correct.
7. *After it screeched to a stop,* I got on the bus and took my seat among the rest of the passengers.

8. I can't eat a hamburger *without pickles.*

9. The sentence is correct.

10. We had to write a paragraph *in our notebooks, and the topic was the weather.*

EXERCISE 3

1. The kids at the party still enjoyed the cake *even though it was baked in an odd-shaped pan.*

2. The sentence is correct.

3. I looked at the baked potato, *loaded with butter and sour cream,* and wondered how I would eat it because I am allergic to dairy products.

4. The sentence is correct.

5. *Unless someone has natural talent,* the violin is almost impossible to learn.

6. *As I was riding on a bus into town,* the sunshine felt warm on my arm.

7. The sentence is correct.

8. I have given up on that comedian *who tells one bad joke after another.*

9. The sentence is correct.

10. I loved *my friends' presents tied with pretty bows.*

EXERCISE 4

1. The sentence is correct.

2. Filled with the perfect amount of air, *the new tires made my car handle really well on the road.*

3. After three weeks of waiting, *I received the textbooks that I bought online. I got them* just in time for the semester to begin.

4. He cooked all of his meals *while he was wearing* his slippers.

5. The sentence is correct.

6. *As we drove past the park,* a ball bounced into the street between two parked cars.

7. *I didn't even want the tiny pieces of that torn quiz paper near me.*

8. The sentence is correct.

9. The sentence is correct.

10. We saw tons of ants walking in the cracks of the sidewalk.

Exercise 5

1. *Because I felt the thrill of a day at the amusement park,* my blisters didn't bother me.
2. My friends and I saw the new tearjerker, *which is full of touching scenes.*
3. The sentence is correct.
4. Practicing for an hour a day, *she improved her piano playing.*
5. The sentence is correct.
6. *While she was sitting on a bench all day,* an idea came to her.
7. They discovered a new outlet mall *on the road to their cousins' house.*
8. *From his parents,* he felt the pressure of trying to get a good job.
9. The sentence is correct.
10. The sentence is correct.

Proofreading Exercise

Corrections are *italicized.* Yours may differ slightly.

As I walked into my neighborhood polling place during the last election, a volunteer greeted me and checked my name and address. *Because it was misspelled slightly on their printout, the volunteer couldn't find my name* at first. I pointed to what I thought was my name. At least upside down, *it looked like mine.* But actually, it was another person's name. *Once the printout was turned toward me,* I could see *it* more clearly. My name was there, but it had an extra letter stuck on the end of it. *With a polite smile,* the volunteer handed me a change-of-name form. I filled it out and punched my ballot. Stuck on my wall at home, *my voting receipt reminds me* to check my name carefully when the next election comes around.

FOLLOWING SENTENCE PATTERNS (PP. 137–141)

Exercise 1

1. Erasto Mpemba (S) is (LV) a big name (Desc) (in science).
2. (In the early 1960s), he (S) observed (AV) an odd phenomenon (Obj).
3. (At the time), he (S) was (LV) a high school student (Desc) (in Tanzania).
4. Mpemba (S) made (AV) ice cream (Obj) (for a school project).

S AV Obj AV Obj
5. He boiled the milk and mixed it (with the other ingredients).

S AV Obj
6. Then he put the hot—not cold—mixture directly (into the freezer).

S AV
7. The hot mixture froze faster.

S AV Obj Obj
8. Mpemba told his teachers and fellow students (about his discovery).

S AV
9. They laughed (at the idea).

S AV Obj
10. Now all scientists call this phenomenon the "Mpemba effect."

Exercise 2

S AV Obj
1. (In late September), the Stade de France (in Paris) hosted an unusual spectacle.

S AV Obj
2. Hundreds (of actors, stunt people, and extras) reenacted the famous chariot race (from the classic film *Ben-Hur*).

S AV Obj Obj
3. The same show included live gladiator fights and a galley ship assault.

S AV Obj
4. Promoters also encouraged participation (from the audience).

S AV
5. Many (of the 60,000 audience members) attended (in traditional Roman costumes).

S AV Obj
6. The stadium sold toga-like robes (in advance) (along with the tickets).

S LV Desc
7. Obviously, the live chariot race was the highlight (of the show).

S AV
8. Participants (in the dangerous race) rehearsed (for nine months).

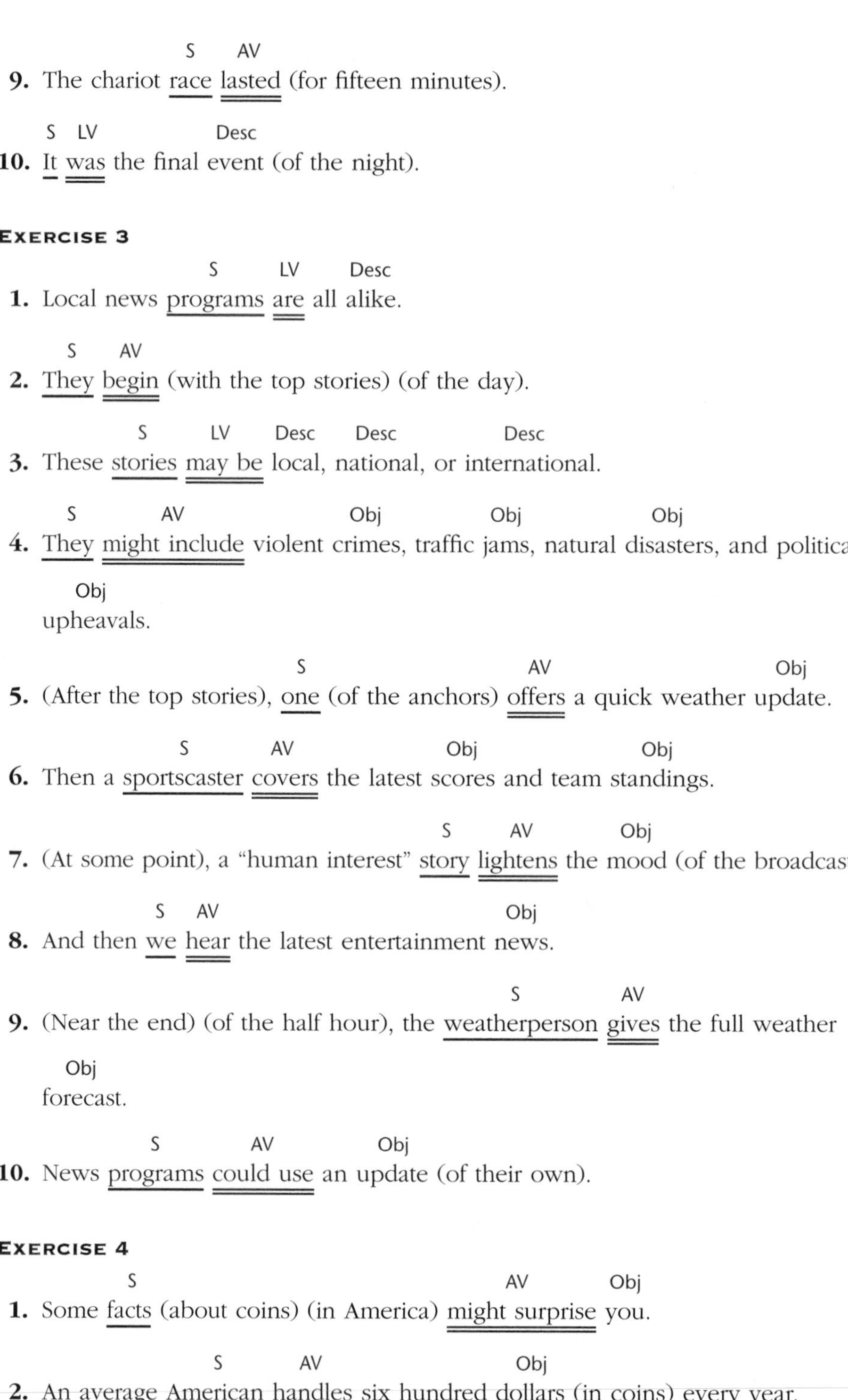

S AV
9. The chariot race lasted (for fifteen minutes).

S LV Desc
10. It was the final event (of the night).

Exercise 3

S LV Desc
1. Local news programs are all alike.

S AV
2. They begin (with the top stories) (of the day).

S LV Desc Desc Desc
3. These stories may be local, national, or international.

S AV Obj Obj Obj Obj
4. They might include violent crimes, traffic jams, natural disasters, and political upheavals.

S AV Obj
5. (After the top stories), one (of the anchors) offers a quick weather update.

S AV Obj Obj
6. Then a sportscaster covers the latest scores and team standings.

S AV Obj
7. (At some point), a "human interest" story lightens the mood (of the broadcast).

S AV Obj
8. And then we hear the latest entertainment news.

S AV Obj
9. (Near the end) (of the half hour), the weatherperson gives the full weather forecast.

S AV Obj
10. News programs could use an update (of their own).

Exercise 4

S AV Obj
1. Some facts (about coins) (in America) might surprise you.

S AV Obj
2. An average American handles six hundred dollars (in coins) every year.

S AV Obj
3. Most Americans keep small stashes (of pennies, nickels, dimes, quarters, half-dollars, and dollar coins) (at home).

S LV Desc
4. The total (of these unused coins) may be ten billion dollars (at any one time).

S AV Obj
5. Researchers have asked people (about their coin use).

S AV Obj
6. Some people use coins (in place) (of small tools).

S AV Obj
7. Others perform magic (with them).

S LV Desc
8. Younger people are more careless (with their coins).

S AV Obj
9. They might toss a penny (in the trash).

S AV Obj
10. Older Americans would save the penny instead.

Exercise 5

S LV Desc Desc Desc Desc
1. Charles Osgood is a writer, editor, TV host, and radio personality.

S AV Obj
2. He has edited a book (about letters).

S LV Desc
3. The book's title is *Funny Letters (from Famous People).*

S AV Obj
4. (In his book), Osgood shares hilarious letters (from history).

S AV
5. Thomas Jefferson wrote (to an acquaintance) (about rodents) [eating his wallet].

S AV Obj
6. Benjamin Franklin penned the perfect recommendation letter.

S AV Obj
7. Franklin did not know the recommended fellow (at all).

S AV Obj
8. Beethoven cursed his friend bitterly (in a letter) one day.

S AV Obj
9. (In a letter) the following day, Beethoven praised the same friend excessively
AV Obj
and asked him (for a visit).

S AV Obj AV Obj
10. Osgood ends the book (with a letter) (by Julia Child) and includes her secrets
(for a long life).

Paragraph Exercise

S LV Desc S
The history (of masks) is one (of [surprising] interest). Nearly every race,
AV
(from the most primitive times) (to periods) (of [advanced] civilization), has found
Obj S AV
some use (for the mask). Perhaps the [painted] face (of a primitive warrior) inspired
Obj S AV Obj
the first mask. (At any rate), many (of the early tribal masks) suggest the abode
(of a fiendish and [warring] spirit). (In tribal and religious ceremonies), (in the
S AV Obj
dance), (in the drama), (in peace and war), the mask has played a unique part.

S LV Desc S
One unusual use (of the mask) was peculiar (to Rome). All families (of
AV Obj S
prominence) preserved waxen masks (of their [distinguished] ancestors). These
LV Desc Desc S AV
were not death masks, but portraits (from life). Many families possessed large
Obj AV
collections and looked (upon them) (with great pride). (On the occasion) (of a
S AV Obj
death) (in the family), they brought forth these masks. (During the elaborate
S AV Obj
funeral ceremonies), certain men impersonated the long line (of [distinguished]
ancestors) (by [wearing these lifelike masks]).

AVOIDING CLICHÉS, AWKWARD PHRASING, AND WORDINESS (PP. 145–146)

Your answers may differ from these possible revisions.

1. Shoppers in today's supermarkets want organic foods. They get excited whenever they see an organic label on a package. I work at a busy supermarket, and I see people with and without a lot of money buying foods grown without pesticides and hormones. People have started to care more about their own and their children's eating habits. Organic eggs do taste good, and it feels good to know that the eggs come from happy, free-ranging chickens. Of course, some people will always care the most about price and won't buy organic foods if they cost more.

2. I just saw a news story about an animal that looks like a mixture of a teddy bear, a little monkey, and a miniature dog. His name is Mr. Winkle, and he has his own celebrity Web site, "mrwinkle.com." His home page flashes questions about Mr. Winkle's identity across the screen while it's loading. Is it an "alien?" a "stuffed animal?" a "hamster with a permanent?" Mr. Winkle is definitely cute. I can see why his owner stopped her car when she saw the strange-looking beast walking along the road and took him home. Since she found Mr. Winkle, she has taken pictures of him posing in quirky little costumes and even running in a hamster wheel. Of course, the Web site sells posters and calendars of Mr. Winkle at reasonable prices.

3. I have a friend who used to be a struggling actor, but now she has become a professional house sitter. First, she joined an organization that advertises house-sitting opportunities. My friend's first house-sitting job was in Malibu. Unbelievably, she was paid to live in a house on the beach, eat free food, and watch free movies. All she had to do was stay at the house and feed the owners' indoor cat. Now my friend is house sitting in Sedona for friends of the owners of the Malibu house. I am thinking seriously of becoming a house sitter myself.

CORRECTING FOR PARALLEL STRUCTURE (PP. 148–152)

Your revisions may vary.

EXERCISE 1

1. Taking a basic grammar class last semester was fun but challenging.
2. I was ready to learn about parts of speech, verb tenses, and dependent clauses.
3. The teacher showed us how to identify subjects and label verbs.
4. We learned the differences between and the uses for adjectives and adverbs.
5. An adjective always adds information to a noun or a pronoun.

6. Adverbs can modify verbs, adjectives, or other adverbs.
7. I know that I learned a lot about grammar but need to practice it in my writing.
8. Before I registered for the grammar class, I had to decide whether to take a full load or to work part time and take only one or two classes.
9. I decided to work at my family's restaurant part time and focus on the grammar class.
10. I waited on tables in the morning, went to class in the afternoon, and studied at night.

EXERCISE 2

1. The Internet is full of information about new gadgets and technology.
2. People want to have the coolest phones, the clearest photos, and the best travel accessories.
3. The sentence is correct.
4. The ring doesn't use technology to help people do something more easily or live more comfortably.
5. Instead, it helps people avoid doing something—forgetting their anniversary.
6. The "Remember Ring" is designed for people who love gadgets but tend to forget special occasions.
7. It includes several hi-tech features: a perpetually charging battery, a clock run by a microchip, and a tiny heating element.
8. The built-in heating element activates at a preprogrammed time and reminds the wearer about an upcoming anniversary.
9. The sentence is correct.
10. The Remember Ring comes in seven styles in both white and yellow gold.

EXERCISE 3

1. The sentence is correct.
2. It has a plush lounge that offers free coffee, cookies, and even pretzels for those who don't like sweets.
3. The sentence is correct.
4. Full plate-glass windows line the front wall of the lounge so that people can see their vehicles being dried and check out the cars of the people around them.
5. For those who don't like to sit down, a full assortment of greeting cards and car accessories lines the back wall of the lounge.

6. To keep things interesting, every hour there is a drawing for a free car wash, but I have never won one.
7. The sentence is correct.
8. Why do people talk on cell phones when they could be resting, and why do some people stand up when they could be sitting on a nice leather sofa?
9. The sentence is correct.
10. It's the modern equivalent of going to the barbershop or getting a new hairdo at the beauty parlor.

EXERCISE 4

1. To begin, decide which person or family you want to focus on.
2. Make a blank chart that includes spaces for all of a person's important information.
3. Then visit a relative who knows a lot of family history and hopefully saves papers and mementos.
4. Plan to spend a lot of time with any such valuable resource.
5. Gather information from and about one individual at a time.
6. Ask about every part of the person's life—marital status, children, religion, occupation, and travel.
7. Thank your resources for providing you with valuable information.
8. Visit the attics or the dusty old cupboards of anyone who has documents relating to your family.
9. Don't forget the local records office in the town where a relative grew up.
10. Purchase books that provide preprinted worksheets and family tree templates to make your family tree come together faster.

EXERCISE 5

1. The U.S. Surgeon General makes the following recommendations for living a healthy and happy life.
2. Try to eat the right amounts of fruits and vegetables, and don't forget to eat meat and dairy products (or their vegetarian equivalents).
3. Be sure to see a doctor regularly and get all the usual tests and check-ups.
4. Learn about any illnesses or health conditions that run in your family.
5. Get enough rest and sleep each night.
6. Keep in touch with your friends and family members.
7. Prevent avoidable injuries by wearing seatbelts and helmets.

8. Limit alcohol and over-the-counter drugs.

9. Try not to smoke or to breathe in second-hand smoke if you can avoid it.

10. The Surgeon General's recommendations and warnings make very good sense.

Proofreading Exercise

Every year in late spring, a long caravan of vehicles arrives at the park in my neighborhood. The caravan consists of a combination of trucks, campers, vans, and trailers full of folded-up kiddy rides. Everyone who lives by or drives by the park can tell that the fair has come to town. It isn't a big fair, but a small, child-friendly one. Most people remember these fairs from when they were growing up. In childhood, the rides seemed huge and scary; in adulthood, they seem small and almost silly. As the fair is being set up in the park for a few days, the kids in the neighborhood look forward to getting on one of those "wild" rides. Their parents look forward to eating the "fair food": the sweet popcorn, the salty popcorn, the mouth-watering corndogs, the deep-fried candy bars, and the juicy snow cones. I can't wait until next year's fair; I'm getting hungry just thinking about it.

USING PRONOUNS (PP. 157–160)

Exercise 1

1. I
2. I
3. he and I
4. I
5. he and I, me
6. I
7. I, I
8. you and me
9. him and me
10. me

Exercise 2

1. *Good parents* give *their* children advice.
2. their
3. it's
4. *Children* often *look* to *their* parents for guidance in difficult times.
5. For instance, a child might have encountered a bully *in elementary school.*
6. The other schoolchildren might tell the child to keep *quiet* about it.
7. A parent would probably offer *the* child very different advice—to speak to the principal about the problem right away.
8. *Bullies* can only get away with *their* activities if everyone else is too scared or too uninformed to stop *them.*

9. their
10. their, themselves

Exercise 3

1. she
2. me
3. You and I
4. she
5. *All* of the participants in the marathon used their own training methods.
6. their
7. he
8. Each of the art students has *a* locker in the hallway.
9. *The neighborhood softball teams* will continue their tournament tomorrow.
10. Each citizen of a democratic country has *a* favorite candidate and can influence the election with *a* vote.

Exercise 4

1. The sentence is correct.
2. I finished my essay and printed it.
3. Angela told Karen, "There's a cup of coffee on top of your car."
4. Hiking over several hills made us all tired and hungry.
5. Hank got permission to drive his father's car to the bank.
6. When she placed her card in the ATM, the card disappeared.
7. Ted told my brother not to go on the field trip.
8. As we were talking on the phone, the lamp fell.
9. The teacher's suggestions help us improve our drawings.
10. Carla asked her new boss, "Why can't I work on weekends?"

Exercise 5

1. I put the finishing touches on my painting, placed my brushes in hot water, and moved my painting to the drying rack.
2. People feel more involved when they join in community activities.
3. My car made a funny noise after I filled it with gas.
4. Rainbows always make me think of my trip to Hawaii.

5. Members of the orchestra invited the music students to sit in the orchestra's seats.
6. The doctor told Steve to put ice on his head.
7. The sentence is correct.
8. As the day got hotter and hotter, the frosting slid off the cake.
9. Some students are enjoying the new computer program, but it is too simple for others.
10. The sentence is correct.

PROOFREADING EXERCISE

Corrections are *italicized.*

Rude drivers have one thing in common: they think that they know how to drive better than anybody else. The other day, as my friends and *I* were driving to school, we stopped at an intersection. A very old man who used a cane to help him walk started across *the intersection* in front of my friends and *me* just before the light was ready to change. So we waited. But while we waited for him, a male driver behind us started to honk his horn since he couldn't see *the old man.* I wondered, "Does *this driver* want us to hit *that man,* or what?" Finally, *the intersection* was clear. *The rude driver* pulled his car up beside ours, opened his window, and yelled at us before *his car* sped away. The old man reached the other side safely, but the *rude driver* hardly noticed.

AVOIDING SHIFTS IN PERSON (PP. 162–163)

PROOFREADING EXERCISE

1. Everyone has seen those game machines that are filled with stuffed animals and *include* a crane-like device to grab hold of one and win. Kids and adults love to play these games, *but a lot of children like them so much that they try to crawl up into them.* Some children are successful. A recent article in the *Chippewa Herald* tells of one seven-year-old boy who made it up into the machine. The boy's father turned his back, and *before he knew it,* his son was sitting inside the game with all the stuffed animals around him. It took firefighters over an hour to rescue the little boy. *The article didn't say whether* he got to take home the stuffed animal that he wanted.

2. I was reading about superstitions for my psychology class, and I learned that a lot of these beliefs concern brooms and sweeping. One superstition says that, whenever *people* change *their* residence, *they* should get a new broom. People should not take their old brooms with them because the brooms might carry any bad luck that was swept up at the old place and bring it to the new one. Also, if *people* sweep dirt out an open door, *they should* make it the back door so that the bad luck will depart forever. If *they* sweep dirt out the front way,

the same bad luck will come right back in again. Finally, *people should* never walk across a fallen broomstick unless *they* never want to get married, for that is the fate for anyone who steps over a broomstick. I bet most people would be surprised by how many things can go wrong when *they* pick up a broom.

3. The paragraph is correct.

REVIEW OF SENTENCE STRUCTURE ERRORS (PP. 164–166)

1. B. s-v agr (The display of textbooks *doesn't* make it easy to find the ones I need.)

2. A. pro (The first person to give a speech was *she.*)

3. A. frag (The total, including food and drinks, *added* up to six hundred dollars.)

4. B. mm (The students could barely hear their professor, *who was speaking very softly.*)

5. B. s-v agr (Either she or I *is* going to receive that scholarship.)

6. A. ro (Meg had a great idea for an ad campaign, so she wrote to the company.)

7. B. shift in person (True friends are not afraid *to tell the truth.*)

8. B. wordy (*We couldn't believe that so many students use the quiet-study area.*)

9. A. mm (When my sister was six, my parents gave her a little violin.)

10. B. frag (*I don't think that it's true.*)

11. A. // (Students were confused by the new room numbers but still *tried* to get to class on time.)

12. B. frag (*I thought that they would be good seats,* but they were too close.)

13. A. ro (Some people like analog clocks and watches; others prefer digital.)

14. B. pro (However, I have better pronunciation than *he [does].*)

15. A. wordy (I received a *gift* when I signed up for my checking account.)

PROOFREADING EXERCISE

Your revisions may differ, but here is one possibility:

Getting Involved

Getting involved in other people's business can be both right and wrong, depending on people's relationships and situations. For example, if one friend is in a bad relationship and the other is concerned, it may be time for the concerned friend to get involved. Stepping in not only shows real friendship but might also lead to solutions.

On the other hand, some people just like to be nosey, and they get involved in other people's business for fun. Such people need to know the details of others' lives to make their own lives more interesting. I have been in situations where peers have tried to learn about my life and problems. All of their discoveries turned into rumors.

Since I have learned from others' mistakes, I would never get involved in other people's business if it could not benefit them in some way. People should better their own lives rather than worry about anyone else's.

PUNCTUATION AND CAPITAL LETTERS

PERIOD, QUESTION MARK, EXCLAMATION POINT, SEMICOLON, COLON, DASH (PP. 168–173)

EXERCISE 1

1. Have you ever had "one of those days?"
2. You wake up feeling great; then you notice that your alarm didn't go off.
3. You take the following steps to avoid being late to your first class: skip your shower, throw on the first clothes you see, and walk out the door without coffee or breakfast.
4. You open your car door, sit in the driver's seat, and turn the key; then you discover that your car battery is dead! (or .)
5. You go back inside the house and call your friend Tracy; she has a reliable car.
6. Tracy's roommate—the one who doesn't like you—answers the phone out of a sound sleep.
7. The roommate mumbles angrily, "She's already gone to school." (or !")
8. You try Tracy's cell phone number; you get her voice mail, as usual.
9. All of your efforts to save the day have failed; there is only one option left.
10. You make yourself breakfast; you sit in front of the television, and you resign yourself to a day on the couch.

EXERCISE 2

1. What have spiders done for you lately?
2. In the near future, a spider may save your life. (or !)
3. Researchers in New York have discovered the healing power of one species in particular: the Chilean Rose tarantula.
4. This spider's venom includes a substance that could stop a human's heart attack once it begins.

5. The substance has the ability to restore the rhythm of a heart that has stopped beating.
6. A scientist in Connecticut is experimenting with the killing power of another arachnid; the creature he is studying is the Australian funnel-web spider.
7. Currently, pesticides that destroy insects on crops also end up killing animals accidentally.
8. The funnel-web spider's venom is lethal to unwanted insects; however, it's harmless to animals.
9. Scientists would have to reproduce the funnel-web spider's venom artificially in order to have enough to use in fields.
10. As a result of these studies into the power of spider venom, you may live longer and enjoy pesticide-free foods.

EXERCISE 3

1. Chang and Eng were a famous pair of conjoined twins; they lived in the 1800s.
2. They were known as the "Siamese twins" because they were born in Siam; Siam is now called Thailand.
3. Chang and Eng traveled the world—as celebrities of sorts—and eventually made enough money to settle down.
4. The sentence is correct.
5. The twins enjoyed the same pastimes: smoking cigars, reading books, and buying clothes.
6. Eng was known for the following: having a calm disposition and playing endless games of poker.
7. Chang—unlike his brother—could lose his temper easily.
8. Chang and Eng married two sisters from the same family: Adelaide and Sarah.
9. The two couples lived together at first; then the twins divided their time between two houses one for each of their growing families.
10. The famous twins had a total of 21 children; their descendents are still a rich part of the Mount Airy community in North Carolina.

EXERCISE 4

1. The sentence is correct.
2. The sentence is correct.
3. One relatively safe place is inside a building that has plumbing pipes or electrical wires; those channels can absorb the electrical energy unleashed by lightning.

4. Of course, once inside such a building, people should stay away from the end sources of plumbing and wiring: faucets, hoses, phone receivers, and computer terminals.
5. Buildings without pipes or wires are not safe shelters during lightning strikes; these might include pergolas, dugouts, and tents.
6. Outside, lightning can move over the ground; therefore, you should be aware of a position that emergency officials call the "lightning squat."
7. The sentence is correct.
8. The sentence is correct.
9. Lightning is electrical energy; consequently, it can travel far from the actual storm clouds.
10. The sentence is correct.

Exercise 5

1. "Am I going to get old like Grandpa?"
2. This question is typical of the ones children ask their parents about aging; luckily, there are books that help parents answer them.
3. Lynne S. Dumas wrote the book *Talking with Your Children about a Troubled World;* in it, she discusses children's concerns and suggests ways of dealing with them.
4. In response to the question about getting old "like Grandpa," Dumas stresses one main point: be positive. (or—be positive.)
5. Too often, Dumas says, parents pass their own fears on to children; parents who focus on the negative aspects of aging will probably have children who worry about growing old.
6. Other subjects—homelessness, for instance—require special consideration for parents.
7. Dumas explains that children carefully observe how parents deal with a person asking for spare change or offering to wash windshields for money.
8. The unplanned nature of these encounters often catches parents off guard; therefore, they should try to prepare a uniform response to such situations.
9. Dumas also suggests that parents take positive action—involving children in charitable donations and activities, for example—in order to illustrate their compassion for the homeless.
10. The most important aspect in communicating with children is honesty; the second and third most important are patience and understanding.

PROOFREADING EXERCISE

The ingredients you will need to make quick, delicious spaghetti sauce include onions, garlic, mushrooms, and canned tomato sauce; meat is optional. First, at the bottom of a big heavy pot on high heat, you should sauté the onions, garlic, and mushrooms in olive oil; then put the vegetables aside and brown the meat, if any. Once the meat has browned nicely, it's time to add the tomato sauce and seasonings. You can use oregano and basil or just salt and pepper. Actually, you can use any blend of spices to suit your taste. Try adding a teaspoon or even a tablespoon of sugar to keep the sauce from being bitter. Next, return the sautéed vegetables to the pot. Cook the sauce mixture over medium heat until it begins to boil. Finally, lower the temperature and simmer the sauce until it achieves the perfect consistency: thick and glossy. Serve the sauce on top of any kind of cooked pasta.

COMMA RULES 1, 2, AND 3 (PP. 175–180)

EXERCISE 1

1. The sentence is correct.
2. We think of funny ways to respond to the "Why did the chicken cross the road?" question, and we endlessly ponder the answer to "Which came first—the chicken or the egg?"
3. The sentence is correct.
4. We try not to visualize the image of the last comparison, but most people understand the reference to a fowl's final moments of frantic activity.
5. Anyone who has heard the story of Mike "the headless chicken" will consider the popular saying differently from that moment on, for it will come to mean having a strong determination to live in spite of major setbacks.
6. The sentence is correct.
7. But after having his head cut off, the rooster didn't die or seem to be in pain, and it continued to act "normally."
8. The sentence is correct.
9. Both *Time* and *Life* magazines ran feature stories complete with photos of Mike in October 1945, and the public became fascinated by the details of Mike's ability to eat, drink, hear, and move without a head.
10. Mike lived for eighteen months after his date with a chopping block and would have lived longer, but he died by accidentally choking in 1947.

EXERCISE 2

1. Whenever I need to borrow some blueberries, an onion, or a teaspoon of ginger, I go next door to my neighbor's apartment.
2. The sentence is correct.

3. Albert always has the season's best fruits, the tastiest vegetables, and the freshest spices.
4. The sentence is correct.
5. He doesn't ask for blueberries, onions, or ginger, but he will ask to borrow a hammer, a wrench, or a Phillips-head screwdriver.
6. The sentence is correct.
7. If I buy myself a new dustpan, broom, or rake, I buy an extra one for Albert.
8. When he visits the farmer's market on Thursdays, Albert picks up an extra basket of strawberries for me.
9. The sentence is correct.
10. The sentence is correct.

Exercise 3

1. As if people didn't have enough to worry about, Melinda Muse has written a book called *I'm Afraid, You're Afraid: 448 Things to Fear and Why.*
2. In her book, Muse points out the dangers of common places, objects, foods, months, days, and activities.
3. If people plan a trip to Vegas, they should worry because paramedics can't get to ailing gamblers, due to the crowds and huge size of the buildings.
4. For another dangerous spot, consider the beauty parlor, where people suffer strokes caused by leaning their heads back too far into the shampoo sink.
5. If new clothes are not washed before they are worn, they may transfer dangerous chemicals to the wearers' eyes, skin, and lungs.
6. Among foods to be avoided, grapefruit juice can interfere with certain medications' effectiveness, and nutmeg contains hallucinogenic substances.
7. Of all the months, July ranks highest in certain kinds of accidental injuries and poisonings, due to Independence Day celebrations and other summer activities.
8. Being linked with more suicides and heart attacks than any other, Mondays are the most dangerous days of the week.
9. The sentence is correct.
10. After reading *I'm Afraid, You're Afraid,* it's possible to be afraid of almost everything.

Exercise 4

1. Speaking of worst-case scenarios, there is a book about how to survive them, and it's called *The Worst-Case Scenario Survival Handbook.*
2. The coauthors of this self-help book are aware that most of us will never have to overpower an alligator or make an emergency landing on an airplane, yet they want us to be prepared nonetheless.
3. In the "About the Authors" section of the book, readers learn that Joshua Piven is a first-time writer, but he has survived encounters with robbers, muggers, and stalled subway trains.
4. About Piven's coauthor, we discover that David Borgenicht has written two other books and has had his share of worst-case scenarios, especially while traveling.
5. Although the overall tone of the book is somewhat humorous because it covers such outlandish topics, the information it shares is deadly serious and could save a life.
6. The sentence is correct.
7. One of the best examples illustrates a way to avoid being attacked by a mountain lion, and that is to try to appear as large as possible, so the drawing shows a man holding the sides of his jacket out wide like bat wings to scare the lion away.
8. If readers wonder whether they can trust the advice on escaping from quicksand, they can just flip to the list of sources consulted for each section, in this case an expert on the physics of natural phenomena at the University of Sydney, Australia.
9. Wisely, Piven and Borgenicht begin the book by warning readers to seek professional help whenever possible instead of trying the survival techniques themselves.
10. The authors know that if people go looking for trouble, they'll probably find it.

Exercise 5

1. Fish may be considered "brain food," but I've never liked it.
2. While everyone is saying how delicious a big salmon steak is or how yummy the shrimp tastes, you'll find me grimacing and munching on a piece of bread and butter.
3. Part of the problem with fish is the smell, but my friends who love to eat fish also love the smell of fish cooking.
4. I always thought that was strange, but it makes sense, doesn't it?

5. If someone hates the taste of onions, that person probably also hates the smell of onions cooking.

6. Come to think of it, my husband hates to eat sweets and doesn't like the smell of them either.

7. When we walk into a bakery together, he practically has to hold his nose the way I would in a fish market.

8. To me, that's odd, but my aversion must be just as odd to someone who loves fish.

9. Our daughter loves the taste of bacon, but she hates the smell of bacon frying.

10. The sentence is correct.

Proofreading Exercise

Use a person's title and last name until you are invited to use first names, which will invariably be immediately. This is not a sign of intimacy; Americans feel that the use of last names is so formal that it is uncomfortable to address others in this manner. You will find that Americans almost always introduce themselves or others using first names, even in business. If you are introduced to someone by his or her first name, then it is perfectly acceptable to use the first name.

Punctuality is important in business. Always phone ahead if you are going to be more than 10 minutes late. Likewise, punctuality is valued for prestigious social engagements. However, punctuality is considerably more flexible for casual gatherings among friends; being a few minutes late is the norm, and it's not unheard of for people to trickle into a casual party among friends anywhere from 15 minutes to an hour after the designated starting time of the party.

Americans are generally very gregarious and welcoming. Frequent smiling is a cultural norm, an important social custom that should not be misinterpreted as superficiality. Maintain a personal distance of at least one arm's length.

Conversation can be animated, quite loud, and refreshingly direct. Although in some situations political correctness obliges people to choose their words carefully so they won't offend anyone, in others you will meet some of the most straightforward people in the world. The freedom to express one's opinions is highly prized in the United States.

Sentence Writing

Here are some possible combinations. Yours may differ.

The final exam was long and difficult, so most students were unable to finish it.

Ever since the gardeners started arriving at 7:00 in the morning and using their lawnmowers and other loud machines, no one in the neighborhood can sleep in anymore.

When I grew up in the 1960s, people rode in cars without seatbelts, without special car seats for children, and without airbags.

COMMA RULES 4, 5, AND 6 (PP. 184–188)

For Exercises 1 and 2, correct sentences remain in the answers without commas for the sake of comparison.

EXERCISE 1

1. This year's graduation ceremony, I believe, was better than last year's.
2. I believe this year's graduation ceremony was better than last year's.
3. The valedictorian's speech, however, was longer than ever.
4. However, the valedictorian's speech was longer than ever.
5. The person who cued the music between speeches fell asleep and missed a cue.
6. Jason Bell, who cued the music between the speeches, fell asleep and missed a cue.
7. The Anime Association, the newest club on campus, showed an inspirational short film.
8. The new Anime Association showed an inspirational short film.
9. And, as usual, no one felt comfortable wearing a mortarboard, so they were flying everywhere.
10. And no one, as usual, felt comfortable wearing a mortarboard, so they were flying everywhere.

EXERCISE 2

1. We hope, of course, that people will honor their summons for jury duty.
2. Of course we hope that people will honor their summons for jury duty.
3. People who serve as jurors every time they're called deserve our appreciation.
4. Thelma and Trevor Martin, who serve as jurors every time they're called, deserve our appreciation.
5. We should therefore be as understanding as we can be about the slow legal process.
6. Therefore, we should be as understanding as we can be about the slow legal process.
7. A legal system that believes people are innocent until proven guilty must offer a trial-by-jury option.
8. The U.S. legal system, which believes people are innocent until proven guilty, offers a trial-by-jury option.

9. With that option, we hope that no one will receive an unfair trial.
10. With that option, no one, we hope, will receive an unfair trial.

Exercise 3

1. Bobble-head dolls, those figurines with heads that bob up and down, have become the souvenir of choice for many modern teams and companies.
2. The sentence is correct.
3. Others say these types of ceramic nodding figures, called "nodder" dolls in Europe, originated there in the 1800s.
4. Much more recently, in the 1960s to be exact, Japan began producing what some call "bobbinheads" as souvenirs to sell at baseball parks in the United States.
5. The sentence is correct.
6. Two of the most famous people of the twentieth century, President Kennedy and Elvis Presley, were immortalized as bobble-head dolls.
7. The sentence is correct.
8. Now some cereal boxes, traditionally the showplaces for athletic triumphs, include tiny bobble-heads as prizes inside.
9. Even William Rehnquist, Chief Justice of the U.S. Supreme Court, had a bobble-head doll in his likeness.
10. The Rehnquist bobble-head, a must-have for any nodding-doll collector, was commissioned by a law journal to encourage people to read about legal issues.

Exercise 4

1. The story of Dracula, the frightening Prince Vlad Tepes, has been fascinating people across the world for hundreds of years.
2. He was held as a prisoner in Bran Castle, a medieval fortress in Transylvania in the 15th century. (This sentence needs only one comma; the end of the sentence is the end of the "scoopable.")
3. Bran Castle, also called Dracula's Castle, has become a popular tourist attraction.
4. The sentence is correct.
5. The sentence is correct.
6. The sentence is correct.

7. It was given to Marie, Queen of Romania, in 1920.

8. The sentence is correct.

9. The sentence is correct.

10. Queen Marie's grandson, Dominic von Habsburg, now owns the castle, along with his two sisters, Maria Magdalena and Elizabeth.

Exercise 5

1. One of the weirdest competitions on earth, the Wife Carrying World Championships, takes place in Finland once a year.

2. These load-carrying races, which may have begun as training rituals for Finnish soldiers, have become popular in the United States and all over the world.

3. Each pair of participants, made up of one man and one "wife," has to make it through an obstacle course in the shortest time possible.

4. The "wife" half of the team has to weigh at least 49 kilos, 108 pounds.

5. She does not have to be married to the man who carries her; she can, indeed, be someone else's wife or even unmarried.

6. The wife-carrying course includes two sections, a part on land and a part in water.

7. The sentence is correct.

8. The wife-dropping penalty, which is fifteen seconds added to the pair's time, is enough to disqualify most couples.

9. Contest officials allow one piece of equipment, a belt that the man can wear so that the "wife" has something to hold on to during the race.

10. The winning couple wins a prize, but the coveted title, Wife Carrying World Champion, is reward enough for most.

Proofreading Exercise

There are two types of punctuation, internal punctuation and end punctuation. Internal punctuation is used within the sentence, and end punctuation is used at the end of the sentence. There are six main rules for the placement of commas, the most important pieces of internal punctuation. Semicolons, the next most important, have two main functions. Their primary function, separating two independent clauses, is also the most widely known. A lesser-known need for semicolons, to separate items in a list already containing commas, occurs rarely in college writing. Colons and dashes have special uses within sentences. And of the three pieces of end punctuation—periods, question marks, and exclamation points—one is obviously the most common. That piece is the period, which signals the end of the majority of English sentences.

SENTENCE WRITING

Here are some possible combinations. Yours may differ.

I think that the average student's life is full of distractions and extraneous information from the Internet and many other forms of media. (or) The average student's life, I think, is full of distractions and extraneous information from the Internet and many other forms of media.

She plans to buy herself an expensive watch by Tag Heuer, her favorite brand. (or) She plans to buy herself an expensive Tag Heuer watch.

Only two people, the manager and a customer, were in the store when it was robbed. (or) The manager and a customer were the only people in the store when it was robbed.

COMMA REVIEW EXERCISE

We're writing you this e-mail, Lena, to give you directions to the reunion this weekend. [4] We know that you will be driving with a few others, but we want to be sure that everyone knows the way. [1] When we contacted some of our classmates over the Internet several of the messages were returned as "undeliverable." [3] We hope, therefore, that this one gets through to you. [5] We can't wait to see everyone again: Michelle, Tom, Olivia, and Brad. [2] Dr. Milford, our favorite professor, will be there to welcome all of the returning students. [6]

QUOTATION MARKS AND UNDERLINING/ITALICS (PP. 191–195)

EXERCISE 1

1. I am reading a book called <u>Don't: A Manual of Mistakes & Improprieties More or Less Prevalent in Conduct and Speech</u>.
2. The book's contents are divided into chapters with titles such as "At Table," "In Public," and "In General."
3. In the section about table don'ts, the book offers the following warning: "Don't bend over your plate, or drop your head to get each mouthful."
4. The table advice continues by adding, "Don't bite your bread. Break it off."
5. This book offers particularly comforting advice about conducting oneself in public.
6. For instance, it states, "Don't brush against people, or elbow people, or in any way show disregard for others."
7. When meeting others on the street, the book advises, "Don't be in a haste to introduce. Be sure that it is mutually desired before presenting one person to another."

8. In the section titled "In General," there are more tips about how to get along in society, such as "Don't underrate everything that others do, and overstate your own doings."

9. The Don't book has this to say about books, whether borrowed or owned: "Read them, but treat them as friends that must not be abused."

10. And one can never take the following warning too much to heart: "Don't make yourself in any particular way a nuisance to your neighbors or your family."

EXERCISE 2

1. "Have you been to the bookstore yet?" Monica asked.
2. "No, why?" I answered.
3. "They've rearranged the books," she said, "and now I can't find anything."
4. "Are all of the books for one subject still together?" I wondered.
5. "Yes, they are," Monica told me, "but there are no markers underneath the books to say which teacher's class they're used in, so it's really confusing."
6. "Why don't we just wait until the teachers show us the books and then buy them?" I replied.
7. "That will be too late!" Monica shouted.
8. "Calm down," I told her, "you are worrying for nothing."
9. "I guess so," she said once she took a deep breath.
10. "I sure hope I'm not wrong," I thought to myself, "or Monica will really be mad at me."

EXERCISE 3

1. "Stopping by Woods on a Snowy Evening" is a poem by Robert Frost.
2. "Once you finish your responses," the teacher said, "bring your test papers up to my desk."
3. I subscribe to several periodicals, including Time and U.S. News & World Report.
4. "Our country is the world," William Lloyd Garrison believed, "our countrymen are all mankind."
5. "Do you know," my teacher asked, "that there are only three ways to end a sentence?"
6. Edward Young warned young people to "Be wise with speed. A fool at forty is a fool indeed."
7. In Shakespeare's play Romeo and Juliet, Mercutio accidentally gets stabbed and shouts, "A plague on both your houses!"

8. "There is no such thing as a moral or an immoral book," Oscar Wilde writes in his novel The Picture of Dorian Gray; "Books are either well written, or badly written."

9. Molière felt that "One should eat to live, and not live to eat."

10. Did you say, "I'm sleepy" or "I'm beeping"?

Exercise 4

1. Women's Wit and Wisdom is the title of a book I found in the library.

2. The book includes many great insights that were written or spoken by women throughout history.

3. England's Queen Elizabeth I noted in the sixteenth century that "A clear and innocent conscience fears nothing."

4. "Nothing is so good as it seems beforehand," observed George Eliot, a female author whose real name was Mary Ann Evans.

5. Some of the women's quotations are funny; Alice Roosevelt Longworth, for instance, said, "If you don't have anything good to say about anyone, come and sit by me."

6. "If life is a bowl of cherries," asked Erma Bombeck, "what am I doing in the pits?"

7. Some of the quotations are serious, such as Gloria Steinem's statement, "The future depends on what each of us does every day."

8. Maya Lin, the woman who designed Washington D.C.'s Vietnam Veterans Memorial, reminded us that, as she put it, "War is not just a victory or a loss. . . . People die."

9. Emily Dickinson had this to say about truth: "Truth is such a rare thing, it is delightful to tell it."

10. Finally, columnist Ann Landers advised one of her readers that "The naked truth is always better than the best-dressed lie."

Exercise 5

1. In his book Who's Buried in Grant's Tomb? A Tour of Presidential Gravesites, Brian Lamb records the final words of American presidents who have passed away.

2. Some of their goodbyes were directed at their loved ones; for example, President Zachary Taylor told those around him, "I regret nothing, but I am sorry that I am about to leave my friends."

3. Other presidents, such as William Henry Harrison, who died after only one month in office, addressed more political concerns; Harrison said, "I wish

you to understand the true principles of the government. I wish them carried out. I ask for nothing more."

4. John Tyler became president due to Harrison's sudden death; Tyler served his term, lived to be seventy-one, and said, "Perhaps it is best" when his time came.

5. At the age of eighty-three, Thomas Jefferson fought to live long enough to see the fiftieth anniversary of America's independence; on that day in 1826, Jefferson was one of only three (out of fifty-six) signers of the "Declaration of Independence" still living, and he asked repeatedly before he died, "Is it the fourth?"

6. John Adams, one of the other three remaining signers, died later the same day—July 4, 1826—and his last words ironically were "Thomas Jefferson still survives."

7. The third president to die on the Fourth of July (1831) was James Monroe; while he was president, people within the government got along so well that his time in office was known as "the era of good feelings."

8. Doctors attempted to help James Madison live until the Fourth of July, but he put off their assistance; on June 26, 1836, when a member of his family became alarmed at his condition, Madison comforted her by saying, "Nothing more than a change of mind, my dear," and he passed away.

9. Grover Cleveland, who had suffered from many physical problems, was uneasy at his death; before losing consciousness, he said, "I have tried so hard to do right."

10. Finally, George Washington, our first president, also suffered greatly but faced death bravely; "I die hard," he told the people by his bedside, "but I am not afraid to go. 'Tis well."

PROOFREADING EXERCISE

We were allowed to choose a book to review in our journals last week. The teacher specified that it should be a short nonfiction book about something of interest to us. I found a great book to review. It's called <u>Tattoo: Secrets of a Strange Art</u>. Albert Parry breaks the contents down into chapters about tattoo legends, techniques, and purposes. A few of the chapter titles are "The Art and Its Masters," "The Circus," "Identification," and "Removal." The book also includes illustrations and photographs of tattoo designs and tattooed people and animals throughout history, including Miss Stella: The Tattooed Lady, The Famous Tattooed Cow, and Georgius Constantine. Parry describes Constantine's tattoos in the following way: "the most complete, elaborate, and artistic tattooing ever witnessed in America or Europe." Parry continues, "There was almost no part of his body, not a quarter-inch of the skin, free from designs." Needless to say, since I love tattoos, I loved Parry's book about them.

CAPITAL LETTERS (PP. 197–200)

In this section, titles of larger works are *italicized* rather than underlined.

Exercise 1

1. I have always wanted to learn another language besides English.
2. Recently, I have been watching a lot of films from India.
3. Some people call them "Bollywood movies."
4. Whatever they are called, I love to watch them.
5. One part of these movies that I love is their language: Hindi.
6. I have to use English subtitles to understand the dialogue most of the time.
7. But sometimes I can catch what's happening without the subtitles.
8. Because of my intense interest in Hindi-language films, I plan to take a Hindi class.
9. I have already bought a book that explains the Devanagari writing system.
10. Now I will enroll in a class and learn Hindi as a second language.

Exercise 2

1. When people think of jazz, they think of *Down Beat* magazine.
2. *Down Beat*'s motto may be "Jazz, Blues & Beyond," but some people think that the magazine has gone too far "beyond" by including two guitarists in the *Down Beat* Hall of Fame.
3. The two musicians in question are Jimi Hendrix and Frank Zappa.
4. Jimi Hendrix was inducted into the Hall of Fame in 1970.
5. *Down Beat* added Frank Zappa to the list in 1994.
6. Since then, readers and editors have been debating whether Hendrix and Zappa belong in the same group as Duke Ellington, John Coltrane, and Miles Davis.
7. Those who play jazz guitar have some of the strongest opinions on the subject.
8. Russell Malone, Mark Elf, and John Abercrombie all agree that Hendrix and Zappa were great guitarists but not jazz guitarists.
9. Others like Steve Tibbetts and Bill Frisell don't have any problem putting Hendrix on the list, but Tibbetts isn't so sure about including Zappa.
10. It will be interesting to see who *Down Beat*'s future inductees will be.

EXERCISE 3

1. I grew up watching *It's a Wonderful Life* once a year on TV in the winter.
2. That was before the colorized version and before every station started showing it fifteen times a week throughout the months of November and December.
3. I especially remember enjoying that holiday classic with my mother and brothers when we lived on Seventh Avenue.
4. "Hurry up!" Mom would yell, "You're going to miss the beginning!"
5. My favorite part has always been when Jimmy Stewart's character, George Bailey, uses his own money to help the people of Bedford Falls and to save his father's Building and Loan.
6. George's disappointment turns to happiness after he and Donna Reed's character, Mary, move into the abandoned house on their honeymoon.
7. Of course, mean old Mr. Potter takes advantage of Uncle Billy's carelessness at the bank, and that starts George's breakdown.
8. In his despair, George places the petals of his daughter Zuzu's flower in his pocket, leaves his house, and wants to commit suicide.
9. Luckily, all of George's good deeds have added up over the years, and he is given a chance to see that thanks to a character named Clarence.
10. When George feels Zuzu's petals in his pocket, he knows that he's really made it home again, and the people of Bedford Falls come to help him.

EXERCISE 4

1. Most people don't know the name Elzie Crisler Segar.
2. Segar was the creator of the comic character Popeye.
3. Segar based Popeye and many of his fellow characters on residents of the town of Chester, Illinois, where Segar was born.
4. Popeye's inspiration was a Chester bartender named Frank "Rocky" Fiegel.
5. Fiegel was a brawler by nature and might have even been a sailor at some point.
6. Segar learned how to draw by taking a correspondence course.
7. One of Segar's bosses at a Chester movie house, J. William Schuchert, was the prototype for Wimpy.
8. Segar introduced Olive Oyl's character in his *Thimble Theater* comic strip.
9. Olive was based on a Chester store owner, Dora Paskel.
10. The town of Chester celebrates the work of Elzie Crisler Segar with a yearly Popeye picnic, the Popeye Museum, a Popeye statue, and Segar Memorial Park.

EXERCISE 5

1. *The New Yorker* magazine has a cartoon contest every week.
2. At the back of each issue, there is a page devoted to the contest.
3. The heading at the top of the page reads "Cartoon Caption Contest."
4. Below the heading is a brief description of the rules involved in the contest.
5. It begins, "Each week, we provide a cartoon in need of a caption."
6. It continues, "You, the reader, submit a caption, we choose three finalists, and you vote for your favorite."
7. Then it specifies the deadline for that week's submissions.
8. At the bottom of the page are three cartoons: one is titled "The Winning Caption," the second lists "The Finalists," and the third shows "This Week's Contest."
9. Winners of the caption contest are named in the magazine, and they receive a signed print of the cartoon that they helped to create.
10. Any U.S. resident who is eighteen or over can enter the contest or vote.

REVIEW OF PUNCTUATION AND CAPITAL LETTERS (P. 201)

1. The Griffith Park Observatory is one of the most famous landmarks in Hollywood.
2. Have you ever read Langston Hughes' essay "Salvation"?
3. Trini and Tracy drove all the way from San Diego to Santa Barbara.
4. "How many years of French have you taken?" my counselor asked.
5. Congratulations, Ms. Thomas, on your recent promotion; you deserved it. (or !)
6. The person who writes the best 100-word description of that car will win it. (or !)
7. I am majoring in art, and my best friend, Lee, is in the nursing program. (or Nursing Program)
8. Due to the low number of completed loan applications in the fall, the Financial Aid office has extended its spring deadline. (Note: The word *its* does not need an apostrophe in this sentence because it does not mean *it is* or *it has*.)
9. The Anime Club needs volunteers to pass out flyers.

10. The man who was selling T-shirts at the concert said the men's medium size is the same as the women's large size, and I believed him.

11. My English teacher always repeats the same little rhyme about commas: "When in doubt, leave them out."

12. Jessie needs a new cell phone; however, she can't afford one right now.

13. "The Road Not Taken" is a famous poem by Robert Frost.

14. Madonna's first children's book was called The English Roses, and since then, she has written several other books for kids.

15. The angry customer stood in front of the cash register and yelled, "I want my money back!" Finally, the cashier called in the manager, who gave the customer a refund.

COMPREHENSIVE TEST (PP. 202–203)

1. (ww) The scary scenes in the movie really *affected* me; I couldn't sleep that night.
2. (sp) The police asked us what time the theft had *occurred.*
3. (wordy and awk) *We can solve our money problems.*
4. (cap) Last semester, I took art history, *Spanish,* and geography.
5. (pro) The department store hired my friend and *me* as gift wrappers for the holidays.
6. (//) In just six weeks, we learned to find main ideas, to remember details, and *to integrate* new words into our vocabulary.
7. (ro) The chairs should be straightened, and the chalkboard should be erased before the next class.
8. (mm) The students noticed *a tiny frog hopping into the room* from the biology lab.
9. (shift in time) He tells the same joke in every speech, and people *laugh.*
10. (pro ref) I bring pies to potluck parties because *pies* are always appreciated.
11. (p) We don't know if the buses run that late at night.
12. (apos) The *women's* teams have their own trophy case across the hall.
13. (dm) *When I turned twenty-one,* my mom handed me a beer.
14. (ro) Their car wouldn't start; the battery was dead.
15. (cliché) I asked the car salesman about the actual price.

16. (wordy) That restaurant serves terrible food.

17. (pro agr) *All of the people* in the audience raised their *hands*.

18. (frag) *We left* because the lines were long and we couldn't find our friends.

19. (cs) I plan to stay in town for spring break; it's more restful that way.

20. (s-v agr) Each of the kittens *has* white paws. (or *All* of the kittens have white paws.)

WRITING

ORGANIZING IDEAS (P. 222)

Exercise 1 Thesis or Fact?

1. FACT
2. THESIS
3. FACT
4. THESIS
5. THESIS
6. FACT
7. THESIS
8. FACT
9. THESIS
10. THESIS

ADDING TRANSITIONAL EXPRESSIONS (PP. 225–226)

Exercise 2 Adding Transitional Expressions

This year, my family and I decided to celebrate the Fourth of July in a whole new way. *Previously,* we always attended a fireworks show at the sports stadium near our house. The firework shows got better every year; *however,* we were getting tired of the crowds and the noise. *In addition,* we were starting to feel bad about our own lack of creativity. The goal this time was to have each family member think of a craft project, recipe, or game related to the Fourth. The result was a day full of fun activities and good things to eat—all created by us! *First,* my sister Helen taught us to make seltzer rockets from an idea she found on the Internet. We used the fireless "firecrackers" as table decorations until late afternoon when we set them off. *Then,* we ate dinner. Mom and Dad's contribution was "Fourth of July Franks," which were hot dogs topped with ketchup, onions, and a sprinkling of blue-corn chips. For dessert, my brother Leon assembled tall parfaits made with layers of red and blue Jell-O cubes divided by ridges of whipped cream. *Finally,* we played a game of charades in which all of the answers had something to do with the American flag, the Declaration of Independence, Paul Revere's ride, and other such topics. We all enjoyed the Fourth so much that the events will probably become our new tradition.

WRITING ABOUT WHAT YOU READ (PP. 241–242)

ASSIGNMENT 17 WRITE A 100-WORD SUMMARY

100-WORD SUMMARY OF "CAT LOVERS VS. DOG LOVERS"

Certain characteristics make people prefer either cats or dogs as pets. The first is whether people seek solitude or companionship. Cat people like to be alone, and dog people like to be with others. Also, studies show that women prefer cats and men prefer dogs. This division goes back to the cave-dwelling days of our ancestors. Obviously, some people like both animals and have no preference. And most people exhibit catlike and doglike qualities in the ways they behave. So there is really no simple answer to whether a particular person would like a cat or a dog the best.

Index